Second Edition

STRATEGIES

Getting and Keeping the Job You Want

Sharon K. Ferrett, Ph.D.
Humboldt State University

New York, New York   Columbus, Ohio   Chicago, Illinois   Peoria, Illinois   Woodland Hills, California

The McGraw-Hill Companies

Strategies
Getting and Keeping the Job You Want, Second Edition

Printed in the United States of America.

ISBN-13: 978-0-07-830509-2
ISBN-10: 0-07-830509-8

8 9 0   VNH/VNH   0 9 8

ACKNOWLEDGMENTS

Special thanks go to the following reviewers whose comments during manuscript development and revision were invaluable.

Carol Brooks
Pittsburgh Technical Institute
Pittsburgh, PA

Kimberly Washington
Cambria-Rowe Business College
Johnston, PA

Gretchen Rummel
Cambria-Rowe Business College
Johnston, PA

Elizabeth Peak-Fortun
Allen County Community College
Iola, KS

Marie Smith
Lasell College
Newton, MA

Jean Rohrer
Hagerstown Business College
Hagerstown, MD

Ed Cole
Indiana Business College
Indianapolis, IN

Amy Zukaukis
Pittsburgh Technical Institute
Pittsburgh, PA

Christopher Caresani
Pittsburgh Technical Institute
Pittsburgh, PA

Anita Brownstein
Long Island Business Institute
Commack, NY

Jean Haley
Southern Ohio College
Fairfield, OH

Viv Dudley
Danville Area Community College
Danville, IL

DEDICATION

To the memory of my dad, Albert L. Ferrett, for teaching me to look ahead.

To my mom, Velma Hollenbeck Ferrett, for teaching me to enjoy every day.

To my husband, Sam, and my daughters, Jennifer and Sarah, for teaching me what is really important.

I would also like to gratefully acknowledge the contributions of the Glencoe editorial staff whose considerable effort, suggestions, ideas, and insights helped to make this text a valuable and viable tool for student success.

Brief Table of Contents

Preface

Appendices

Index

Table of Contents

CHAPTER 3

Your Résumé

CHAPTER 4

Cover Letters and Applications

CHAPTER 5

Preparing for the Interview

CHAPTER 6

The Interview

158

CHAPTER 7

Following Up

188

CHAPTER 8

Job Success Strategies

Appendices

Index

PREFACE

From the Author

For many students, making job and career decisions can be overwhelming. When I began thinking about *Strategies: Getting and Keeping the Job You Want*, I sat down to consider how I could guide job seekers through the exciting but often stressful steps of the job search. As I began writing, I asked myself, "What are the most important skills for getting and keeping the *right* job?"

After many discussions with colleagues and students past and present, I concluded that *confidence*—in yourself and in your ability to make good decisions and sound choices—is crucial for any successful job search. Moreover, using the concrete strategies and guidelines presented in this book can help you:

- Assess and define your current skills in a meaningful way.
- Plan a systematic job search that gets results.
- Feel secure about networking.
- Create résumés that put your best foot forward.
- Write positive, confident cover letters.
- Feel good about interviewing.
- Keep up your morale and energy.
- Build professional rapport.
- Make the right choices, using critical thinking and problem solving.
- Keep your job and get promoted.

New to the Second Edition

The second edition of *Strategies: Getting and Keeping the Job You Want* has been thoroughly updated and revised, based upon many helpful comments and suggestions of adopters and reviewers in the field. Our goal is to give you effective job-search tools and to help guide you through the job-search process so that you will succeed in finding and getting the job you want. The text also offers current information and strategies for keeping and advancing in your present job.

Some job-search techniques, strategies, and acceptable practices have changed since the publication of the first edition. Job seekers need to understand and keep pace with ways to navigate the job market with new tools, such as the Internet, and methods of research, networking skills, and applications. This new edition of *Strategies: Getting and Keeping the Job You Want* offers expanded emphasis in areas such as self-assessment, sending electronic résumés, dressing for success, and the career portfolio. The second edition examines the shifting job market and workplace trends through features, such as *BusinessWeek Career Directions*, so that all job seekers can keep the winning edge.

Features

Net Advantage – This **NEW,** chapter-related Internet feature provides specific tips to aid the job-search process and highlight the extensive resources available on the Web for job hunters. It includes a question that encourages you to tap into the Internet—and also directs you to the new *Strategies* Web site at **strategies.glencoe.com.**

Stress Savers – This **NEW** margin feature is designed to help you feel less overwhelmed by the job-search process. A short list of stress-saving tips tied to chapter content will help you to cope with the job hunt.

BusinessWeek **Career Directions** – This **NEW** feature focuses on workplace trends. Excerpts from *BusinessWeek* articles highlight current issues important to employees and employers, such as technology, training, diversity, etc. A brief case study of a job seeker presents a problem correlated to the article content. A critical-thinking question helps you apply what you learn from the article and chapter.

Staying Power – This **NEW** feature helps you recognize and deal with the difficulties, setbacks, and frustrations of the job-search process. The second part (Try This) offers solutions and tips on keeping a positive attitude and getting results.

Your Career Portfolio – This **NEW** worksheet on last page of each chapter is designed for you to fill out and add to your own career development portfolios. The information you gather and document on these practical worksheets can be used throughout your career when applying for jobs or seeking promotions.

Take Charge!

As you begin your search for the right job now, and as you move into future jobs, remember the following empowerment strategies:

1. Be a lifelong learner. By learning new skills throughout your life, you'll stay current with changes in developments in your field, and you will increase your value to current and potential employers.

2. Be a problem solver. All jobs require problem-solving skills and creativity. Take the time to explore creative options when faced with a problem.

3. Use critical thinking. The best jobs go to those who can use critical thinking to make sound decisions.

4. Network. Build a strong network of contacts and supporters, in and out of your field.

5. Develop personal qualities. Being dependable and reliable, keeping a positive attitude, and being an enthusiastic team player who practices honesty and integrity are personal qualities you can refine and build.

6. Focus on the benefit factor. Employers hire you for what you can do for them. Highlight what you have to offer. Once you get a job, continually ask yourself how you can add value to the company.

7. Do your homework. Develop a broad and current knowledge of your industry by becoming aware of trends in the field.

8. Focus on the big picture. Be aware of major projects, competitors, goals, new products, and customer concerns within your company or within a company where you would like to work.

9. Be prepared. Be ready to look for a new job at any time. Keep your résumé up-to-date and feel confident about your job-search skills.

10. Stay positive. Develop a resourceful, confident, and determined state of mind. Stay enthusiastic and persistent.

USING THE TEXT

This book is designed for you to learn and be successful in your job search and beyond. *Strategies,* Second Edition, uses the following integrated learning system to help you accomplish this:

Concept Preview – Each chapter's opener introduces key concepts to be learned.

Concept Development – Each chapter's text explains the concepts in a structured, visible format.

Concept Reinforcement – Each chapter's text provides examples, graphics, and special features to enhance and strengthen your learning.

Concept Review and Application – Each chapter's ending review, questions, and activities encourage you to apply what you have learned.

Concept Preview

Winning Points list strategies and points related to the chapter concepts that are designed to give the winning edge to job seekers.

The **opening photograph** previews the chapter's content.

Quotes set the tone for the chapter to follow and offer further insight on the chapter topic.

CHAPTER 5

Preparing for the Interview

"Being good at something is only half the battle. The other half is mastering the art of self-presentation, positioning, and connecting."
—Adele Scheele
Author

Winning Points

* Do your homework and be prepared.
* Research yourself.
* Research the company.
* Research the industry.
* Research interview questions.
* Research all details of the interview.
* Dress professionally and appropriately.
* Rehearse your interview until you are comfortable.

Introduction

The moment of truth in the job-search process is the all-important interview. This chapter will help you prepare for it as you look at the planning process for the interview within the larger context of the job-search process. Remember, your résumé and cover letter got the potential employer's attention; your job interview will get you the job. Strategies and techniques will help you to market your work experience, education, personal qualities, and skills, and create an overall positive image.

Chapter 5 also highlights creative problem solving and critical thinking as important abilities you will want to demonstrate during the interview. By preparing, getting organized, and learning verbal and nonverbal communication skills, you will stand out from the crowd.

If you follow the strategies in this book, you can turn an interview into a job offer. Mastering the art of interviewing may also help you get promoted faster, make great presentations, and have high self-esteem.

Chapter 5 Objectives

After you have completed this chapter, you will be able to:

* Explain the purpose and importance of the interview
* Explain the importance of preparation as a key to success
* Describe essential factors of the interview process
* Research likely questions and prepare good answers
* Describe how to plan a professional image
* Explain the importance of rehearsing the interview

Concept Development

Skill Check is designed to highlight a job-search strategy/skill that is presented in the text. These "skills" are compiled into a list in the Chapter Review section at the end of each chapter.

Exercises are in-chapter, consumable worksheets throughout each chapter. You apply job-search strategies and practice techniques by doing these exercises as you read each chapter and apply what you learn.

Positive Attitude

Your attitude at the beginning of an interview is the one factor that will most affect its outcome. Chapter 2 discussed the importance of motivation and positive attitude for building contacts, staying enthusiastic, and making a good first impression.

It is also critical to create a relaxed and positive mental state before and during the interview so that you will **project a confident, positive, and professional image.** If you have a negative outlook or go into an interview with a sense thinking but also your body lang behavior. Learn to relax by prep and taking deep breaths.

Warmth and Humor

People who have a knack for bui They are able to laugh at themse ease by bringing a light atmosph warmth, and a sincere smile crea

Respect and Etiquett

It is important to **be respectful** look at a few points of etiquette t essential for an effective interview

Arrive on time. If you're late too much. Being late indicates yo serious about the job. If an emer Make certain you arrive at the o scheduled interview. Use that ext read notes on bulletin boards, ge mirror, and relax. Use the power tive thoughts, and calmly review check in with the receptionist if y Check in about 5 to 10 minutes receptionist; turn in an applicatio one. Be pleasant and positive.

Remember to get a good nig enough to have a healthy breakfa less rushing.

It is best to go on interviews invited to a special event, bringin fessional. Also, it might indicate to project.

Be respectful. While you und tant to be sensitive to the intervi bit nervous, too. Civility means re

EXERCISE 6.2 **Connecting Traits and Experiences**

Review the list of personality traits in the previous section. On the lines provided, write your responses. The following is an example that demonstrates the personal trait of *initiative:*

> I helped my auto shop instructor grade papers and worked with him in the shop during labs. One time he didn't show up for class. I knew his wife was overdue on her delivery date for their first child. This was a night class and no administrators were on campus. I felt comfortable meeting the class. I gave the class several sample problems. I also gave them a demonstration on motor repair since that is my area of specialty. My instructor was very appreciative that I took the initiative to go ahead with the class. The students said they enjoyed the demonstration and were kept on target with the class schedule. Because of this experience, I am more confident. I am careful not to overstep my bounds of authority, but I also know there are times when it is important to take the initiative to get the job done.

1. The personal trait I most want to highlight is:

2. I have demonstrated this trait in the following ways:

3. Because of this quality, my work was affected in the following manner:

Copyright © Glencoe/McGraw-Hill

Concept Reinforcement

Figure references in the text guide you to illustrations and charts for concept reinforcement.

Figures highlight and help you understand important chapter concepts. Figure captions and questions also help preview and reinforce concepts you are learning.

No Specific Job in Mind?

In many cases, you may not be applying for a specific job, but you want to write to companies where you would like to work, or you want to follow up on contacts you have met through networking. The "blind" cover letter in **Figure 4.4** is a response to a networking contact.

"Blind" Cover Letter

October 29, 2003

Mr. John Tempis
231 Brook Street
John's Texaco Station
Bennet, ME 01223

Dear Mr. Tempis:

It was a pleasure to talk with y
time to discuss the field of auto
your review and evaluation. As
occupation and my passion. I ha
and have developed a reputatio
earned a certificate in foreign c

Your station has grown in the la
customer-service oriented. In ac
demonstrated a willingness to h
My accomplishments include:

- Designing a customer satisfa
- Increasing sales by 25 perce
- Never being late for work i
- Earning a reputation for be

I have hands-on experience wit
business and with increasing sa
company or other opportunitie
let me know. Thanks again for

Sincerely,

Thomas R. Kason

Thomas R. Kason

Enclosure

Figure 4.4
Contacting Your Network
Networking can provide great sources for job opportunities. You can use a blind cover letter to follow up your initial contact. *What are the differences between a blind cover letter and a standard cover letter?*

Questions to Ask

1. How does my position fit with the mission of the organization? What are the key responsibilities of this job?

2. What are the major challenges or concerns that face this organization in the near future?

3. Is the company planning major changes in the future? If so, how would they affect my department? My position?

4. With whom would I be working most closely? Does this company use working teams?

5. Ideally, what would you like me to contribute to this organization? What skills and personality characteristics are most important for success at this company?

6. How would you describe the corporate culture at this organization? The management style?

7. Who are your major competitors?

8. What is the major difference between this company and your competitors?

9. What do you wish you had known about this company when you interviewed for your position? What is it about the company that attracted you or has caused you to stay?

10. How do you view company morale? What is the company's philosophy about motivating employees?

11. Besides making a profit and offering good service, what values are most important at this company?

12. I have read your mission statement. How do you manifest this philosophy on a daily basis for your employees and customers?

13. I plan on working hard and contributing to the company. What advancement do you see for me in five years if I have proven myself?

14. What are the major goals of this company in the near future?

15. How many people have held this job in the last ten years? Where did they go?

Figure 6.3
The Right Questions Asking the right questions will not only give you needed answers, but it will also tell the interviewer that you're a serious, well-informed candidate. *Think of a particular job you might want. Which of the sample questions in this figure would most apply in an interview?*

the question and attempt to determine what the interviewer is trying to get you to reveal. Remember, the employer is trying to find a "fit"—someone who will be an integral part of the team. Given that most employers have honorable intentions, get beyond the question to what they really want to know.

Laws change, but the following are some sensitive areas that are taboo or at the very least inappropriate.

1. **Age:** Federal law protects against age discrimination. *How old are you? How old are your children?* or other questions that attempt to determine age are inappropriate and taboo. Special laws, however, do exist for

Special Features

Net Advantage is a chapter-related Internet feature providing specific tips to aid the job-search process and to highlight the extensive resources available on the Web for job hunters.

Stress Savers is a margin feature designed to help students feel less overwhelmed by the job-search process. This brief feature gives succinct suggestions and shortcuts for dealing with the job-search process.

***BusinessWeek* Career Directions** focuses on current workplace trends using excerpts from *BusinessWeek* articles that deal with chapter-related issues important to employees and employers, such as technology, training, diversity, and so on. A brief case study of someone in the job market dealing with a problem correlated to the article content.

Staying Power helps you recognize the difficulties, setbacks, and frustrations of the job-search process. This feature addresses the barriers along the way and offers solutions.

Net Advantage

Nonverbal Communication How you communicate during an interview plays a critical role in winning over the interviewer. According to communication experts, only 10 percent of our communication is represented by what we say, 30 percent by our sounds, and 60 percent by body language. Proper preparation for an interview can help you feel and appear more relaxed and ready to answer challenging questions.

For interview preparation techniques, go to strategies.glencoe.com for links to Web sites that provide useful tips.

What aspect(s) of nonverbal communication would you improve so that y̶̶̶̶̶̶̶̶̶̶̶̶̶̶ view process?

Stress Savers

Review and Interview

When you go to your interview, remember these important tips:

- Be 15 minutes early.
- Bring your résumé.
- Bring any supplementary documentation.
- Dress conservatively, even if the office attire is casual.
- Ask 2–3 prepared questions when you are given the

Career Directions   BusinessWeek

The Tender Issue of Age?

It is generally illegal in a job interview for employers to ask questions—even indirect ones such as when you got ͏hool diploma— ͏sed to determine ͏ys employment ͏uis DiLorenzo, ͏he labor depart- ͏d, Schoeneck & ͏cuse, N.Y. But ͏smart to stand up ͏ in the middle of ͏ if you really ͏ is another issue. ͏Discrimination in ͏t Act (ADEA) ͏ers from using ͏s for hiring, ͏ther employment ͏ns, such as pro- ͏ compensation. ͏ion generally ͏orkers age 40 and ͏ndividual states ͏s that protect even younger employees.

There are some fuzzy areas, however. An employer can ask you when you graduated from college if the question is related to the job.

Otherwise, sniffing around to find an employee's age is pretty much verboten.

Of course, if you're persuaded that you have been discriminated against because of your age, then you may want to seek counsel or file an EEOC complaint. One thing to remember, though, is that discrimination in hiring cases is among the hardest to prove.

"It's definitely in a candidate's best interest to be as honest as possible," says Bobbi Moss of Management Recruiters International. Moss thinks the best way to deal with an employer's concerns is to anticipate them and counter them in an interview.

—By Eric Wahlgren

Excerpted from December 17, 2001, issue of BusinessWeek Online by special permission, copyright © 2000-2001, by The McGraw-Hill Companies, Inc.

Career Case Study As a reentry student majoring in marketing, Ron Villarosa was excited about a new career. Previously, he had managed a supermarket for 15 years. After graduating, he went to a job interview at a company that sold video games. However, he was greeted coolly by the 28-year-old supervisor. Ron expected to be viewed as being older but believed his skills could overcome doubts about his ability to relate to a younger market. *What do you think Ron said to persuade the prospective employer to hire him?*

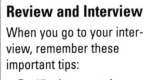

STAYING POWER

Listen and Relax

*C*ongratulations! A potential employer has responded to your cover etter and résumé, and you have just scheduled an interview. Unfortunately, what you've been trying so hard to arrange now seems like your biggest nightmare. You begin to wonder if it's the job you really want. ou may even begin to doubt your qualifications—and have a sneaking suspicion that the person who called you must have made a mistake.

These are all normal symptoms of anxiety about job interview. However, it's important not to let the fear of failure r "stage fright" cause you to dwell on your fears and imagining worst-case scenarios. Create the impression you want o make by visualizing a successful, confident job interview as you take inventory of the qualities and qualifications that make you the right person for the job.

It's important to be clear about what you want o say but you can also project a relaxed, respectful attitude by paying attention to the interviewer. You can use shyness to become an effective listener. When you focus on making the interviewer eel comfortable and concentrate on the interview, your self-consciousness may disappear.

Try This...

Being comfortable during your job interview can suggest to a prospective employer that you will be comfortable in the working environment. Focus on these strategies:

- Make sure your body language shows that you are attentive and respectful of the interviewer.
- Make eye contact as you listen to questions and give answers.
- Don't overact or fawn, but listen with genuine curiosity and attentiveness.
- Observe the way people around you speak. Be a better listener every day, and you will be a better listener during interviews.
- Decide what habits and techniques work well for you and practice them.

Concept Review and Application

Chapter Review is an end-of-chapter review designed to help you focus on and assess what you've learned.

Skill Check Recap is a bulleted list of strategies and skills relevant to chapter topics. Each skill is also highlighted throughout each chapter and signposted in the margins.

Self-Check List is a list of questions to remind you what you need to do to cover the job-search process.

Review Questions include 8 review questions, 1 critical-thinking question, and 1 cooperative-learning activity.

Strategies at Work presents real-world case studies of problems that require students to apply skills using a standard 10-question method.

Your Career Portfolio is a worksheet on last page of each chapter designed for you to fill out and add to your own career development portfolios. The information you gather and document on these practical worksheets can be used throughout your career.

CHAPTER 6 *Review*

SKILL CHECK

Skill Check Recap
* Relax and overcome fear, anxiety, and shyness.
* Project a confident, positive, and professional image.
* Be respectful and use good business etiquette.
* Build rapport by being a good listener.
* Respond with good answers.
* Demonstrate how you will benefit the company.
* Ask your prepared questions.
* Review, assess, and close your interview.

Self-Check List
Keep track of your progress. Read the following and mark *yes* or *no*.

	Yes	No
* I have practiced relaxation to overcome fear.	___	___

Review Questions *Questions*

1. What are eight factors used to evaluate you as a prospective employee?

2. What are three ways to overcome major anxiety?

3. Which four strategies will you use for establishing rapport?

4. What is the interviewer's purpose behind asking basic questions?

5. When the interviewer's questions become more intense and probing, what is his or her question behind the question?

6. What are six things to remember during a lunch or dinner interview?

CHAPTER 6 *Strategies* **AT WORK**

Anticipating the Interview

Gary is 20 and has just graduated from a community college with an associate of arts degree in heating, air conditioning, and technology. He is eager to start working full-time and wants to work at the same company where he has worked part-time while attending school. He has put together a résumé and a good cover letter and has prepared good questions and answers for an interview.

Gary is well prepared. However, he is very shy and has always avoided any kind of public speaking. He is terrified of the interview and breaks out in a sweat just thinking about it. He is afraid that his anxiety may overshadow his qualifications and other personal qualities during his interview—and that he won't get the full-time job.

Problem Solving The following ten questions are designed to help solve problems and make sound decisions. You can use these questions to find solutions to your own problems. Put yourself in Gary's place and consider these questions from his point of view.

* What is the problem?
* Do I have enough information?
* Can I make the decision by myself?
* Have I brainstormed alternatives?
* Have I looked at likely consequences?
* Have I identified all the resources and tools needed?
* Have I developed and implemented an action plan?
* Have I identified the best solution?
* Have I assessed the results?
* Have I modified the plan, if necessary?

What solution would you suggest to Gary? Write your answer on the lines below.

The Interview   185

STRATEGIES Online
Find out more about building confidence for your interview by visiting this book's Web site at strategies.glencoe.com

---

Your *Career* Portfolio

Interview Rehearsal

Practice interviewing out loud and as often as possible with friends, with career-center staff, and on tape. Review how you perform and ask others for feedback.

* Do you have good eye contact?

* How is your body language?

* Do you reveal self-confidence?

* How is your ability to answer questions?

* Make a list of questions to ask the interviewer.

* On the lines provided, write down the points you wish to improve and

Strategies Skill-Check List

The skills in this chart correspond to those highlighted in each chapter. As you work through the steps of the *Strategies* job-search process presented in this book, keep track of your progress and commitment to getting and keeping the job you want by using the chart below.

Chapter	Skill Check	Action date
1	Create a career portfolio.	
	Practice creative problem solving.	
	Start self-assessment.	
	Create a database.	
	Discover your strengths, weaknesses, and skills.	
	Discover your natural personality and learning styles.	
	Examine your attitude.	
2	Set immediate and long-term goals.	
	Research jobs through traditional and nontraditional sources.	
	Assess your network.	
	Build your network.	
	Expand your base.	
	Write networking letters.	
	Set up informational interviews.	
3	Organize your database to use in your résumé.	
	Write a job objective.	
	Translate experiences into job skills.	
	Contact your references.	
	Prepare a chronological résumé.	
	Prepare a functional résumé.	
	Choose the best format.	
4	Send a cover letter with every résumé.	
	Write a standard cover letter.	
	Write a tailored cover letter.	
	State your job objective.	
	Indicate that you know about the company.	
	Relate the needs of the employer to your skills.	
	Organize a database to use for job applications.	
	Make your job application neat and correct, and follow directions carefully.	

Chapter	Skill Check	Action date
5	Research companies before your interview.	
	Research the industry before your interview.	
	Prepare your answers for standard interview questions.	
	Prepare your interview wardrobe.	
	Rehearse an interview.	
6	Relax and overcome fear, anxiety, and shyness.	
	Project a confident, positive, and professional image.	
	Be respectful and use good business etiquette.	
	Build rapport by being a good listener.	
	Respond with good answers.	
	Demonstrate how you will benefit the company.	
	Ask your prepared questions.	
	Review, assess, and close your interview.	
7	Review and reassess the interview.	
	Follow up with a thank-you note.	
	Follow up with good record keeping.	
	Continue to network.	
	Follow up with phone calls.	
	Find out the expectations and essential details of the job.	
	Negotiate the best possible salary.	
	Reevaluate and readjust regularly.	
8	Learn the corporate culture.	
	Listen, be aware, and ask questions.	
	Develop a positive attitude and work habits.	
	Be professional.	
	Be a lifelong learner.	
	Improve communication and listening skills.	
	Be ethical and take responsibility for your actions.	
	Create effective work relationships.	
	Increase your visibility.	
	Continue to network.	
	Manage your performance reviews.	
	Increase your energy and balance.	

CHAPTER 1

Self-Assessment and Your Future

> *"*The future belongs to those who believe in the beauty of their dreams.*"*
>
> —Eleanor Roosevelt
> Former first lady, author

Introduction

The job-search process involves taking stock of your strengths, areas where you want to improve, personal qualities, values, goals, abilities, and skills. In this chapter, you will learn to take a pro-active role in your job search and to plan in a systematic and organized manner. This includes creating a career development portfolio. You will also learn the importance of critical thinking and how to apply it to creative problem solving and decision making. By using self-assessment, you will be able to determine your:

- Skills
- Abilities
- Personality styles
- Learning styles

Assessing your strengths and values will help you lay the foundation for choosing your major and career, building skills in networking, exploring jobs, writing your cover letter and résumé, and interviewing. As you complete this course, you will see the connection between these activities and getting and keeping the job you want.

Chapter 1 Objectives

After you have completed this chapter, you will be able to:

- List the steps involved in the job-search process
- Explain how to compile a career portfolio
- Explain the importance of critical thinking
- Describe how to creatively solve problems
- Explain how to make decisions
- Explain the importance of self-assessment
- Identify how to determine your personality and learning styles
- Describe how to explore majors and careers
- Explain the importance of developing personal qualities, a positive attitude, and self-esteem.

The Job-Search Process

Seeing the big picture of the job-search process and mapping out a step-by-step guide to getting a job will make the process less mysterious and overwhelming. This clear focus is essential for taking control of your job search.

The job-search process can be broken down into three major stages: preparation and planning, action, and follow-up.

Stage One: Preparation and Planning

Preparation is essential during the planning stage and is the foundation of the entire job search. Preparation involves self-assessment and reflection. Once you have assessed your values, interests, strengths, abilities, and needs, you can set goals. Defining what you want in a job is the first step in getting it.

The planning stage also involves creating a database that will help you prepare your résumé, a list of networking contacts, and good answers to interview questions.

Planning involves setting up a daily schedule and monitoring your progress. It includes creating a quiet place to reflect, set goals, return calls, compose your résumé and cover letters, prepare interview questions and answers, and keep your records. You must make a commitment to make an effort, keep a positive attitude, and deal with rejection or negative feedback. You must also prepare yourself to keep detailed records that will help you focus and follow up on the required tasks.

Stage Two: Action

Taking action involves actively researching jobs and possible careers. It also involves networking and making contacts and phone calls. The preparation of the first stage will help you during the action stage while you are creating a résumé and cover letter and filling out applications. The action stage also involves conducting your interviews. This is the stage when it is important to keep busy. Inactivity is the number one cause of failure.

Stage Three: Follow-Up

Follow-up involves attending to a variety of details and is important from day one of your job search. You need to follow up on your self-assessment and preparation and make certain you are on track, have returned phone calls, updated your data system, and followed up on all leads. Following up with phone calls, writing thank-you notes, and following up on job leads can give the leading edge to successful job hunters.

"The indispensable first step to getting the things you want out of life is this: Decide what you want."

—Ben Stein
  Writer, TV host, lawyer

Creating a Career Portfolio

The key to getting and keeping a job is to have an organized system for collecting and keeping information about you and your job prospects. Your career portfolio is a valuable tool that can help you get a new job or advance in your current career. **Create a career portfolio** that includes these elements:

- Your work philosophy
- Career goals
- Values, interests, strengths, and areas of growth
- Copy of your résumé
- Copy of a general cover letter
- Samples of your work
- Letters of recommendations
- Documentation of community service
- Documentation of work experience, critical skills, and abilities
- Examples and documentation of personal qualities (e.g., motivation, honesty, ability to work with people)
- Academic plan of study, degrees, certificates, awards, and transcripts
- Documentation of professional memberships

As you research job prospects and go about applying and interviewing for possible positions, you will have all your necessary information and documents readily accessible in your portfolio. Use a loose-leaf binder, some colored pens, and tab dividers. You can organize your career portfolio by dividing it into seven sections: Assessment and Planning, Documentation, Market Information, Networking, Documents, Interviews, and Follow-Up:

SECTION 1: ASSESSMENT AND PLANNING
- Assessment of skills, values, interests, and personal qualities
- Assessment of strengths and weaknesses
- Autobiography
- Work philosophy
- Career goals
- Time log of job-search activities

SECTION 2: DOCUMENTATION
- Documentation of skills and competencies
- Documentation of personal qualities
- Work experience, related skills, competencies, and personal qualities
- Work samples
- Community service and leadership experiences

SECTION 3: MARKET INFORMATION
- Job listings
- Job and industry trends
- Standard salaries, benefits, and job descriptions for your field

SECTION 4: NETWORKING
- List of all personal and professional contacts (instructors, advisors, former employers, minister, etc.)
- Professional memberships
- Possible service clubs to join
- References and letters of recommendation
- Time log of initial and follow-up contacts

SECTION 5: DOCUMENTS
- Résumé
- Cover letter (to be adapted as needed)
- Copies of degrees, transcripts, diploma, certifications, awards, etc.

SECTION 6: INTERVIEWS
- List of interviews and background of companies
- Correct names, spelling, and pronunciation of interviewers
- Address, phone number, and directions to interview site
- Possible interview questions with brief responses
- Your own questions
- Match of job description with your skills and experiences
- Summary of interviews (strengths, weaknesses, and questions)
- Record of questions and responses

SECTION 7: FOLLOW-UP
- Copy of thank-you notes
- Copy of follow-up letters
- List of companies to contact again
- Acceptance letters

As you finish each chapter in this book, turn to the last page of each Chapter Review and complete the Your Career Portfolio exercise. This activity is designed to supplement, provide information for, and be included in your own personal career portfolio.

Critical Thinking

In this chapter and throughout the book, you'll read about critical thinking, problem solving, and the ability to make decisions. Why are these terms so important? They are lifelong skills that carry over from school into the world of work. In fact, mastering these skills will also help you in the job-search process.

Critical thinking is required throughout the job search to see problems clearly and to make sound decisions. In your career, it is important that you be able to assess a situation as it really is and not how you wish it were. Critical thinking is a skill that uses facts, logic, and reasoning to help you make decisions and solve problems. A critical thinker is someone who has the willingness and ability to analyze, explore, probe, question, and examine issues before a decision is made. Critical thinkers use facts and reasoning to make sound decisions and solve problems. Critical thinking is a valuable job and life skill that helps us to analyze, reason, question, and suspend judgment until facts are gathered and weighed.

CHARACTERISTICS OF A CRITICAL THINKER:
- Able to suspend judgment
- Willing to analyze and reason
- Able to ask pertinent questions and examine beliefs, assumptions, and opinions against facts
- Has knowledge and awareness of common errors in judgment
- Uses facts and logic instead of biased, illogical, or wishful thinking

Problem Solving

What Is Creative Problem Solving?

Creative problem solving is the ability to explore new approaches, see the problem in a new light, and resolve an issue by using a step-by-step system. Effective problem solving is an essential job skill. In fact, many employers say that problem solving is one of the most desired qualities in employees. How good are you at solving problems? **Practice creative problem solving** by drawing upon your creative resources and critical-thinking skills to help you solve problems, such as how to find a job and make sound decisions. Creative problem solving can help you during the self-assessment stage by clarifying and exploring new approaches. Too many job searchers give up their dreams, ignore their values and interests, and take the traditional, no-risk path to finding a job. Effective problem solving involves both a creative and a systematic approach.

Be creative and have fun. Some people approach problem solving in a creative and playful manner. They use imagination to explore new ideas, try out fresh solutions, and break through traditional thinking. They see problems as puzzles to solve and use creativity to search for innovative approaches. As children, most of us were enthusiastic, inventive, and creative. As we grew up, however, many of us became reluctant to challenge the rules and now may feel overwhelmed by problems or deny that they exist. There is a tendency among many people to play it safe and follow established procedures rather than explore new ideas.

Think of new ways to assess your skills and weaknesses, research, and network. Don't automatically adopt a standard résumé, cover letter, or personal image. Look for creative ways to clearly communicate your strengths while still creating a professional style. Don't just copy rote answers to interview questions. Develop a verbal and nonverbal image that is distinct, sincere, credible, and professional.

Use a logical systematic approach. Problem solving will not be overwhelming if you break the process into several steps.

- Identify the problem.
- Gather information.
- Explore resources.
- Brainstorm alternatives.
- Look at likely consequences.
- Identify necessary resources and tools.
- Develop and implement an action plan.
- Select the best alternative.
- Make a commitment to ensure success.
- Evaluate your decision and progress.
- Modify your plan if necessary.

Decision Making

At each stage of the job search, you will be faced with making decisions. Within each broad decision, there will be smaller decisions and problems to solve. Problem solving and critical thinking are needed for the decision making you'll do as part of your job search. Here are ten questions to consider as you go through the job-search process:

1. Do I know my career objective? (Have I assessed my skills, values, strengths, interests, and abilities?)
2. What information can I gather that would help me decide what jobs are available and to what companies I would like to apply?
3. What traditional or nontraditional resources can help me explore jobs and find out more about certain companies?
4. Have I explored many jobs and companies—small companies, large companies, international companies?
5. If I apply to certain companies, what would be the likely consequence? (Would I be more likely to gain more responsibility in a small company? Would a large company fit my values and needs?)
6. Have I created an outstanding résumé and cover letter that highlights my accomplishments? (What other job-search tools would help me be more successful?)
7. Have I developed an action plan and set goals and daily priorities?
8. Have I narrowed my search to jobs that most match my interests, values, skills, and background?
9. Have I evaluated my job search? (Am I meeting my goals and objectives? Am I getting interviews? Am I getting job offers?)
10. How should I modify my job search in order to ensure success?

In order to solve a problem, you have to make decisions. Therefore, it is important to develop the ability to assess the possible consequences of your actions and become skillful at predicting cause and effect. Critical thinking and effective decision making are essential job skills.

Self-Assessment: A Foundation

Before you even start to look for a job, it is important to decide what you want to do, what you like to do, and what skills and abilities you have to offer. Self-knowledge means understanding your skills, strengths, capabilities, feelings, character, and motivations. It involves serious self-assessment and reflection about what is important to you and the values by which you want to live your life.

How Do I Get Started?

Start self-assessment by focusing on the following questions:

- What are my skills, values, and abilities?
- What do I want to do?
- What is out there?
- What job best matches my skills?
- What tools can help me best market myself?

Know Yourself

"Know thyself," Socrates advised, and self-assessment is truly the foundation for the job-hunting process. The more you know about yourself and your skills, values, attitude, and the type of work you like best, the easier it will be to market your skills. It is indeed the fortunate person who loves what she or he does—and gets paid to do it. Your entire job search will be faster and smoother if you take time for self-assessment:

- Identify your most marketable skills.
- Assess your strengths and weaknesses.
- Review your interests.
- Assess your values and life purpose.
- Assess your self-esteem and attitude.
- Identify creative ways that you solve problems.
- Identify ways to use critical thinking in making decisions.
- Determine your goals.

Net Advantage

Self-Assessment Online If you haven't already discovered the advantages of using the Internet to help your job-search activities, start now. Besides having a multitude of sites where you can post your résumé and get job listings, the Web is a great resource for related job-search tools, such as self-assessment tests.

For self-assessment tests, go to strategies.glencoe.com for links to Web sites that provide free, interactive tests.

What other types of job-search assistance would benefit you?

Think of your life as a series of stepping stones or growth experiences and events that have shaped you into the person you are today. Write the following items on the lines provided. You will discover values, accomplishments, strengths, and weaknesses. This exercise may also help you answer the typical interview question: "Tell me about yourself."

Interests, hobbies, challenges, and lessons that you have learned _____

_____

_____

Jobs in which you learned responsibility and earned money _____

_____

_____

Events that point out strengths and weaknesses _____

_____

_____

Volunteer work and community service _____

_____

Internships _____

_____

Sports, special activities, or clubs _____

_____

_____

Achievements and awards _____

_____

Challenges, setbacks, and disappointments _____

_____

_____

Problems, decisions, and how you handled those decisions _____

_____

_____

What you have learned from your choices _____

_____

_____

Strengths as you see them _____

_____

Weaknesses as you see them _____

_____

_____

Your Database

Take time to organize essential information for your résumé and job application. **Create a database.** Use this form to compile and update your information.

Identification

Last name   First   Middle

Date/Place of birth

Present address

City   State   ZIP

Home phone   Business phone

Previous or permanent address

In case of emergency, notify: Name   Relationship

Address

Home phone   Business phone

Education

Primary—Name/Location

Years attended

High School—Name/Location

Years attended   Date graduated

College/Technical

Years attended   Date graduated

Major

Specific training, seminars

What subjects did you like best and why?

What extracurricular activities were you most involved in and which did you most enjoy?

Did you form good working relationships with teachers, administrators, and students? Explain.

(Note: You may also be requested to provide your Social Security number.)

continued

Work Experience (List your complete employment record.)

Employer—Name/Address
_____

Job title
_____

Duties
_____

Reason for leaving

Internships

Job title
_____

Duties
_____

Name of supervisor
_____

Dates

Volunteer Work

Job title
_____

Duties
_____

Name of supervisor
_____

Dates

Work-Study/Part-Time Jobs

Job title
_____

Supervisor
_____

Dates

Military Experience

Dates
_____

Rank
_____

Duties
_____

Education or training

References

Name
_____

Address

Discover Your Strengths, Weaknesses, and Skills

Another goal of self-assessment is to **discover your strengths, weaknesses, and skills** in an effort to find jobs for which you are best suited. You can also discover areas to improve. Review Your Autobiography and Your Database on pages 10 and 11. What strengths and abilities have helped you so far? What qualities or personal strengths helped you to achieve your accomplishments? Win awards? Succeed in school or in other jobs? When did you make unsound decisions that you later regretted? What did you learn from them? Were there times when you ignored problems or chose the quick solution? Look at these experiences honestly and determine what the real problem was, the weaknesses you observed, and the lessons you learned.

You can also discover your strengths by examining the skills you've acquired throughout your life. Skills can be divided into two broad categories: job skills and transferable skills. Job skills are specialized and generally learned through study, on-the-job training, or job experience. They involve specific knowledge and enable you to perform a specific type of job, such as fixing a car or cooking a meal. Transferable skills are general skills that can be used and transferred to many jobs. Employers look for candidates who have both specific job skills and transferable skills.

Taking Stock

EXERCISE 1.3

What strengths do you bring to your job search? What weaknesses do you need to face and overcome? Make lists of your traits on the lines provided.

Examples of Strengths
Self-starter
Positive attitude
Good communication skills
Willing to learn
Education
Advanced skills

Examples of Weaknesses
Little work experience
Weak presentation skills
Unemployed
Frequent job changer
Little training
Lack of skills

Strengths	Weaknesses	Skills	Interests
_____	_____	_____	_____
_____	_____	_____	_____
_____	_____	_____	_____
_____	_____	_____	_____
_____	_____	_____	_____
_____	_____	_____	_____

Connecting Skills With Interests

Generally, your skills match your interests. There are exceptions, however. You may be very good at computer skills, but sitting at a computer for eight hours leaves you cold. For most people, skills and interests fall into five areas. Knowing your skill area is helpful in narrowing down your choice of career areas. Few people fit into just one area. In fact, you may find you have interests in all five.

1. **People skills**   You like to work with people to help, train, cure, develop, inform, and interact. You are a team player and are sensitive to the feelings of others. *Examples:* counselor or teacher
2. **Information or data skills**   You like to work with data, details, and clerical information. *Examples:* computer programmer or secretary
3. **Mechanical skills**   You prefer to work with machines, tools, plants, animals, and objects or to work outdoors. *Examples:* forester or veterinarian
4. **Creative skills**   You have artistic, creative, or intuitive skills and like unstructured, imaginative, innovative situations. You are a creative problem solver. *Examples:* artist or writer
5. **Motivational skills**   You like to work with people, motivating, persuading, influencing, or leading them for organization or economic gain. You like to solve problems and make decisions in a logical and systematic way. *Examples:* public speaker or administrator

Which of the following job skills and transferable skills interest you the most?

Examples of Job Skills

Working with computers	Wallpapering
Typing	Bookkeeping
Gardening	Cooking
Overhauling an engine	Plumbing
Repairing equipment	Painting a house

Examples of Transferable Skills

Communicating	Persuading
Problem solving	Managing
Critical thinking	Negotiating
Creativity	Analyzing
Interpreting	Using numbers
Organizing	

Personality and Learning Styles

In this chapter, we will explore several ways that you can identify and develop your ability to learn and relate to others. You will accomplish more at school and at work when you understand and **discover your natural personality and learning styles** . There are many theories about personality types and about how we process and learn information.

The concept of temperaments and personality types is not new. Hippocrates (the father of modern medicine) classified people according to personality types. The Enneagram, a study of the nine basic types of people, dates back many centuries.

In 1971 psychologist Carl Jung proposed that people are fundamentally different but also fundamentally alike. He theorized that people are made up of two basic types with specific characteristics:

Extroverts	**Introverts**
Outgoing, social	Quiet, reflective
Energized by people	Energized by time alone
Gregarious	Have fewer, closer friends

Jung also defined two ways in which people gather information. He classified them with certain characteristics:

Sensing	**Intuitive**
Practical	Speculative
Concrete	Abstract
Uses direct experience	Relies on hunches
Sees details	Likes big picture

Jung also defined two types of evaluating information with specific characteristics:

Thinking	**Feeling**
Uses facts and logic	Focuses on personal values and people
Values analysis and principles	Values harmony and wholeness
Lineal	Thrives on praise and is sensitive to criticism
Impersonal and critical	

He further classified two ways of relating to the outer world and assigned them certain characteristics:

Judging	**Perceiving**
Organized	Flexible and spontaneous
Decisive	Tentative
Creates closure	Open-minded
Sets goals	Lets life unfold
Meets deadlines	Procrastinates

Jung suggested that differences and similarities among people could be understood by combining personality preferences. Although people cannot be classified exclusively one way or another, he maintained that they have basic preferences, just as you have a preference for right-handedness or left-handedness. Jung's work inspired Katherine Briggs and her daughter Isabel Briggs-Myers to design the Myers-Briggs Type Inventory. Their work in the 1940s put Jung's type theory into practical use, and since then over 20 million people have completed the MBTI.

Just as there is no one best way to learn, there is no one assessment or inventory that can categorize how you learn. A learning-style assessment is only a guide. However, if you review a variety of assessments, you will build a profile of how you relate to other people and how you process and learn information.

The Four-Grid Personality and Team-Style Profile on pages 20–21 is a simple assessment, yet provides valuable clues for determining how you work and relate to others and learn information. The learning-style assessments offered in this chapter have been adapted from Jung and the Enneagram, and involve 25 years of research. The purpose of any inventory is to provide a guide, not to categorize you into a specific box.

More About Personality Styles

The following four personality and team-style descriptions will help you clarify your preferred style. Keep in mind that your style will vary depending on whether you are an extrovert or introvert.

ANALYZER STYLE

People with a dominant analyzer or thinker style tend to be logical, thoughtful, loyal, exact, dedicated, steady, and organized. They like detail work, follow directions, and work at a steady pace. They prefer to work alone and are independent thinkers. As sensation-type learners, they prefer routine and order. They search for precise details when solving a problem and like to work with established facts rather than look for new possibilities. The key word for this style is *thinking*.

Analyzer's most commonly asked question: *What are the facts?*

Effective Traits	Ineffective Traits
Objective and perceptive	Too cautious and indecisive
Logical	Stubborn
Thorough	Obsessive-compulsive
Dependable	Abrupt and judgmental
Alert to details and observant	Aloof and distant
Disciplined	Unimaginative and serious
Precise	

In the workplace, analyzers work best when they can be organized, logical, and think through ideas. They like to evaluate facts and come to a precise conclusion. They seek intellectual recognition and are disciplined. They like to assimilate information and tend to be more concerned with abstract ideas and concepts than with people. They like to read and listen to what experts think and prefer working alone. Analyzers tend to be introverts.

They relate to bosses and coworkers who are systematic, know their facts, present information in a logical and precise manner, and are on time. They like to work with things and make models of theories.

Possible Majors	Possible Careers
Accounting	Computer programmer
Mathematics	Bookkeeper
Computer programming	Accountant
Research	Insurance agent
Military	Librarian
Manufacturing technology	Technician
	Engineer

RELATOR STYLE

People with a dominant relator style tend to be supportive, cooperative, honest, sensitive, warm, and understanding. They value harmony and are informal, approachable, and tactful. Preferring to work with people, they tend to be good listeners and supportive in groups. They are good at viewing situations from many different perspectives. The key word for this style is *feeling*.

Relator's most commonly asked question: *Why is this important and how does it relate to me?*

Effective Traits	Ineffective Traits
Understanding and helpful	Unassertive
Generous	Resentful
Pleasant and tactful	Insecure
Appreciative	Passive and indirect
Sensitive and attuned to others	Forgetful
Supportive	Procrastinates

In the workplace relators work best when they are in jobs where they can be helpful and that add meaning and clarity to their lives. Preferring to function in the here and now, they like working in teams. They want to feel useful and like to listen, share, and be involved. They relate to bosses and coworkers who are warm and sociable, tell interesting stories, and are loyal, and are approachable. They like to feel accepted.

Possible Majors	Possible Careers
Counseling	Counselor
Social work	Elementary school teacher
Elementary school education	Nurse
Home economics	Therapist
Nursing	Social worker
Human resource management	Home health caregiver
	Physical therapist
	Personnel manager

CREATOR STYLE

People with a dominant creator style are innovative, flexible, spontaneous, creative, romantic, and idealistic. They are intuitive and love drama, style, ideas, and imaginative design. They like the abstract, as well as fresh ideas and concepts, and have passion for their work. When they are involved in a creative process, they may work alone and can work on creative projects for hours. The key word for this style is *intuitive*.

Creator's most commonly asked question: *What if?*

Effective Traits	Ineffective Traits
Imaginative	Unrealistic
Innovative	Self-absorbed
Enthusiastic	Unreliable
Expressive	Inconsistent and unfocused
Creative and curious	Impulsive
Visionary	Self-destructive
Idealistic	
Charming and fun-loving	
Quick and confident	

In the workplace creators enjoy work that is creative. They can see the big picture and like to start up projects. However, once a project is up and running, they may lose interest. They do not like routine. They like to talk about dreams and visions. They relate best to enthusiastic bosses who have a passion for their work and coworkers who are imaginative, flexible, present interesting ideas, and are open-minded. Often good public speakers, they can be creative and persuasive.

Possible majors	Possible Careers
Art	Writer
Creative writing	Cartoonist
Public speaking	Politician
Theatre	Musician and composer
Music	Artist
Design	Public speaker
Science	Journalist
	Craft worker
	Landscape designer
	Florist
	Small business owner
	Scientist

DIRECTOR STYLE

People with a dominant director style tend to be confident, practical, self-directed, energetic, dynamic, decisive, risk-takers, and results-oriented. They are decisive, efficient, assertive, and competitive; prefer action, act with authority; like to solve problems; and are self-starters. They like to be the leader of groups. The key word for this style is *doing*.

Director's most commonly asked question: *How can this be applied?*

Effective Traits	Ineffective Traits
Confident	Dominating and overpowering
Results-oriented	Controlling
Assertive	Overly competitive
Doers	Vain and pretentious
Hands-on	Aggressive
Risk-takers	Uncaring and self-centered
Effective leaders	

In the workplace directors like hands-on, direct experience and prefer to try things out for themselves. They are often self-employed, entrepreneurs, or business executives. They like jobs where they can solve problems and be physically active and challenged, preferring hands-on activities, the outdoors, and leadership roles. They relate to bosses and coworkers who are clear, to the point, on time, results oriented, and organized. They like tasks that are relevant and practical. Preferring to be active and involved, they want to see the results of their work. They tend to be disciplined and motivated.

Possible Majors	Possible Careers
Business	Manager
Outdoor recreation and administration	Small business owner
	Entrepreneur
Small business management	Sales manager
Sports	Lawyer
Natural resource management	Police officer and detective
	Athlete
	Consultant
	Politician
	Public relations specialist
	Salesperson
	Marketing specialist

The Four-Grid Personality and Team-Style Profile

The following questions are designed to indicate your preferences regarding working with others, making decisions, and learning new information. Read each question with its four possible answers, then rank the answers as follows:

4 – the answer MOST like you

3 – the answer second most like you

2 – the answer third most like you

1 – the answer LEAST like you

1. I learn best when the material is
   ____ a. systematically organized.
   ____ b. fun and people oriented.
   ____ c. interesting and creative.
   ____ d. hands-on and experiential.

2. When I'm at my best, I'm described as
   ____ a. organized, studious, logical, and objective.
   ____ b. understanding, loyal, charming, and harmonious.
   ____ c. imaginative, optimistic, open-minded, and creative.
   ____ d. confident, assertive, practical, and results oriented.

3. I respond best to instructors and bosses who
   ____ a. are consistent and clear with me about what they expect.
   ____ b. expect me to be involved, active, and get results.
   ____ c. encourage creativity and flexibility.
   ____ d. show appreciation and are friendly.

4. When working in a group, I tend to value
   ____ a. objectivity and correctness.
   ____ b. consensus and harmony.
   ____ c. originality and risk taking.
   ____ d. efficiency and results.

5. I am most comfortable with people who are
   ____ a. informed, serious, and accurate.
   ____ b. supportive, appreciative, and friendly.
   ____ c. creative, unique, and idealistic.
   ____ d. productive, realistic, and dependable.

6. Generally, I am
   ____ a. methodical, efficient, trustworthy, and accurate.
   ____ b. cooperative, genuine, gentle, and modest.
   ____ c. high-spirited, adventurous, easily bored, and dramatic.
   ____ d. straightforward, conservative, responsible, and decisive.

7. When making a decision, I'm generally concerned with
   _____ a. collecting information and facts to determine the right solution.
   _____ b. finding the solution that pleases others and myself.
   _____ c. brainstorming creative solutions that feel intuitively correct.
   _____ d. quickly choosing the most practical and realistic solution.

8. In one word, you could describe me as
   _____ a. analytical.
   _____ b. caring.
   _____ c. innovative.
   _____ d. productive.

9. I excel at
   _____ a. reaching accurate and logical conclusions.
   _____ b. being cooperative and respecting people's feelings.
   _____ c. finding hidden connections and creative outcomes.
   _____ d. making realistic, practical, and timely decisions.

10. When learning at school or on the job, I enjoy
    _____ a. gathering facts, technical information, and being objective.
    _____ b. making personal connections, being supportive, and working in groups.
    _____ c. exploring new possibilities, creative tasks, and flexibility.
    _____ d. producing results, problem solving, and making decisions.

Add the totals for each letter answer:

	Answer a	**Answer b**	**Answer c**	**Answer d**
1.	_____	_____	_____	_____
2.	_____	_____	_____	_____
3.	_____	_____	_____	_____
4.	_____	_____	_____	_____
5.	_____	_____	_____	_____
6.	_____	_____	_____	_____
7.	_____	_____	_____	_____
8.	_____	_____	_____	_____
9.	_____	_____	_____	_____
10.	_____	_____	_____	_____
Totals	_____	_____	_____	_____
	Analyzer	**Relator**	**Creator**	**Director**

Scoring: To determine your style, add up the total in each column. If you have the highest number in the *Answer a* column, you are an analyzer. If you have the highest number in the *Answer b* column, you are a relator. If you have the highest number in the *Answer c* column, you are a creator. If you have the highest number in the *Answer d* column, you are a director. You may be fairly close in two areas, but most people tend to fall into one or two areas rather than all four. Remember that all inventories only provide clues. People change over time and react differently in different situations.

More About Learning Styles

Each student has his or her own unique set of abilities, perceptions, and needs, and so learning styles may vary widely. Knowing your preferred learning style can increase your effectiveness in school and on the job, as well as enhance your self-esteem. (See **Exercise 1.5.**)

VISUAL LEARNERS

If you are a visual learner, you prefer to see information and read material. You learn more effectively with pictures, graphs, illustrations, diagrams, time lines, photos, pie charts, and visual design. You like to contemplate concepts and summarize information in writing. Make certain your notes highlight main points and use different color markers. Use arrows, pictures, and bullets to highlight points. You will want to make certain that you have important information in writing. When you take study breaks, look at art, read a chapter of something light, or write a letter. Visual learners are often holistic and reflective learners.

AUDITORY LEARNERS

If you are primarily an auditory learner, you rely on your hearing sense and are verbal. You like lectures, tapes, music, and listening to information. You will want to set up study teams, have phone conversations, and meet with people to discuss what you have learned. You like to talk and recite and summarize information aloud. You may want to create rhymes out of words and play music that helps you concentrate. When you take study breaks, listen to music to relax.

KINESTHETIC LEARNERS

Almost everyone learns better when they do a task. Whether you are primarily a visual or auditory learner, you can enhance your learning potential by making learning more physical. Collect samples, write out information, spend time outdoors, and actually relate to the material that you are learning. For example, try relating abstract material to something concrete in nature.

Using Both Sides of Your Brain

We have learned that people have different personality and learning styles. People also differ in which side of the brain they tend to use for acquiring new information. Research indicates that the brain classifies information with two systems or "sides" of the brain. The left side is language based; the right side is visually based. Psychologists and neurologists suggest that some people are left-brain dominant and use a logical, rational, and detailed approach, while others are right-brain dominant and use an intuitive, insightful, and holistic approach to solving problems and learning new information. Knowing which side of the brain you are inclined to use makes it easier to understand and use your natural learning and working styles. It's possible, however, to nurture both sides of the brain and integrate the best of both.

Your Learning Style Inventory

Circle either **a** or **b** to determine your main learning preference:

1. I learn best when I
   a. see information.
   b. hear information.

2. For pleasure and to relax, I love to
   a. read.
   b. listen to music and tapes.

3. To remember a ZIP code, I like to
   a. write it down several times.
   b. say it out loud several times.

4. In a classroom, I learn best when
   a. I have a good textbook, visual aids, and written information.
   b. the instructor is interesting and clear.

5. I study for a test when
   a. I read my notes and write a summary. I often study alone.
   b. I review my notes out loud and talk to others. I like group work.

6. I have
   a. a strong fashion sense and pay attention to visual details.
   b. fun telling stories and jokes.

7. I like to
   a. write on place mats and napkins in restaurants.
   b. talk out loud when working on a math problem.

8. I often
   a. remember faces, but not names.
   b. remember names, but not faces.

9. I remember best
   a. when I read instructions and use visual images to remember.
   b. when I listen to instructions and use rhyming words to remember.

10. When I give directions I might say,
    a. "Turn right at the yellow house and left when you see the large oak tree. Do you see what I mean?"
    b. "Turn right, go three blocks, and left at Buttermilk Lane. OK? Got that? Do you hear what I'm saying?"

Total answers for **a** _____
Total answers for **b** _____

Scoring: The highest total for **a** indicates a visual learning style.
The highest total for **b** indicates an auditory learning style.

Exploring Majors and Careers

Self-assessment is key in determining and clarifying your interests, values, skills, and abilities, and then aligning them with your college major and career goals. Many students change majors several times. Knowing what you do well and what you enjoy doing will help you choose the right major. The assessment inventories in this chapter can provide guides to exploring majors and careers that best match your personality. Explore other personality inventories as well.

Tips for Choosing a Major

1. **Experience general education classes.** General education (G.E.) classes are a great way to experience a variety of disciplines and professors and, at the same time, meet college requirements for graduation.

2. **Perform self-assessment.** Spend time assessing your interests, values, strengths, likes, dislikes, abilities, skills, and personality. Take various personality inventories. Your campus career center may provide these assessments. For example, the Strong Interest Inventory matches your interests with careers.

3. **Take introductory classes.** Most departments have orientation classes that review specific majors and also discuss possible career options. Look through the catalog and circle classes and descriptions that appeal to you. Do you find a common thread in your choices?

4. **Talk with instructors and your advisor.** Instructors from various departments and your academic advisor will be glad to discuss majors and possible careers with you.

5. **Talk with students.** Most majors have clubs you can attend to get more information about a major. Fellow students may also be eager to discuss their majors. Ask them why they like the major they chose and what careers they plan to explore.

6. **Talk with professionals.** Talk with professionals in various fields in which you are interested and discuss the related majors. Ask them what they like and dislike about their jobs and what classes they would have taken in college if they could go back.

7. **Explore campus resources and get the facts.** The library, advising center, and career center are tremendous resources for information on various majors and careers. Find occupational facts and explore what careers are new. Make an appointment with a career counselor. Also, most campuses have a majors fair and a career day.

8. **Get job experience.** A part-time job, volunteer work, or internship can provide valuable experience and help you determine if a certain major or career path is right for you.

9. **Explore other options.** Many campuses offer an interdisciplinary major that allows students to create their own majors. Most campuses also offer a general liberal arts major. These majors are ideal for students who find it difficult to choose just one traditional major.

STRATEGIES Online

Remember, one of your best resources is strategies.glencoe.com

10. **Set goals.** Don't allow the fact that you are undecided to get in the way of setting goals. A general liberal studies degree or a degree in any major is valuable both personally and professionally. Getting a college degree, whether at a two-year or four-year college, is a worthwhile career and life goal. It will help you in a variety of jobs, and you will have the option of either transferring to a four-year college or going on to graduate school.

Defining Your Values

Self-assessment also helps you define your values. Values are the emotional reasons for how we commit our time and energy. Values are the *whys* of life and are what make a job fulfilling, satisfying, and inherently valuable to you. Values need to be given high priority in deciding on a career or a job. Some people value freedom, time off, or status more than a high salary. No one can give you the *right* values. Only you can determine what is right for you. Do you prefer jobs that allow you to:

- Help others?
- Make lots of money?
- Have freedom?
- Live where you want to?
- Have flexible work hours?
- Be creative?
- Supervise others?
- Work alone?
- Work with details?
- See the big picture?
- Take risks?
- Work outdoors?
- Achieve fulfillment and potential?
- Use power and authority?
- Gain recognition?
- Solve problems?
- Learn new skills?
- Be a recognized expert?
- Spend a lot of time with your family?

To clarify your values, take a moment to review the key points in your life that you wrote about earlier. Look at **Exercise 1.1** Your Autobiography on page 10, and study the situations in which you achieved recognition or pushed yourself to achieve a goal. When you have reviewed your life for patterns, consider these questions:

- What experiences brought me the most joy and satisfaction?
- What values are most important in my job?
- Is it important to make a contribution to the world or to help society in my job?
- Do I want to help people by working in small groups or directly on a one-to-one basis?
- Is it important for me to make decisions or influence people?
- Is interesting, creative work essential to my happiness, or can I find my creative expression outside my job?
- Do I need security, independence, variety, prestige, excitement, artistic involvement?
- Do I want job security or am I a risk-taker?

Stress Savers

Focus on the Employer

Presenting yourself as an asset to an employer is a good way to get and keep the job you want. You can quickly focus on what an employer wants through self-assessment by asking yourself these questions:

- What do I have to offer an employer?
- What could I do to benefit a company?
- What do I have that satisfies a need for a company?

Exploring Careers and Making a Match

Now that you have assessed your interests, skills, strengths, and values, it is time to explore careers. Since you will be spending much of your time at work, it is important that you choose a career that you'll love and in which you can succeed. (See **Figure 1.1** and **Appendix 2** for examples of different occupations.) In Chapter 2, researching jobs and networking will be covered. Both can help you explore the careers that are growing as well as the skills and qualities necessary to succeed.

Figure 1.1

Growing Occupations The occupations on this chart are expected to account for 38 percent of all new jobs requiring at least a bachelor's degree. *Do your interests and skills match any of these careers?*

Fastest Growing Jobs (1998–2008)

Occupation	Percent increase	Job number increase (thousands)
Computer engineers	108	323
Computer systems analysts	94	577
Database administrators	77	67
Physician assistants	48	32
Residential counselors	46	88
Engineering, natural science, and computer and information systems managers	43	142
Securities, commodities, and financial services sales agents	41	124
Speech-language pathologists and audiologists	38	40
Social workers	36	218
Biological scientists	35	28
Occupational therapists	34	25
Physical therapists	34	41
Teachers, special education	34	137
Medical and health services managers	33	74
Computer programmers	30	191
Management analysts	28	98
Interior designers	27	15
Designers, except interior designers	27	91
Teachers, preschool	27	92
Electrical and electronics engineers	26	93

SOURCE: *Fall 2000 Occupational Outlook Quarterly*

The Fastest Growing Jobs

1. **Information Technology** The entire field of information technology will offer the fastest growing occupations. Computer engineers and scientists have grown by 112 percent since the year 2000. There will also be a growing number of opportunities in network services or systems. For example, one hot job will be for an online multi-media content developer. This is a professional who will enhance products with textual, visual, and audio life.

   Since the year 2000, software programming jobs have grown by more than 30 percent to more than 700,000. Programmers are needed in almost all industries to program a variety of systems. As CD-ROMs continue to be the fastest growing segment of the $20 billion-a-year software industry, programmers with multimedia training will be highly prized.

   A systems analyst is a programmer who specializes in corporate databases to project future needs, solve problems, and reach goals. Since the year 2000, the number of systems analysts has increased by over 100 percent.

2. **Electronic Communications** Professionals, such as online services marketers, will work in the field to train users with the software and to monitor customer relations. This will be a growing field as electronic communications continues to grow. Related careers include customer-support jobs and sales.

3. **Health Care Professionals** Health care has grown by almost 47 percent since 2000 and will move out of hospitals and into community- and home-based settings. Physical therapists, geriatric care managers, and nurse practitioners or physician assistants (registered nurses with advanced training) will be growing specialties. The field of physical therapy has increased dramatically. Related careers include athletic and physical trainers and exercise physiologists. There will also be a growing need for speech-language pathologists, audiologists, and occupational therapists. The need for health assistance for an aging population will also increase. Geriatric care managers are social workers or nurses who work for families to provide care for the elderly. Since 2000, almost 36 million people have become 65 or older.

4. **Human Services** The helping professions have also increased. Corporate human service occupations include human resources managers, professionals, labor-relations specialists, employee assistance program counselors, and marketing, advertising, and planned-giving officers. These professionals offer assessment skills and expertise in treatment, training, compensation, and diversity management. Other industry focus areas will include customer service, public relations, and fund-raising.

5. **Teachers** Part of the growth in the helping professions will be generated by the need for teachers at the elementary and secondary levels.

Special-education teachers will be most in demand to work with children who have developmental disabilities or physical or emotional impairments. Other growing occupations in the helping professions field will include psychologists, counselors, occupational therapists, and social workers.

6. **Financial Services** The investment service area will see a growth in such occupations as portfolio managers, trust managers, bank financial-service marketers, and independent financial planners. Professional women are the fastest growing group of investors in the personal-finance industry.

7. **Travel and Tourism** The travel and tourism industry is also expected to increase. There will be a growing need for hotel managers, leisure-time managers, destination marketers, tourism managers, tour guides, and travel agents.

Career Directions

BusinessWeek

Résumés: Beware of Getting "Creative"

Officially, the average period a person is unemployed right now is 13.1 weeks, up from 12.1 weeks a year ago, according to the Bureau of Labor Statistics.

This doesn't mean that your only hope is to don a hair net and flip burgers. But you must be prepared financially for many weeks, if not many months, of pounding the pavement. "You want to be able to make a good decision relative to your career change," says Robert Veasey, a certified financial planner. "A lot of times, when people get laid off, they take the first thing they can get because they don't have a cushion."

Of course, you won't need as much cash in the bank if you can get a new job quickly.

In this tight labor market, networking is more important than ever because with fewer positions to go around, companies are less likely to hire an unknown.

Brushing up on your skills, or developing new ones, is another way of making yourself stand out.

At least 50% of your time should be spent talking to people who might actually be able to hire you, says Louise Kursmark, President of Best Impression Career Services. An additional 20% would be well spent networking with associations, while no more than 15% should be focused on Internet searches, and no more than 15% talking to recruiters. "You have to balance things that are easier with things that are harder."

By Eric Wahlgren

Excerpted from October 30, 2001, issue of BusinessWeek Online by special permission, copyright © 2000-2001, by The McGraw-Hill Companies, Inc.

Career Case Study Maria Costanza, a Web designer, recently experienced the effects of downsizing and was laid off. She has an excellent track record designing for several Internet companies. However, after 11 weeks of sending her résumé to dozens of companies found on the Web, she's received little response. ***What suggestions would you give to Maria to increase her chances of getting more responses from prospective employers?***

8. **Environment** Those in industry will continue to hire consultants and engineers to help them comply with environmental regulations. Such occupations are environmental engineers, managers specializing in environmental ethics, and geographic information systems practitioners.

9. **Law** Growth occupations in law include paralegals, legal assistants, law-firm marketers, labor and employment lawyers, property lawyers, and environmental attorneys. More companies are hiring attorneys to translate complex labor laws and comply with new regulations.

10. **Corrections** Jobs for corrections and security professionals will increase to help prevent crime. These careers will include corrections officers, counselors, health care providers, computer-security specialists, high-tech security guards, and white-collar crime law-enforcement experts.

Developing Personal Qualities, Attitude, and Self-Esteem

People are hired for many reasons. Sometimes candidates demonstrate specific skills that the organization needs. In other cases, the employer wants a person who can solve problems; make sound decisions; is a team player; or has a motivated, enthusiastic attitude. Personal qualities—such as a positive attitude, initiative, honesty, willingness to work hard, loyalty, creativity, the ability to solve problems, and willingness to learn—can be just as important as education or technical skills. Chapter 7 will examine personal qualities for career success.

The Role of Self-Esteem

How you feel about yourself can affect you at every stage of the job-search process and can directly affect your success on the job.

Characteristics of people with high self-esteem may include:
- A willingness to learn new skills.
- Self-trust.
- The ability to be self-directed.
- A sense of competency.
- A resistance to dependencies and addictions.
- The ability to cope with stress, adversity, and problems.
- A basic sense of well-being and happiness.

Characteristics of people with low self-esteem may include:
- A basic feeling of unworthiness and lack of self-respect.
- The inability to form solid, healthy relationships.
- Vulnerability to peer pressure and lack of inner trust.
- Possible tendency to abuse drugs or alcohol.
- Lack of confidence in ability to perform in school or at work.

Knowing yourself through self-assessment can help you set goals and work out a plan for learning new skills and overcoming weaknesses. It will also prepare you for the task of writing your résumé and shining during the interview. You will be able to organize and give structure to your job-search process, putting yourself in a good position to creatively explore options and begin using critical thinking to help make solid choices.

Creating a Positive Attitude

You may see the job-search process as a boring, frustrating, and discouraging process that you will drop as soon as you get the first job that comes along. What if you approached the job search with a sense of adventure and could see it as an ongoing process that involves exploring, investigating, and discovering more about yourself and your career?

Examine your attitude. If your attitude is negative, it could sabotage your chances of job success. It could also decrease your energy so that you become discouraged. If your attitude is positive, people will want to brainstorm job opportunities with you and will feel good about recommending you for jobs. You will also have the strength to handle setbacks.

A positive attitude is fundamental to job success. Being able to project confidence and enthusiasm, and have assertive communication skills will make an enormous difference in how others see you. These are the qualities that you have some control over and that can work for you. It is important to try to overcome the frustrations and discouragement that are part of the job-search process and of life itself. Two strategies that can help make a big difference in your attitude and self-esteem are self-talk and imagery.

Self-Talk and Imagery

What you say to yourself all day and the mental images that you create have a powerful effect on your attitude. Positive self-talk and images can improve your attitude and self-image, and can empower you. At worst, negative self-talk can send you into a self-sabotaging downward spiral. For example, you may wake up one morning and say, "I don't want to prepare for this job interview. I am very shy and uncomfortable in interviews. I know I'll blow it. It's no use anyway. There are no good jobs out there. I might as well go back to sleep."

Self-talk is often accompanied by images. In the above example, you may see yourself failing in a job interview, and you may actually get butterflies just thinking about talking with employers. Imagery is just that—visualizing yourself in certain situations, talking and behaving in either a positive or negative way. These images can help produce confidence, enthusiasm, and success, or they can focus on fear, worry, and failure.

As with self-talk, your mental images can go on unnoticed unless you consciously stop and assess them.

You can practice choosing positive thoughts, self-talk, and imagery, and improve your attitude. By changing your behavior, you can take charge of your life and career. Positive self-talk and images can help you overcome doubt, increase your confidence and self-esteem, and help you focus on reaching your goals.

Improving Your Self-Talk, Self-Image, and Imagery

EXERCISE 1.6

Most people are unaware of the amount of negative thoughts, self-talk, and images that go through their minds each day. For now, don't try to change your thoughts; just observe and record them in a detached manner.

1. Assess your self-talk and imagery for a few hours. On a separate sheet of paper, write down all your negative and positive self-talk and imagery. Then translate your self-talk and imagery from negative to positive. For example:

    Negative: I will never get a job. The economy is bad, and there are too many people to compete with. I am afraid of rejection.

    Positive: I am confident and self-assured. I am taking time every day to assess my values, abilities, skills, and likes, and to explore careers.

2. Write down what attitudes or personality traits you would consider important for success in a job. By changing your attitude, you can produce the results you want in all areas of your life.

3. Review Your Autobiography on page 10 for moments in your life when you were positive, enthusiastic, and motivated. When did you push yourself to achieve a goal? Perhaps it was achieving an award in speech, debate, or drama club; running for school office; participating in Girl or Boy Scouts; or excelling in a sporting event. Write down responses to the following:

   * Describe how you felt, your body language, self-talk, and so on.
   * What do you consider to be your most valuable attitudes and personal qualities?
   * List times when you've demonstrated a few of the above personal qualities. Which of these attitudes and personal qualities would you use in your ideal job?
   * What is your attitude toward work? What do you like and dislike about work?

Once you start exploring the good things about having a job, you can become clear on why you want a job.

Image Counts

As the old saying goes, "You never get a second chance to create a good first impression." It only takes a few minutes for others to form either a positive or negative impression of you, and careers can be made and lost based on first impressions. Therefore, throughout the job-search process, you will want to create an image that projects a confident, neat, well-groomed, friendly, and professional impression. Your appearance, dress, body language, tone of voice, and eye contact all combine to communicate your style. Never underestimate the power of image.

Take time to honestly assess your appearance and image. Appearance refers to the total visual impression you make and takes into account clothing, shoes, hair, accessories, nails, makeup, eye contact, body type, posture, body language, smells, and color. If you are going to school, you may not see the need to start thinking about image. No one expects you to dress as if you were a top executive. However, you can dress for school and still begin to build a professional wardrobe. If you are working part-time, have an internship, are in a co-op program, or even do volunteer work, you should dress in a professional and appropriate style.

By assessing your image, you can be more aware of what image you are projecting. Review **Figure 1.2** and ask yourself these questions:

- Is my clothing professional and appropriate for the job? Do I have one basic suit or suitable outfit for interviews?
- Are my clothing and shoes neat, clean, stylish, and of good quality?
- Are my nails, hairstyle, makeup, perfume/cologne, and color scheme, flattering, neat, professional looking, and in good taste?
- Are accessories, such as jewelry, ties, and pen, professional looking?

Chapter 5 will discuss more about the importance of first impressions.

Figure 1.2

Dressing for Success Creating a positive visual impression can communicate your professional attitude to an employer. *What else do you imply by presenting an appropriate image to an employer?*

The Best Impression	
Do	**Don't**
Wash and comb you hair.	Don't use excessive hair spray.
Shower and use deodorant.	Don't use perfume or aftershave cologne.
Trim and groom fingernails.	Don't wear bright nail polish.
Shave.	Don't wear heavy makeup.
Wear clean, newer shoes.	Don't wear sandals.
Wear conservative and appropriate clothing, neatly pressed.	Don't wear clothes that wrinkle easily.

STAYING POWER

Maintaining a Positive Attitude

The job-hunting process can be a lengthy and difficult task that needs total commitment. Few job hunters expect the amount of work and time required for a successful job search. Many people do not realize that looking for a job is a full-time job. Be prepared for moments of self-doubt and discouragement.

You may become discouraged if you know of someone who was hired even though he or she was less qualified than other applicants. You may not have been hired for a job even though you were very well qualified. You may have also noticed that people are sometimes promoted or not promoted based on reasons other than ability or competence. Keep in mind that some people seem to have a knack for creating great résumés. Other people may be able to create a spark during the interview process, despite being weak on experience.

Some people keep a job for years, until they decide to leave, while others are forced into the job-hunting process overnight through no fault of their own. With corporate reorganizations and reduced profits for many small businesses, it's reasonable to expect more job seekers in the market with more competition.

Try This… Starting the day off right is one way to deal with times when you may be losing energy or you feel discouraged. Using an affirmation or positive statement to help you reset your mind can produce positive results. One of the most effective times to use imaging and positive self-talk is when you first awaken.

- Set the alarm a few minutes early to allow time to gradually wake up.
- Review your priorities for the day as you awaken and see yourself achieving them. For example, see yourself going through the day accomplishing your main goals with confidence and calm.
- Write affirmations before you start the day, such as "I can see the importance of each step in the job-search process."

CHAPTER 1 Review

Skill Check Recap

- Create a career portfolio.
- Practice creative problem solving.
- Start self-assessment.
- Create a database.
- Discover your strengths, weaknesses, and skills.
- Discover your natural personality and learning styles.
- Examine your attitude.

Self-Check List

Keep track of your progress. Read the following and mark *yes* or *no*.

	Yes	No
I have thought about the kind of job I want.	____	____
I have assessed the skills I have.	____	____
I have assessed my personal qualities and attitude.	____	____
I have assessed my values and what is most important to me in life.	____	____
I have taken time to dream about the job I would really like.	____	____
I have assessed my interests.	____	____
I have assessed my problem-solving abilities.	____	____
I have assessed my education and training and the areas in which I excel.	____	____
I have assessed my work experience and the jobs I have enjoyed most.	____	____
I have assessed the areas in which I need to improve and learn new skills.	____	____
I have assessed my sense of self-worth.	____	____
I have adopted ways to increase my self-esteem.	____	____

Review Questions

1. What are the three stages of the job-search process?

   _____

   _____

2. What are the seven sections of a career portfolio?

   _____

   _____

3. What is creative problem solving?

   _____

   _____

4. What are the characteristics of a critical thinker?

   _____

   _____

5. What are the first five steps in logical problem solving?

   _____

   _____

6. Why is it important to do self-assessment before choosing a major?

   _____

   _____

7. What are the four main personality styles?

   _____

   _____

8. Why is self-esteem important in your job search?

   _____

   _____

Critical Thinking

9. Reread the characteristics of people with high self-esteem. How do you think these characteristics translate into on-the-job excellence?

   _____

   _____

Cooperative Learning

10. Work in groups of two or three students. Each group will choose one of the ten fastest growing fields. In your group, discuss, brainstorm, and develop answers to these questions:

    a. What college major(s) are most suitable for this field?

    b. Which one of the four personality types best suits this job field?

    c. How would good self-esteem be an asset in this field?

    d. Discuss your findings with the entire class.

Making Career Decisions

Jason has always loved working with people. He is an extroverted, action-oriented person. He's also a good organizer and leader. Jason likes to motivate others and manage events and activities. He coordinated a campaign in high school that resulted in his being elected president of his senior class. He also loves the outdoors and is an avid rock climber.

Jason recently entered a small private college with a major in business. His father operates an accounting business in a large city, and Jason will have a job waiting for him when he finishes college. However, after taking several general education courses and reflecting on his interests, goals, and values, Jason has realized that he does not want to sit behind a desk every day. Because he enjoys the outdoors, he's now considering a career in forestry, but he still wants to make a good living and likes the challenge of the business world.

You can see Jason's problem. Should he get an accounting degree that would ensure him a good job and please his parents, or should he explore a job related to forestry?

Problem Solving   The following ten questions are designed to help solve problems and make sound decisions. You can use these questions to find solutions to your own problems. Put yourself in Jason's place and consider these questions from his point of view.

- What is the problem?
- Do I have enough information?
- Can I make the decision by myself?
- Have I brainstormed alternatives?
- Have I looked at likely consequences?
- Have I identified all the resources and tools needed?
- Have I developed and implemented an action plan?
- Have I identified the best solution?
- Have I assessed the results?
- Have I modified the plan, if necessary?

What solution would you suggest to Jason? Write your answer on the lines below.

_____

_____

_____

_____

_____

STRATEGIES Online

Find out more about making career decisions by visiting this book's Web site at strategies. glencoe.com

Your *Career* Portfolio

Assessing Careers

Complete the following exercises to help you discover, self-assess, and choose a career path. Add this page to your career portfolio.

- Go to the library or career center and find ten careers that interest you. List them below. Then use the Internet to explore one or more.

    _____   _____

    _____   _____

    _____   _____

    _____   _____

    _____   _____

- List your skills and interests. Then list several careers that match these skills and interests. Create names for careers if they are unusual.

Skills/Interests	Possible Careers
_____	_____
_____	_____
_____	_____
_____	_____
_____	_____

- Review your list of skills and interests. What stands out?

    _____

    _____

    _____

    _____

- Describe an ideal career that involves the skills you enjoy using the most. Include the location of this job and the kinds of people with whom you would work (e.g., coworkers, customers).

    _____

    _____

    _____

    _____

Exploring and Networking

Winning Points

- Explore traditional and nontraditional methods.
- Build your confidence and sense of worth.
- Create a network of professional and personal contacts.
- Be persistent and positive.
- Set goals and daily priorities.

Introduction

Just as you learned the value of self-assessment, you will now learn how to take action. We will look at specific strategies for setting goals, which will help you focus your job search and clarify your career path. Then we will explore researching jobs and creative ways to find jobs, using the following traditional and nontraditional resources:

- Newspapers
- Job-Search Web sites
- TV and radio
- Campus recruiters
- Employment agencies
- Library
- Phone book
- Community
- Organizations
- Observation

Finally, you'll learn about the importance of internships and networking. You'll see that networking is not only a part of job research but also an ongoing career skill that can enhance your personal and professional lives.

Chapter 2 Objectives

After you have completed this chapter, you will be able to:

- Explain the importance of setting goals
- Describe how to set goals
- Explain how to research jobs in a traditional way
- Explain how to research jobs in a nontraditional way
- Identify how to creatively solve problems
- Explain how to network

Focusing Your Job Search by Setting Goals

In Chapter 1 you assessed your strengths, weaknesses, attitudes, needs, values, and interests. You learned various strategies for creatively solving problems and understood the role of critical thinking in decision making. You also learned how knowing your learning and personality styles can guide your decisions. Now you are ready to focus on your job search.

Some job searchers feel discouraged, even though they have been working hard and are involved in lots of activities, because their efforts have been scattered and disorganized, producing few results. A major reason some job searchers become sidetracked and discouraged is lack of goals. They may not have devoted much time to thinking about what they would really like to do. They may have drifted into a major or career as a result of a part-time job, joined the family business, or pursued a certain career because of money or status. Other people may resist setting goals because they think goals will lock them into certain decisions. It is important to remember that a goal is simply a guide. A goal is like a road map: It gives you a sense of direction. You can change your direction and destination at any time. You will find it easier to keep a positive attitude and maintain high energy if you have a focus for your job search and you set immediate and long-term goals.

Goals can help you to:
- Clarify what you want and determine specific results.
- Gain a sense of direction, energy, and focus.
- Gain a feeling of accomplishment and competency.
- Produce results by doing first things first.
- Have a more positive attitude and increased self-esteem.

Goal-Setting Steps

1. **Determine what you want to accomplish.** The first step is to decide what you want to accomplish. Goals should be put in writing, prioritized, and reviewed often. A goal that is not written is just a wish or dream. Write a specific job objective that you want to achieve now. Then expand your thinking and set long-term goals. Start with 1-year, 5-year, and 10-year goals. Then write down your lifetime goals. Remember, these can be revised and changed as your circumstances, experience, opportunities, and preferences change.

2. **Establish a time line.** Next, allocate a certain amount of time for both your long- and short-term goals. Set a year-long time line and monthly and weekly target dates. Creating a time line for accomplishing your goals helps align everyday actions with your long-term goals and your life's purpose. It also helps you visualize what needs to be done and when it should be accomplished.

3. **Set Priorities.** To be a successful with your job search, you need to learn to do first things first. Setting daily priorities by using a "to-do list" will help you put abstract goals into immediate action. (See **Figure 2.1**.) Begin each day with a list of tasks to be achieved. Review your list to make certain the tasks are related to your goals and are not just frantic activity. You need to allocate enough time for tasks to ensure that you are doing important things, things that lead to accomplishing your goals. Prioritize each task by assigning it a #1 for most important, #2 for next important, and so on. Make it a daily habit to start with first things first and work through your list.

Your To-Do List

Job Search To-Do List

Goals	Priorities

Continuing-Attention Items

To See or Call

Awaiting Developments

What	Who	When

Figure 2.1
Daily Priorities Organize your job-search goals and tasks for each day. *Which tasks should you complete first?*

4. **Assess results.** Periodically evaluate your progress. Assess the results of your activity and determine what factors are contributing to your success and what factors are wasting time. Are you spending your high-energy time on your most important goals, or are you doing the easiest tasks first and spending leftover time on high-priority tasks? You may need to reassess your day and adopt new, positive habits that will help you to overcome procrastination and focus on your goals. By applying the following goal-setting tips, you may be able to achieve the results you want.

GOAL-SETTING TIPS

- Take time to plan and reflect.
- Put your goals in writing.
- Write specific goals.
- Write both short- and long-term goals.
- Assess the benefits of reaching your goals.
- Determine which goals overlap.
- Determine which goals are incompatible.
- Establish a schedule and time line.
- Set specific deadlines for accomplishing your goals.
- Establish daily priorities and tasks.
- Break large goals into small tasks.
- Do first things first.
- Consolidate similar tasks.
- Use idle time to accomplish tasks.
- Learn to say no to distractions and stay on target.
- Overcome procrastination: Get started.
- Review goals and progress often.
- Reward yourself for accomplishing your goals.

HAVEN'T A CLUE?

If you still don't know what you want to do, skip **Exercise 2.1** on the next page. Explore the sections in this chapter: *Researching Jobs* on page 45 and *Informational Interviews* on page 61. Then come back and complete the exercise. Don't worry if you have trouble writing a clear and specific goal. It is not an easy task. In fact, your present and future goals may change. Many people find they need previous job experience to give them direction and help them sort through all the job possibilities. Getting started with determining your goals is the biggest step. You'll find that you can fine-tune your goal statement as you go through your job search. Also, as you gain more information and experience, your goals may become more clarified. You can copy **Exercise 2.1** and revise it as needed. The more practice you have in writing goals, the easier it gets.

Your Present and Future Goals

1. My immediate job objective is:

   _____

   _____

   _____

2. My major goal this year is:

   _____

   _____

   _____

3. My major goal in 5 years is:

   _____

   _____

   _____

4. My major goal in 10 years is:

   _____

   _____

   _____

5. Other life goals are:

   _____

   _____

   _____

6. The most important goal in my life, or my life's purpose, is:

   _____

   _____

   _____

Goal Assessment

After you have thought about your goals, answer these ten questions:
1. How important is your major goal?
2. Is your major goal in conflict with your other goals?
3. Which goals are top priorities?
4. How do you feel about achieving your major goal?
5. What are the benefits to achieving your major goal?
6. What alternatives are available if you don't achieve your major goal?
7. How do your goals relate to your life's purpose and your values?
8. Are your goals realistic?
9. What barriers might you have to overcome to achieve your goals?
10. What resources are available to help you achieve your goals?

Action Plan

Consider the smaller steps necessary to reach your major goal and objective. For example:

Major goal: To graduate from college

Action plan:

1. Pick up college schedule.
2. Talk with an advisor.
3. Enroll in a class.

Keep an action form to monitor your progress. (See **Figure 2.2**).

Barriers

Consider the barriers that could prevent you from reaching your goal. Can you plan to overcome these barriers? For example:

Barrier to overcome: Lack of follow-through

Solution: I will keep a detailed checklist of each step necessary and review it every day to ensure that I follow through on each step.

Creating a time line can help you overcome barriers to reaching your goals. **Figure 2.2** illustrates a sample time line to help you plan your year.

Action Form and Time Line

Figure 2.2

Keeping Track Once you know your goals, you can plan the right steps to take by using an action form. Plotting a time line will also help you envision your goals and accomplish them over a certain period of time. *How would you modify these samples to fit your goals?*

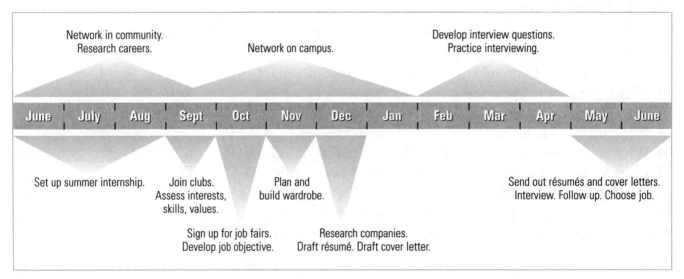

Date:	Weekly Action Form		
Goal	Deadline	Completed	Notes
Complete résumé.	October 23	October 21	Prepare list to send.

	June	July	Aug	Sept	Oct	Nov	Dec	Jan	Feb	Mar	Apr	May	June	

Network in community.
Research careers.

Network on campus.

Develop interview questions.
Practice interviewing.

Set up summer internship.

Join clubs.
Assess interests,
skills, values.

Plan and
build wardrobe.

Send out résumés and cover letters.
Interview. Follow up. Choose job.

Sign up for job fairs.
Develop job objective.

Research companies.
Draft résumé. Draft cover letter.

Researching Jobs

Once you've set goals and thought about what kind of job you'd like at this time in your life, the next step is to research where you can find this job. There are a variety of methods you can use for job hunting (see **Figure 2.3**).

Knowing how to research jobs and companies is crucial to a successful job search. There are two main paths for discovering what jobs are available. One is the traditional path using newspaper ads, advertisements, and employment agencies. However, there are literally thousands of jobs in a variety of fields that take some creative exploring to uncover. Most are not listed in the classifieds, many are not advertised, and some may not have specific titles. In fact, it has been estimated that between 70 and 90 percent of available jobs can be found in the hidden job market. The nontraditional path for exploring the job market includes networking through both professional and trade organizations and researching jobs through various publications. It is important to explore and research jobs through traditional and nontraditional sources to ensure a successful job search.

Students who participate in professional and trade organizations will have a head start on building contacts and relationships. There is no substitute for the grapevine. You can find out which companies are growing, which have new products, and how frequently they hire or lay off employees.

Ways That People Get Jobs		
Percent of total job seekers using the method	Method	Effectiveness Rate
66.0%	Applied directly to employer	47.7%
50.8	Asked friends about jobs where they work	22.1
41.8	Asked friends about jobs elsewhere	11.9
28.4	Asked relatives about jobs where they work	19.3
27.3	Asked relatives about jobs elsewhere	7.4
45.9	Answered local newspaper ads	23.9
21.0	Private employment agency	24.2
12.5	School placement office	21.4
10.4	Asked teacher or professor	12.1

Figure 2.3
Job Searching This chart shows the success rates of different job-search methods. *What appears to be the least effective method of getting a job? What method would you use?*

Researching jobs through various publications is also important. You can learn more about the market, key players, and trends in particular fields. (See **Figure 2.4** on page 50 for a list of current job opportunities.) In addition, companies often list job announcements in trade journals. You can determine the employer's preference by noting style, key words, and expectations through job announcements. Use this information to create a targeted résumé and cover letter and to help you prepare for the interview.

Traditional Sources

Newspapers

Few people get jobs by answering newspaper ads. However, you should still explore this source because it will give you information about companies, who is hiring, and what kinds of jobs are available, and you may find jobs that you want to pursue. Don't just read a few local papers. Look at the *Wall Street Journal*, the *New York Times*, *National Employment Weekly*, and large newspapers in your area. Sunday papers are especially helpful.

In addition, read the business section for job leads. Investigate companies that have hit new sales records, are developing new products, are expanding into new territory, or have merged with other companies. Look for articles about managers being promoted or employees who are leaving to take other jobs. This means the company will be going through some changes. These articles are, for your purposes, job ads and are worth following up with a cover letter and résumé or phone call.

You also may find a company that really appeals to you. Even if they say they are not hiring, it's worth a visit; or you can send a cover letter and résumé to the head of the department in which you are interested. Don't worry if the ad is six months old. Most companies move very slowly with hiring, and most will consider an applicant even after the closing date has passed. All companies experience unplanned turnover, and if your letter creates interest, you may find yourself at the right spot at the right time.

Job-Search Web Sites

The Internet has quickly become a popular resource for job listings and a forum for posting your résumé and making contact with prospective employers. It's important to keep in mind, however, that many job placements still occur through networking. Investigate online resources as well as newspapers and magazines, which often highlight up-to-date job trends. Access the Internet—a vast resource network with information about all types of industries, organizations, and job trends.

Stress Savers

Earn While You Search

Ideally, you'll be job hunting while you're currently employed. However, what if you find yourself out of work due to layoffs, termination, going to school, or personal reasons? Explore these options for interim income or experience until you find your niche:

- State unemployment insurance
- Temporary agencies
- Freelance or part-time work
- Campus job, if you're a student
- Paid internships, if experience is needed
- Job-training programs

TV and Radio

Listen to the news and you'll find many stories about business successes, expansion, new production, franchises, new growth in the community, and local job opportunities. There are also TV shows on job opportunities, such as specials on business trends and job forecasts. Commercial spots on TV and radio will also give you a clue about which businesses are marketing their products and creating new products.

Campus Recruiters

A job-recruitment program on campus is not always a major job source because only a few companies recruit at schools. However, you should explore this source to learn more about specific companies that interest you, to practice interviewing, and to explore various jobs within the company.

You can use these strategies when taking advantage of your school's job-recruitment program.

1. **Start a file of job openings.** Check out all campus and community job postings. The specific job may not appeal to you, but you may be interested in the company.
2. **Talk to a company representative.** This is a great way to learn more about the company. Get the name, title, and phone number of the company representative so you can follow up with more questions.
3. **Keep a log of names.** Ask for names and titles of the managers who head the departments in which you are most interested.

Employment Agencies

Employment agencies can be effective in finding jobs. They can also help you with résumé writing and interviewing skills; help you assess your skills and interests; and help you match your skills and interests with available jobs. Employment agencies charge a fee, which is usually paid by the company that hires you. Look in the Yellow Pages for a list of employment agencies in your area.

STRATEGIES Online

Remember, one of your best resources is
strategies.glencoe.com

Nontraditional Sources

Library

The library is a treasure of information about available jobs, occupations, industries, and companies. While you can use the library as a traditional resource for looking through newspapers, you can also use it as a nontraditional resource for research and browsing through trade journals. Trade journals discuss new trends and also list professional organizations in related fields. Get to know your librarian, ask for specific trade journals, and check out the following references:

- *Dictionary of Occupational Titles*
- *Guide for Occupational Exploration*
- U.S. Department of Labor Occupational Books
- *The Occupational Outlook Handbook*
- *Almanac of American Employers*
- *Business Periodical Index*
- *The Wall Street Journal Index*
- *Dun & Bradstreet's Million Dollar Directory*
- *Standard Industrial Classification*
- *Career Placement Directory*
- *College Placement Annual*
- *Ulrich's International Periodical Directory*
- *Gale Directory of Publications*
- *Standard Periodical Directory*
- *National Directory of Addresses and Telephone Numbers*
- *Consultants and Consulting Organization Directory*
- *The Wall Street Journal*
- *Washington Post*
- *New York Times*
- Manufacturing directories
- Trade journals and magazines

Phone Book

Most libraries have phone books from across the country. Look in the phone book in the Yellow Pages under broad areas that interest you and in the business section. Make a list of the companies that interest you and call them to request more information—annual reports, sales projections, brochures, growth projections, future plans, and so on.

Also use the Yellow Pages to find agencies that can help you research jobs. Here are a few resources that can help:

- Career placement offices
- Civic clubs
- List of local businesses
- List of schools, colleges, and universities
- Employment agencies
- Employment security office (state or federal)
- State job-service offices

Community

Investigate and research your community. Find out who the mayor is and who the local business leaders are, and look at the programs offered by the Rotary and Kiwanis Clubs. Keep a file marked *Community* in which you gather information regarding company profiles and job opportunities from a variety of community sources, such as:

- Chamber of Commerce directory
- Local directories of businesses
- Professional organizations
- Small Business Administration
- Rotaries
- Local college placement offices

Organizations

Investigate and research organizations. In the networking section of your job-search notebook, keep a file of clippings from newspapers and magazines and information you gather from organizations. Be sure to include annual reports, flyers, brochures, employee packages, applications, and telephone directories.

Observation

Now that you have some leads, take your job search to the streets. Look for new businesses, new products being advertised, new buildings, or other signs of expansion. New products may indicate growth for a department, and the company may be hiring new employees. If you notice new branches of a business being built, write to the corporate headquarters or talk to the local manager. By increasing your observation skills, you may find new products in stores and discover what businesses are growing.

Use the following guide to do the detective work necessary to find out what types of jobs are available.

1. **Investigate the company.** When you find a company that appeals to you, find out as much as you can about it. Request an annual report; find out about future plans and new products from the sales office. There may be great opportunities in new organizations or in small companies that are easy to overlook.

2. **Ignore job specifications.** A company may say they are looking for a candidate with a master's degree, a high grade-point average, a degree in a specific area, or a certain number of years of experience. Apply even if you don't meet all the stated requirements. If they are impressed with you, they may discuss other job opportunities.

3. **Take action.** Find out what jobs are open and to whom you would report. Call the department and tell the secretary you are going to be sending a letter (don't say résumé, or you may be directed to personnel) and that you want to check the spelling and title of the director of the office. Address the person who has the authority to hire you.

4. **Send a cover letter.** Write a cover letter that describes your interest in the company, includes company information that indicates you have done research on the company, and explains how you can benefit the company. Chapter 4 will discuss cover letters in more detail.

Figure 2.4

Hot Jobs The U.S. Department of Labor forecasts the fastest growing job opportunities for job seekers with bachelor's degrees. *Why do you think these careers are experiencing growth?*

Top Ten Job Opportunities Requiring a Bachelor's Degree or Higher Through 2005

Occupation	Average Annual Openings
General managers and top executives	100,320
Teachers, secondary school	71,070
Teachers, elementary school	46,490
Systems analysts, electronic data processing	43,710
Financial managers	29,490
Accountants and auditors	28,370
Lawyers	24,370
Teachers, special education	23,850
Marketing, advertising, and public relations managers	19,190
Physicians and surgeons	18,590

Internships

Job experience is important to employers. Internships, cooperative education programs, and volunteering can give you experience, help you explore careers, and help you learn good job skills and habits. Internships are usually unpaid jobs that require several hours per week of your time. Another type of internship is called an externship. Externships can be paid and have a regular 40-hour work week. They are wonderful ways to build contacts and get your foot in the door of a company. Internships provide opportunities to start networking while you are still in school.

Internships—paid or unpaid apprentice-type positions—are priceless. They are another way you can demonstrate that you can "hit the ground running." Students find internships valuable because they can link theory with real-world application. Many companies view internships as a recruiting tool. This experience gives employers the opportunity to actually test a person's skills and see if he or she fits in. Especially during recession times or in competitive job markets, employers want graduates who have job experience. Not only will you gain valuable experience, but you also will be able to demonstrate to the employer that you took the initiative to research internships and learn more about the business world.

A successful internship can provide several benefits:
- Places you in an entry-level job
- Provides excellent firsthand experiences and work experience for your résumé
- Helps you in career planning and decision making

- Provides knowledge about the field and gives you the opportunity to develop useful skills
- Establishes contacts with professional people
- Allows you to shadow other jobs at the same company
- Provides an opportunity to gain greater responsibility

The internship is, indeed, an important strategy for building a network, for career planning, and for getting a job. When you plan your internship, think about what you want to gain as well as what you can contribute. Consider the following questions:

- What kind of work, responsibility, advancement, exposure, location, and possibility for job placement does the internship offer?
- Is it a paid internship? Does your school offer credit for it? Is there a grade-point requirement? Is it formally structured, or will you have some independence?
- Do you want to spend the summer in an internship, take a semester off school to intern full time, or intern part time?
- In what setting would you like to intern: urban area, rural area, resort, or foreign country?

To find out what opportunities exist, talk to instructors, the career placement center, your academic advisor, and internship coordinators, and call various companies that interest you.

Once you get an internship, make certain to present yourself as a professional. Treat this experience as a real job. Dress appropriately, use effective communication skills, act maturely, show that you're dependable and responsible, and give it a 100-percent effort. You don't want to be treated as a student. You want to be regarded as a coworker. Your dress, image, and overall appearance will project you as either a serious career professional or a student who is just putting in the time to get credit for an internship.

Job Opportunities and Creative Brainstorming

EXERCISE 2.2

Cast a wide net and brainstorm from a broad perspective. This exercise will help you eliminate companies or jobs that don't match your tastes and interests and help you pinpoint potentially interesting job opportunities. You have a job objective, but there may be many jobs and companies that could creatively use your talents. Creative problem solving starts by asking questions. Don't be concerned if you can't immediately pinpoint the exact job or company or even industry that you want. You can narrow your search as you get into the critical-thinking stage. You will want to consider size, location, growth potential, training programs, professional level of staff, and so on.

Based on information you've been able to gather from resources up to this point, ask yourself the following questions as you fill in the worksheet.

continued

1. Which companies will help me advance in my field and meet my career goals?

_____   _____
_____   _____
_____   _____
_____   _____

2. Which companies and jobs are in areas of the country I prefer?

_____   _____
_____   _____
_____   _____
_____   _____

3. Which companies and jobs have good training and education programs?

_____   _____
_____   _____
_____   _____
_____   _____

4. Which companies and industries are expanding? Which are shrinking?

_____   _____
_____   _____
_____   _____

5. Which companies are about the right size for me? Would I prefer working in a small or large company?

_____   _____
_____   _____
_____   _____
_____   _____

6. Which companies seem to share my values? (e.g., high ethical standards, concern for the environment, quality products, customer service)

_____   _____
_____   _____
_____   _____
_____   _____

Networking for Job Success

There is no doubt about it: Effective networking produces jobs and is vital for lasting career success. Good jobs are all around you, but most—at least 80 percent—are never listed in the want ads. This "who-do-you-know" method of hiring is common. Therefore, the more you talk to people, the better your chances of finding a job in the hidden job market. It's important to **assess your network.**

Building a community of professional people is your greatest resource for gaining access to jobs, getting referrals, and getting promoted. Networks create the vital link between you and the people who have the authority to hire you. They also provide personal and professional benefits, such as fulfillment and fellowship. Networking is the best way to communicate your goals, skills, qualifications, and personal qualities to others.

Career Directions — BusinessWeek

For Gen X, It's Schmooze or Lose

A recent survey by outplacement firm Drake Beam Morin reveals that members of this latté-swilling crowd [born from 1965 to 1981] rely more heavily on recruiters and job announcements than do other job seekers who network.

In the survey, 36% of Gen Xers said they found new jobs through networking, compared with 46% of Boomers and 51% of mature workers.

"By networking, you are telling the employer what you want before the opportunity presents itself," says Pettenon [of DBM], who adds that the meeting-and-greeting way of job searching is the best way to build a successful career. "If you respond to an ad, there is going to be a remote possibility that the job is going to be exactly what you are looking for."

With layoffs rising, fewer jobs are available at the moment, so networking is becoming more important. Pettenon suggests that job seekers join professional associations and reach out to friends and university networks.

One other place jobs don't seem to be materializing quickly is the online job boards. Pettenon is hardly surprised. Most employers hire first from within, he says, especially for plum positions. If they can't find what they want on the inside, they look for referrals from current employees. Only after those two methods fail do they consider hiring via the Internet or using other forms of classified advertising. "It's a lot more meaningful for employers to bring on someone they know and trust already."

By Eric Wahlgren

Excerpted from August 28, 2001, issue of BusinessWeek Online by special permission, copyright © 2000–2001, by The McGraw-Hill Companies, Inc.

Career Case Study Rob Jordan has been looking for a job since graduation six months ago. He just read about something called the "hidden job market" but thought the term referred to a job-search Web site that was hard to find. After talking to a career counselor, he discovered that it includes unlisted available jobs that are filled by referrals. He wondered if he had his own network for referrals. ***Who are some of the people Rob might include as part of his network?***

Make a list of people you relate to professionally and people you know personally who may have job contacts. Don't evaluate who could best help you or whom you should call. At this time, just concentrate on categorizing any name that comes to mind. Fill in this list of possible network sources:

- Former classmates _____

  _____

- Members in professional associations _____

  _____

- Family members and relatives _____

  _____

- Friends of family members _____

  _____

- Present colleagues and coworkers _____

  _____

- Past colleagues and coworkers _____

  _____

- Present boss or former bosses _____

  _____

- Customers and previous customers _____

  _____

- Neighbors _____

  _____

- The local chamber of commerce staff _____

  _____

- Newspaper editors and writers _____

  _____

- Fellow members of clubs or associations _____

  _____

- Members of professional clubs and meetings _____

  _____

- Placement officials _____

  _____

- Professional acquaintances who are bankers, accountants, real estate brokers, insurance agents, elected officials, doctors, small-business owners, instructors, professors, and so on _____

  _____

  _____

  _____

Defining Your Network

Networking means talking to and building rapport with qualified people. Networking is relationship building. Networks are the web of people you know from all walks of life. They may not be managers, company presidents, or owners of small businesses but they know someone who can introduce you to people who do the hiring. Networking builds a resource bank of professionals who can give you support, advice, and encouragement, and it also increases your visibility.

Networking is also an important job skill that will help you do well in your job, help you get promoted, and enhance your personal and professional lives.

SUPPORTERS

Look at **Figure 2.5** and determine who supports you on a daily basis. We'll call these people your supporters. They may be secretaries, student assistants, administrative assistants, clerks, advisors, typists, classmates, friends, family, or support staff. In the space provided in **Exercise 2.4** on page 57, write down the names of the people in your life who help you get things done. They are at the core of helping you with your job search.

PROFESSIONALS

In the space provided in **Exercise 2.4,** write down the names of professionals in related areas or fields who have expertise and whom you respect. If you are a student, these professionals may be counselors, professors, teachers, administrators, and support staff. If you are a salesperson, they might be hotel workers, suppliers, or staff in the main office. If you are a writer, these people might be editors, publishers, or artists. They may also be professional contacts whose services you use and whom you would recommend to others.

Network Resources

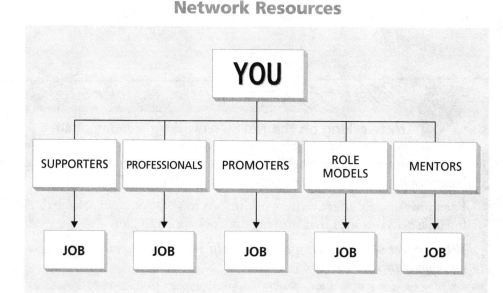

Figure 2.5
Building Relationships You may already have a built-in network of people whom you can call for assistance. *Why do you think networking is one of the best ways to find a job?*

PROMOTERS

Other contacts may be people who have already helped you with your career. They encourage and promote your career. They give you advice and can help you look at your career direction. If you are a student, these professional experts may be club or academic advisors, instructors, professors, coaches, career counselors, and so on. They may be your good friends, a favorite uncle, a next-door neighbor, a minister, or your family doctor. If you are in business, these people may be co-workers, chairs of committees, members of professional organizations, customers, clients, sales staff, and colleagues in other organizations. These people are great sources of information and ideas.

ROLE MODELS

Which successful people could serve as your role models? They may or may not work in your area of interest. List them in the role-model section of **Exercise 2.4.** You may or may not know some of these people personally, but they nevertheless provide inspiration and an example to follow. Role models might be instructors, professors, community leaders, authors, and noted experts in their profession. They may have demonstrated tremendous courage, resilience, creativity, or sheer hard work. Collect stories about successful people you admire and how they became successful.

MENTORS

You may have a small number of people who are not only promoters and coaches but who also provide opportunities and concrete guidance on a personal basis. Mentors can be role models, or they can be professionals outside your career area who take an interest in your career. They are generally well established and successful in their own careers. They make suggestions, inform you of opportunities, introduce you to key people, help you become more visible, and guide your career. They help you set goals and assist you as you face important career decisions. They provide connections to other important people and refer you to essential resources. List these contacts under mentors in **Exercise 2.4.**

Net Advantage

Networking on the Net   Networking is an important resource when searching for jobs. It builds your contact list and can provide you with leads for new job opportunities. Networking is a large part of your career success.

For more tips on effective networking, go to strategies.glencoe.com for links to Web sites that provide networking strategies.

What aspect of networking can best help you as you explore job opportunities?

Identifying Your Network

Write the names of people in your network.

Supporters

_____   _____

_____   _____

_____   _____

Professionals

_____   _____

_____   _____

_____   _____

Promoters

_____   _____

_____   _____

_____   _____

Role Models

_____   _____

_____   _____

_____   _____

Mentors

_____   _____

_____   _____

_____   _____

Network Strategy #1: Get Organized

It is important to keep your network system organized. Here are a
few tips:

- Keep names of contacts in a notebook or on your computer and
  update your list often.
- When you meet a new contact, ask for a business card or write
  down the information on a note card. If possible, get the person's
  home phone number.
- When you have a moment, jot down information about this person
  on the back of the card: shared interest, ideas, projects he or she is
  working on, and possible opportunities. Put the cards in your
  record-keeping system (see Chapter 1).
- For all your contacts, set up worksheets like the one in **Figure 2.6**
  on page 58. This allows you to see the growing network you are
  creating.

Contact Sheet

	Name	Company	Phone	Date Called	Call Back	Result	Other Information
1.	Cathy Barnes	ABC, Inc.	822-2938	9/1/02	9/2/02	Interview	Sent literature
2.							
3.							
4.							
5.							

Figure 2.6
Making Contacts Worksheets are very helpful for organizing your network and adding to it. *Can you think of at least five contacts to add to your network?*

Network Strategy #2: Build Your Network

You should now have listed contacts in **Exercise 2.2** on pages 51 and 52 and organized them into categories in **Exercise 2.3** on page 54. Review your lists and see where you need to build contacts. You may discover that you need to go to professional meetings, get more involved in the community, or reestablish contact with old friends and classmates.

Think of fresh ways you can **build your network.** Use creative problem solving to come up with new contacts. For example, brainstorm ideas with a friend: "Mark, didn't your roommate in college have an uncle in banking?" "Lily, isn't your niece dating someone whose father works for a large computer firm?" "Jan, does your brother work for an auto firm in Detroit?"

One effective way to build your network is to contact personal and professional friends and take them out for coffee or lunch. Ask them for other contacts in your field or contacts that they might have at a company in which you're interested. Be prepared to invest time, positive feedback, and money in giving back to people something for their time and help. Take people to lunch, send them interesting articles, and introduce them to people you think would help their own careers. Remember, the more people who know that you want a job, the greater your chances of landing a job you want. Don't assume that even your best friends or coworkers know your skills, past job experiences, accomplishments, or career goals.

The main point to remember is that networking doesn't just happen. Like anything else in life, you must cultivate and nurture your contacts if they are to expand and support you. See every contact as a means to gaining information, building professional and personal associations, and advancing in your career.

Successful job searchers can start to network in high school and continue when they go to college. While attending college, you can begin networking by participating in various activities:

- Do an internship.
- Do volunteer work.
- Work part time.
- Help your instructors with projects.
- Get to know students in your classes and exchange phone numbers.
- Join professional organizations.
- Get to know professionals and ask them about their careers.
- Use the guidance of instructors, career counselors, and advisors.

Get involved in the field of your interest and build your network. For example, if your field is environmental planning, join environmental clubs and volunteer your services to a state or federal agency. If your field is in computers, find a part-time job at a computer store or a campus or high-school computer lab; or ask local businesses if you can help set up a computer system or teach staff. If you have a chance to work for a company, don't be afraid to take an entry-level job.

NETWORKING WITH THE INTERNET

Internet and various online services can plug you into a network without your actually having to meet professionals in the field. Buy an Internet directory at a bookstore. However, remember that blatant self-marketing is inappropriate when using any medium.

Network Strategy #3: Expand Your Base

Go beyond the initial contacts you've listed and **expand your base.** Many of the people you contact may not know of openings but may recommend that you see or call someone else. It helps if you have a mutual acquaintance whom you can say has referred you. Expand your network by asking all the contacts on your initial list if they can recommend five people to contact. Ask them for their counterparts at other companies. If you start with 50 names, and each one gives you five more names, you will quickly see the layers of your network build up. Building a strong network is time-consuming, but it is helpful for getting a job and will benefit your career as well.

Network Strategy #4: Write Networking Letters

The purpose of networking letters is to help you build *long-term* professional and personal contacts, to keep people informed about your career, and to gather information for your file. These letters will help you build your network to generate job leads.

It is important to let people know you are looking for a job or about to make a career change. **Write networking letters** to friends, family, professional acquaintances, business associates, and to people on your contacts lists who may provide information, advice, and referrals. Whenever possible, turn these letters into telephone calls and face-to-face meetings. (See **Figure 2.7** on page 60 for sample letters.)

Figure 2.7
Keeping in Touch These letters help you establish your contacts to get jobs. *What's the difference in tone between the first and second letters?*

July 5, 2003

Linda Sanders
Director of Marketing
J.C. Systems Inc.
531 Bay Avenue
Seattle, WA 98772

Dear Linda:

It has been nearly three years since we last talked at the National Conference on Marketing in Santa Fe. You were most helpful in helping me clarify my career goals.

I'm leaving Consumer Programs after three years of increasingly responsible marketing experience. I have enjoyed my job but very much want to return to Seattle.

Do you know of any employers in the Seattle area that would be interested in my marketing and computer background? Do you have suggestions as to whom I might call for further contacts?

I'll call you next week to discuss any ideas you may have. I very much appreciate your help and support.

Sincerely,

Jay Turner

Jay Turner

December 12, 2003

Dear Bob,

Merry Christmas! This should be one of your earliest greetings. Will you be going back to visit your family in Idaho?

I'm writing to ask your support and advice. As I told you in my last letter, I am ready to start thinking about a job change. Can we meet for coffee or dinner at the FAPPS Conference in January? I want to give this next career move some real thought, and I don't want to jump into anything too quickly. You've always given me invaluable support and advice for my career. I think I want to stay in sales, but this may be a good time to launch myself into an entry-level marketing position.

I'm sending you a copy of the speech I gave at a local seminar and an updated copy of my résumé so you can see the kinds of projects I have been involved in this last year.

I look forward to hearing from you soon. Give Mary and the girls my best.

Warm regards,

Jay

Jay

Network Strategy #5:
Go to Informational Interviews

Informational interviews are just that, interviews that help you find out more about your career field, or about a certain company, from a professional in that field. Most of these interviews will be the result of referrals. Referrals get your feet in the door and give you a common connection—even if it is several times removed.

In most cases, an informational interview is not a formal interview for a specific job, so don't do a hard sell. Most professionals enjoy taking a few minutes to talk to someone just going into a field, and they feel flattered that you have asked for their advice about career issues.

Prepare a personal approach when you **set up informational interviews.** Write out a brief script that focuses on your purpose. You don't want to sound cliché, but you also don't want to ramble aimlessly and waste people's time. Practice on a tape recorder until you have a relaxed speech that sounds friendly, direct, and professional. The following are sample openers for breaking the ice:

- *Hello, Ms. Whitney. Thank you for taking the time to meet with me. I think I'd like to be in sales someday for a large company, too. I'd like some advice on getting started in this field from someone who has made it.*
- *Hello, Mr. Wells. My name is Sandra Wooley. May I speak with Ms. Whitney?*
- *I have been told by a mutual friend, Joe Nettles, that Ms. Whitney would be an excellent person with whom to discuss a career decision. When could I see her for a short meeting?*

Get to your informational interview a few minutes early. This will give you time to relax, and you may find out information about the company or the job. If the secretary is not busy, ask if you may have a copy of the annual report or company publication. Have a list of questions prepared. You might want to ask the following questions during an informational interview:

- To what trade journals should I subscribe?
- What professional organizations should I join?
- May I have a copy of the latest annual report?
- What are the advantages and disadvantages of this field?
- What community groups would be good to join?
- Who are other top leaders in this field?
- If you had it to do over again, what would you do differently to succeed in this line of work?
- What companies do you think would be best to apply to?
- What specific advice would you give me that would help me advance in my career?
- Can you give me the names of five other people to contact?

Have another list of questions prepared in case the conversation focuses on the company itself and a possible job opportunity:

- What skills and abilities are most important for this field and for the company?
- What are the biggest concerns and problems facing this company?
- What is the corporate culture? (values, or set of norms)
- Is this a good company in which to learn the field and get promoted?
- What is the company's mission and philosophy of management?
- What are the most common day-to-day problems?
- Does this company encourage training and learning new skills?

NETWORKING TIPS

Whether speaking with your network contacts, going to an informational interview, or cold-calling, keep in mind the following suggestions for successful networking.

1. **Be prepared.** Know what you want and have a list of questions. Don't waste other people's time.
2. **Be positive.** Have a positive attitude and show enthusiasm. Don't complain about former employers.
3. **Be generous.** Send ideas, articles, and names of contacts to others. Share ideas and remember that networking is a two-way process.
4. **Be a risk taker.** Set goals for networking and build them into your everyday life. Talk with people you don't know at meetings, and introduce yourself at various events. Stretch your comfort level.
5. **Be respectful.** Be brief and respectful and don't ask for too much. You don't want to appear insensitive or too bold.
6. **Be trustworthy.** Never betray another person's confidentiality or trust. Never gossip.
7. **Be a doer.** Follow up on leads.
8. **Be courteous.** Send thank-you notes to people who have given you support, advice, time, and referrals.

FOLLOWING UP

It's important that you follow up any type of networking meeting. Write a note thanking the person for taking the time to talk with you either by phone or in person. A handwritten note is more personal than a typed letter and shows that you have taken the time to be gracious. This is not just good manners; it also serves as one more memory jogger about who you are. Don't forget the receptionist and/or secretary. She or he often has influence with the boss. Write a handwritten note showing appreciation for his or her arranging the meeting, the professional manner with which you were treated, the coffee, and so on.

Networking Strategy #6: Cold Calling

Cold calling (calling someone you don't know without a referral) is useful for gaining informational interviews. I suggest you do it, but it does require a positive attitude and the willingness to risk rejection. Since most people would rather help someone who is a friend or at least a friend of a friend, you may encounter some resistance when you call a total stranger. The key to success in cold calling is to be pleasant and to practice. Don't do a hard sell, but ask to discuss the field, your career, or questions you have about the company. When you make calls every day or several times a week, you improve your technique. With persistent effort, you will get interviews. Remember, you control the number of calls you make and your state of mind. Don't take rejection personally. This take-charge attitude will also contribute to your success on your new job.

Sometimes you will hear of an opening or have an interest in a company or a specific office. You may hear that the arts center at a college just lost its graphic designer, and you want to explore the possibility of working for them. Go for it! Follow these guidelines for cold calling:

- Get as many details about the position as you can from the source.
- Call the company and find out who the department supervisor is in charge of the department. This is the person with the authority to hire you.
- Get the person's correct name, spelling, pronunciation, and phone number.
- Get the person's secretary's name, spelling, pronunciation, and phone number.
- Call the secretary. The conversation should go something like this:

    Hello, Ms. Timmons. My name is Jan Foss. May I speak with Ms. Little, please?

The secretary may ask what the call is about. If so, say something such as:

This regards a career question. I would like to speak to him this week if possible. (If he is not available, ask if you can arrange a short meeting at his convenience.)

Notice that you are not asking *if* you can meet with the decision maker, but *when*. Also notice that you did not tell the secretary you are looking for a job. Most secretaries will steer you to the personnel office or protect the boss from people who are trying to get jobs. You are asking for career advice and a chance to show what you can do for the company. Limit the information you are giving out. (Never answer questions that haven't been asked.) Your goal is to either meet with the person who has the authority to hire or to at least engage in a phone conversation. If you don't get a call back, call again in a few days. Be courteous, but persistent.

Don't feel as if you are wasting someone's time by asking for an informational interview. As long as you keep your meetings short and you are respectful, most professionals are flattered that you want to know about their field or that you are interested in working for the company.

Writing a Cold-Call Script

Write out a script so you know what you are going to say and what your goals are for the phone conversation. For example, your goals may be to gain information, discuss career options, find out information about the company, or inquire about job openings.

Goals:

_____

_____

_____

_____

_____

_____

_____

_____

Phone Script:

_____

_____

_____

_____

_____

_____

_____

_____

_____

_____

_____

_____

_____

_____

_____

_____

_____

Network Strategy #7: Alumni Contacts

Once you graduate, use the alumni office to match your interests with alumni who are working in related fields. Then call alumni and introduce yourself.

You'll be surprised at the positive response you will get. Even alumni who have graduated years before you will most likely be delighted to talk with you about career planning. Ask for a short interview either by phone or in person, so that you can ask specific questions about job openings and what their jobs involve. Describe the job you are interested in, discuss the skills you have to offer, and ask for five or six professional contacts. Ask them what professional associations they would suggest you join. Make certain you contact every person recommended and ask that person for five more contacts. Your network will grow, and you will be amazed at how valuable these contacts will be for you throughout your career. Not only will they open up new opportunities, but you will enrich your professional contacts and build friendships.

Network Strategy #8: Other Sources

SERVICE

Community service can provide the connection between school and the real world. You can demonstrate that you are an involved person, a problem solver, and a doer. You will stand out from other candidates who may have a degree but whose excuse is that they didn't have time to contribute. The benefits are both personal and professional. You will gain contacts and high visibility (helping expand your network) and learn on-the-job skills. The real benefit, however, is knowing you are giving something back to society. Get involved in the community and campus. There are many agencies that can use your talents:

Community

Hospitals	Junior League
Nursing homes	Literacy programs
Homeless shelters	Animal support work
Schools	Girl Scouts
Nonprofit agencies	Boy Scouts
Red Cross	Senior citizen centers
Cancer Society	Animal shelters

Campus

Campus ministry	Journalism clubs
Environmental clubs	Multicultural clubs
Sports	Student volunteers
Theatre clubs	Tutoring

How Networking Produces Results

Josh decided to call his good friend, Adam, who attended West Technical Business College in Massachusetts and worked one summer as an intern in the alumni affairs office. Josh asked Adam if he knew anyone in the computer business in the Boston area. Adam referred him to Anne Springer. Anne is the director of software at Compco Computer Company. After several phone calls, Josh talked directly to Anne who gave Josh a couple of contacts and told him to keep her posted. He called the contacts, and in a few weeks, Josh had an incredible network of professional contacts in the Boston area. (**See Figure 2.8** for a map of Josh's network.)

He also used traditional sources for finding jobs. In fact, the lead that resulted in his final job offer came from an ad, but it was the network of referrals that helped him finalize the job he wanted. Josh was not only rewarded for his hard work by landing a job, but he was able to begin a professional network that could result in many lifelong professional associations.

Networking is one of the most powerful tools you can use in your job search. It is also a valuable job-success tool that will pay off throughout your professional career. Networking is a give-and-take process that involves helping others and building solid relationships based on mutual respect.

Figure 2.8
Effective Networking Traditional sources for jobs can be very effective in your job search. However, networking can also support and enhance job opportunities from traditional sources. *How important was networking as a job-search tool for Josh and why?*

Josh's Network

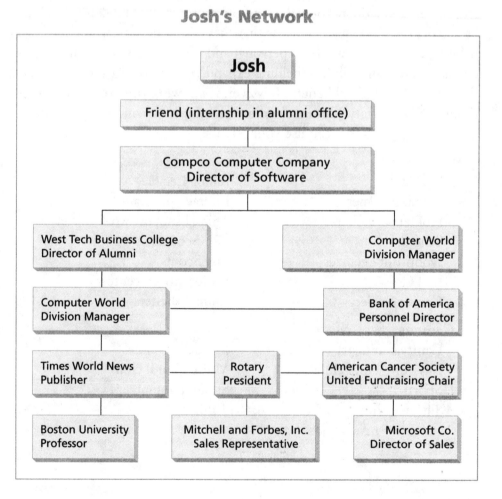

STAYING POWER

Overcoming Shyness

*a*re you able to talk to people you don't know? Can you introduce yourself calmly and confidently? What type of impression do you give when you first meet someone? Does your body language send the right message? Not everyone feels comfortable when talking to strangers, making cold calls, or networking with unfamiliar contacts. Even sending an e-mail to a stranger can be stressful when a job depends upon it.

Not everyone is a perfect communicator. Remember, even world-class public speakers, who are paid to make commencement speeches or to emcee award shows on television, must practice to overcome discomfort and "the jitters." Coaches, politicians, professors, and actors all take time to perfect their presentation skills. If you spend some time practicing communication skills, you will feel less anxiety when making necessary contacts.

Your improved skill will be an asset, which will also give you confidence during a job interview. View your situation in a positive light. Become aware of the opportunity to overcome shyness and improve your communication skills while you gain valuable relationships, build your network, and eventually get a job.

Try This...

- Practice talking to new people outside of your job search, and focus on your successes.
- Think of specific improvements you can make. They can range from staying calm and taking your time when speaking to simply smiling more.
- Ask friends what they like about your personality and build your presentation around those points.
- Think of the attributes you admire in the people around you. How do they express themselves and invite interaction? Try to emulate those qualities.
- Role-play telephone calls, networking situations, and job interviews.

CHAPTER 2 *Review*

Skill Check Recap

- Set immediate and long-term goals.
- Research jobs through traditional and non-traditional sources.
- Assess your network.
- Build your network.
- Expand your base.
- Write networking letters.
- Set up informational interviews.

Self-Check List

Keep track of your progress. Read the following and mark *yes* or *no*.

	Yes	No
I have set goals and priorities.	___	___
I have written a specific action plan.	___	___
I have explored job options using traditional methods.	___	___
I have explored job options using nontraditional methods.	___	___
I have explored job options using creative problem solving.	___	___
I have explored job options using critical thinking for decision making.	___	___
I have assessed and expanded my network.	___	___
I have set goals and set up informational interviews.	___	___
I have explored internships.	___	___
I have kept in touch with my network.	___	___

Review Questions

1. What are the five advantages of setting goals?

   _____

   _____

2. What are the four steps in setting goals?

   _____

   _____

3. What are the traditional paths for discovering available jobs?

   _____

   _____

4. What are the five primary nontraditional resources you can explore?

   _____

   _____

5. What are some advantages of internships?

   _____

   _____

6. What are eight networking strategies?

   _____

   _____

7. Briefly, what is the purpose of an informational interview?

   _____

   _____

8. What are eight tips for networking?

   _____

   _____

Critical Thinking

9. Look at the eight networking strategies in this chapter. Which two strategies would be most difficult for you to do? How can you best ensure you do them?

   _____

   _____

   _____

Cooperative Learning

10. In groups of three or four, pick one of the ten career fields listed in Chapter 1. Brainstorm to develop a networking strategy for that specific field. Report back to the whole class.

CHAPTER 2 *Strategies* AT WORK

Which Job-Search Method?

Leticia will graduate in a year with a degree in computer technology from a business school in Ohio. She is just starting to plan her job search. She is enjoying the traditional method of researching jobs and companies and creating a résumé. She has been told that it is "who you know" that counts when finding a job. Leticia has friends who attend professional conferences, volunteer in the community, set up information meetings with business leaders, and make cold calls to professionals.

Leticia's problem is that she is shy and doesn't feel she has the confidence, personality, or skill to explore nontraditional job-search methods. Should Leticia stick with the traditional methods of job hunting that are more comfortable for her or explore nontraditional methods as well?

Problem Solving The following ten questions are designed to help solve problems and make sound decisions. You can use these questions to find solutions to your own problems. Put yourself in Leticia's place and consider these questions from her point of view.

- What is the problem?
- Do I have enough information?
- Can I make the decision by myself?
- Have I brainstormed alternatives?
- Have I looked at likely consequences?
- Have I identified all the resources and tools needed?
- Have I developed and implemented an action plan?
- Have I identified the best solution and done everything possible to ensure success?
- Have I assessed the results?
- Have I modified the plan, if necessary?

What solution would you suggest to Leticia? Write your answer on the lines below.

_____
_____
_____
_____
_____
_____
_____
_____

STRATEGIES Online

Find out more about job-search methods by visiting this book's Web site at strategies. glencoe.com

Your Career Portfolio

Researching Jobs and Networking

Part A

Now that you have assessed your skills, interests, strengths, personal qualities, and values, you can start researching your options. This exercise is important throughout your entire career. Use the following questions as a guide as you research and explore job and career options. Add this page to your career portfolio.

• What national trends may have an effect on our economy and job opportunities?

_____

_____

• What industries would best fit my personality, skills, interests, values, and educational background?

_____

_____

• What industry trends are hot right now?

_____

_____

Part B

Networking is critical for lifelong career success. The following will help you build contacts for networking.

• Make a list of some professional organizations you could join that would benefit your job search.

_____   _____

_____   _____

• Make a list of possible references.

_____   _____

_____   _____

CHAPTER 3

Your Résumé

Winning Points

- Make your résumé short, concise, and neat.
- Focus on skills, achievements, and the ability to solve problems.
- Show a clear relationship to the available job.
- Be sure your résumé is honest, simple, and free of errors.
- Print your résumé on quality paper and send with a cover letter.

Introduction

The résumé is a critical tool to help you get your foot in the door. In this chapter, we will look at the overall image and specific factors involved in writing an effective résumé. You will also get practical advice and practice translating your skills into specific benefits for a company.

Now that your strategic planning is done, you can organize that information into a résumé that stands out and says who you are. Your autobiography and the self-assessment exercises in Chapters 1 and 2 will pay off now. In these exercises, you've begun to discover what you have to offer. Now you can begin showing connections between your strengths, accomplishments, and skills, and the needs of a company or your targeted employer.

First impressions really do count. Often your résumé is the first contact the employer will have with you. Your résumé can make or break you. You want your résumé to stand out, look professional, and highlight your skills. Whether you choose a functional or chronological résumé format, your résumé should accomplish the following objectives:

- Demonstrate that you are capable of performing the job.
- Highlight your accomplishments.
- Show a connection between your skills and how they have benefited other companies.
- Highlight your education and skills.

Chapter 3 Objectives

After you have completed this chapter, you will be able to:
- Describe the characteristics of a good résumé
- Write a job objective
- Highlight your experience in your résumé
- Apply action words in your résumé
- Identify how to choose the best résumé format

The Importance of a Résumé

There is a lot of controversy about the effectiveness of a résumé for landing a job. The purpose of a résumé is to get you an invitation to an interview. It is the interview that will get you the job, not the résumé. Résumés are often used to screen out applicants, so you want your résumé to stand out, be easy to read, be general enough to reach a large market, and be specific enough to clearly indicate your skills. The résumé is useful for many other reasons:

1. **Self-assessment.** Writing a résumé requires a process of self-assessment that sets the tone and the foundation for the entire job-search process. It defines your skills, accomplishments, and experiences as they relate to a job and helps you to bring your job objective into focus.
2. **Standard policy.** Many companies have standard hiring procedures that require a résumé when you apply for a position. Even if the company knows you well, a résumé may be required "for the file."
3. **Interview questions.** In most cases, you will be asked to send or bring your résumé, even if you're invited personally to meet with the employer. The interviewer will scan your résumé and ask questions about your past performance based upon your experience, skills, and qualifications. You must be able to explain and elaborate on your résumé at the interview.
4. **Memory jogger.** A résumé can serve as a reminder or memory jogger to the employer after you have been interviewed. This is perhaps one of the most important aspects of the résumé.
5. **A reflection of you.** The résumé is not only a reflection of your skills and experience, but of your style, sense of organization, and neatness.
6. **Increasing your chances.** Although personal contact is always preferred over a piece of paper or a phone interview, direct contact with the hiring authority is not always possible. By sending your basic résumé and specific cover letter to many companies, you may increase your chances of getting the job you want.

You can see that a résumé is an important and necessary tool in the job-search process. Job-search strategies are all tools that complement each other and work together. It bears repeating: A résumé is not only a summary of your skills, experience, and education, but it also reflects who you are and what you can do. To be effective, a résumé must stand out.

Definite vs. Maybe

Most employers are busy and don't take the time to read the vast number of résumés they receive. They skim through them, read a few lines, and put them into piles. They toss out those that are not right for the job, those that lack the necessary education or training, and those that are messy or have misspelled words. There is a pile of "maybes" and a pile of "definite interest." Those résumés in the definite interest pile get a closer look, and those applicants are invited to come for an interview. You want your résumé to be in the definite interest pile, and you want to be invited for an interview. Nothing happens until you meet face-to-face with the employer. Remember, a good résumé will get you the interview.

The effective résumé is designed to highlight your experience, education, skills, interests, and talents in a clear, organized manner. It represents you and must therefore sell you. Keep in mind that you are selling yourself, not your degree, major in school, or present job title. Therefore, your résumé needs to be planned, organized, and polished to reflect your unique accomplishments and skills.

Characteristics of an Effective Résumé

The key to an effective résumé is to organize the information about your experience and skills in a clear, concise, easy-to-read, and appealing manner. **Figure 3.1** on page 76 is an example of a functional résumé that will get read. A functional résumé may be effective for people with little work experience for the job in question. A chronological résumé features work experience in the first section after the job objective and lists jobs chronologically.

Now that you have filled out the personal inventory in the database exercise in Chapter 1 on page 11, have reflected on your strengths, achievements, and skills, and have researched companies, you have taken the first steps to writing an effective résumé. Your investment in self-assessment will add focus and clarity to your résumé. Now **organize your database to use in your résumé.** Take the information in your inventory and organize it into basic sections.

Guidelines for a Letter-Perfect Résumé

A letter-perfect résumé is an easy-to-read presentation of your skills, experiences, and accomplishments. Choose the format and style that best reflects your experiences and background and follow these guidelines.

1. Keep your résumé to one page for an entry-level job.
2. Focus on skills and achievements.
3. Use action words to define duties.
4. Keep it formal and businesslike.
5. Make certain it is grammatically correct and free of errors.
6. Keep it clear, concise, and easy to read.
7. Present data in reverse chronological order (most recent first).
8. Print it on good-quality paper.
9. Make certain all information is correct and verifiable.

An Effective Résumé

KATIE J. JENSEN

Present address
1423 10th Street
Arlin, MN 52561
(313) 724-2896

Permanent address
812 La Jolla Avenue
Burlingate, WI 53791
(401) 792-1928

JOB OBJECTIVE: To obtain an entry-level job as a travel agent.

EDUCATION
Arlin Community College, Arlin, MN
    Associate of Arts in Business, June 2001
        Magna cum laude graduate
Cross Pointe Career School, Arlin, MN
        Certificate in Tourism, June 1999

HONORS AND AWARDS
Academic Dean's List
Recipient of Burlingate Rotary Scholarship, 1999

WORK EXPERIENCE
UNIVERSITY TRAVEL AGENCY, Arlin, MN
Tour Guide, August 2000–present
- Arrange tours to historic sites in a four-state area. Responsibilities include contacting rail and bus carriers, arranging for local guides at each site, making hotel and restaurant reservations, and providing historical information about points of interest.
- Develop tours for holidays and special events. Responsibilities include pre-event planning, ticketing, and coordination of travel and event schedules.
- Specialized tour planning resulted in 24-percent increase in tour revenues over the preceding year.

BURLINGATE AREA CONVENTION CENTER, Burlingate, MN
Intern Tourist Coordinator, December 1999–June 2000
- Established initial contact with prospective speakers, coordinated schedules, and finalized all arrangements. Set up computerized database of tours using dBase 1V.
- Organized receptions for groups up to 250, including reserving meeting rooms, contacting caterers, finalizing menus, and preparing seating charts.

CAMPUS AND COMMUNITY ACTIVITIES
- Vice President Tourist Club, 2000–2001
- Co-chaired 1999 Home-tour fund-raising event for Big Sisters

PROFESSIONAL MEMBERSHIP
Burlingate Area Convention and Visitors Bureau

KATIE J. JENSEN
References

Ms. Jan A. Tostee
Instructor of Business
Cross Pointe Career School
Arlin, MN 49002
(313) 555-1728

Mr. John D. Rogers
Instructor of Business
Arlin Community College
Arlin, MN 49003
(313) 555-8924

Mr. Thomas Jones
Supervisor
University Travel Agency
Arlin, MN 49002
(313) 555-3845

Ms. Janice Hines
Coworker, Sales
Burlingate Area Convention Center
Burlingate, WI 53702
(401) 555-5423

> A separate reference list should also be available, such as the one shown here.

Electronic Résumés

Many companies scan résumés into their computers when they receive them. That is, they copy and store them electronically so that when they need to hire new employees, they can do a quick electronic search of the résumés. Additionally, when employers search job Web sites where thousands of résumés may be posted, they will narrow their choices by scanning for keywords as well. They often look for words that describe skills or job experience that they require, such as *food service*, *mathematics*, and *Spanish*.

Here are some guidelines for making your résumé "scannable":

1. Keep the résumé clean.
2. Use a crisp, dark, sans serif font.
3. Make sure the letters do not touch each other.
4. Avoid italics, underscores, and other fancy type.
5. Use white paper.
6. Use keywords in describing your experience.

Résumé Sections

A functional résumé and a chronological résumé include much of the same information. The difference between them is the arrangement of data. The following résumé section descriptions appear in the same order used for a functional résumé.

Net Advantage

Résumés on the Web   When you apply for a job online, you must send your résumé electronically. While this can be convenient, there are certain steps you must take to do it right.

Your résumé might look better being sent as an attachment, but it might not be read. Increasingly, companies only view résumés that are cut and pasted onto an e-mail, or through a job Web site, to prevent receiving viruses. Prepare your résumé in simple text or ASCII with no bullets or special fonts. Even though the style or appearance of your résumé might change during the process of cut and paste, the standards do not. Your résumé is still the crucial first impression you make.

For strategies on applying to jobs online, go to strategies.glencoe.com for links to Web sites that provide helpful tips.

How can you still add personal style to your résumé when sending it online?

Identification

Write your name, address, and telephone number. Don't use a nickname. If you have a temporary or school address and phone, you will want to include a permanent address and phone number as well.

(one inch from top)

ROBERT L. LEWIS
378 Park Lane
Lake Pleasant, Michigan 48092
(810) 724-1876

Never include a picture of yourself. Adding gimmicks or fluff only detracts from the essential information and clutters up your résumé. Keep information to the essentials. However, if you decide that your hobbies are relevant to your job objective or indicate a skill or personal quality, put them at the end of the résumé or on a separate sheet of paper that you can take with you to the interview.

Job Objective: Plus or Minus?

It is not essential that you include a job objective on your résumé. The rule of thumb is to **write a job objective** if you will only accept a specific job. The rationale is that you don't want to limit yourself. Most new graduates want to gain experience and will accept various jobs in a company. For example, you might really want to be an editor with a publishing company, but the company may want you to work in field marketing or sales so you that you will gain valuable experience and get to know the service area. If you state your job objective as an editor on your résumé, you may not get called back—even if the company is impressed with your skills and abilities and has openings in sales.

Instead of writing a specific job objective on your résumé, you can use the cover letter to relate your résumé to the specific job for which you are applying. (See Chapter 4 for examples.)

However, if you want to use a job objective on your résumé, you can change the job objective for each résumé that you send out. You have researched jobs in order to relate your skills and interests to the type of work that best suits you. Your goal now is to define a job objective—a specific statement of the type of job for which you would like to apply. If you are having trouble writing a job description, review resources listed in Chapter 2, such as the *Occupational Outlook Handbook*.

Write a specific job objective if you have a specific job target, such as a dental assistant. Keep it general if you are willing to accept different jobs, such as an entry-level position in sales, marketing, or management.

JOB OBJECTIVE

To obtain an entry-level position as an occupational therapist. *(specific)*

To obtain an entry-level position in business administration that will utilize my computer, organizational, and accounting skills. *(general, but not too broad)*

Writing a Job Objective

Complete this exercise even if you have decided not to include a job objective on your résumé. Once you have targeted your job objective, you will add more direction to your job search.

1. What kind of job do you want?

_____

_____

_____

2. Write your own job objective.

_____

_____

_____

Education

List your education in reverse chronological order (most recent degree first). Write the degree in full. List school, city and state, your degree or certificate, major, date of graduation, and GPA (if over 3.0).

EDUCATION
Michigan State University, East Lansing, MI
Bachelor of Science in Mechanical Engineering, 2003

Lake Harbor Community College, Lake Harbor, OH
Associate Degree in Business, 2001
Major: Accounting
GPA: 3.6

Some formats list date, school, location, degree, and GPA:

| 2001 | San Jose Career College | San Jose, CA |
| | Bachelor of Arts in Business | GPA 3.5 |

If you have a college or career-school degree or certificate, don't list your high school. If you are still in college or career school, you can list your high school if you prefer.

Bennett Career School, Burlingate, WI
Associate of Science in Respiratory Therapy
Expected date of graduation: June 2002

La Jolla High School, Burlingate, WI
High School Diploma, June 2000

List your minor area of study, specific courses, workshops, seminars, or training programs if you think they are relevant and will help you get the job. Otherwise, keep your education section brief. You can expand on your education in your cover letter, application, or in the interview by explaining how certain courses relate to a specific job.

CERTIFICATION, LICENSURE, OR ADVANCED TRAINING

Under "Education" list certificates and licenses you have earned, as well as any advanced training you have received. For consistency, follow the same format for dates.

CERTIFICATION

1994	Certificate in Food Management and Sanitation
1999	Certificate in CPR

LICENSURE

Registered Emergency Medical Technician, 2000

Rehabilitation License in Nursing for the State of Wyoming, 1999

1994   E.C.C. Radiotelephone Third-Class Operator License

University of Illinois, Chicago, IL
Continuing Education Management Series, June 2001–2002

HONORS AND AWARDS

If you received college honors or a fellowship, you will want to list these as part of your education regardless of how long you have been out of school.

HONORS AND AWARDS
- Academic Dean's list
- National Honor Society

EXERCISE 3.2　　　　　**Education and Honors**

List your information on the lines provided.

1. Educational experiences

   _____

   _____

   _____

   _____

   _____

   _____

2. Certificates

   _____

   _____

   _____

   _____

3. Honors and awards

   _____

   _____

   _____

   _____

Work Experience

List your work experience in reverse chronological order, starting with your most recent job.

- List the dates (year is sufficient).
- List the name and location (city and state) of the company.
- List your job title.
- Describe your duties and responsibilities. **Translate experiences into job skills.**
- Don't forget internships, apprenticeships, on-the-job training programs, part-time and summer job experiences that relate to the prospective job.

← SKILL CHECK

EXPERIENCE

2000–present   ADAMS ELECTRIC COMPANY   Seashore, FL
Electrician

- Calculated plans in compliance with latest N.C. codes and regulations.
- Implemented plans for wiring diagrams.

Or use this order:

Tour Guide
GLOBETRAVEL
Englewood, NJ
August 2002–present

- Coordinated tours to historic sites.
- Developed new holiday tour package, resulting in 24-percent increase in revenues.

Job Descriptions

List three or four key duties under your most recent job and two or three for previous jobs. For many people, this is a difficult part of writing the résumé. Review your job duties and choose action verbs and short statements to describe them. Don't use complete sentences. Whenever possible, be clear about how you have benefited the company, using keywords and skill descriptions. (See pages 82–83.) Here are some examples:

- Created automated accounting system, resulting in 40-percent cost savings.
- Developed sales promotions, negotiated and wrote sales contracts. Increased revenue by 33 percent during first year.
- Provided customer service to store patrons.
- Responsible for window displays. Won 2000 Creative Advertisement Award.
- Revised reporting procedures to comply with government regulations.
- Provided administrative services for department.
- Supervised a staff of six volunteers.
- Drafted reports and edited papers and articles.
- Collaborated with clinicians on proper treatment.
- Coordinated activities and prepared daily reports.

ACTION VERBS

The personality and team-style exercise in Chapter 1 on page 20 helped you determine your dominant style. That exercise can also help you choose action words to use in the experience section of your résumé. Review your dominant style and choose the action words, or verbs, that best highlight your style, indicate your diversity, and are most appropriate in relation to the particular job. You may have more than one style.

Director	Creator	Thinker	Relator
Persuaded	Created	Compiled	Adapted
Administered	Designed	Calculated	Served
Organized	Coached	Analyzed	Cared for
Negotiated	Visualized	Set criteria	Teamed with
Ordered	Attracted	Evaluated	Supported
Controlled	Invented	Formulated	Communicated
Carried out	Demonstrated	Reviewed	Balanced
Developed	Engaged	Regulated	Coordinated
Established	Entertained	Monitored	Assisted

OTHER ACTION VERBS

Here is a list of general action verbs to use for appropriate jobs and activities.

Acted	Coordinated	Keynoted
Adjusted	Created	Led
Administered	Delegated	Licensed
Analyzed	Demonstrated	Maintained
Applied	Designed	Managed
Appraised	Directed	Mediated
Arranged	Discovered	Monitored
Assembled	Edited	Motivated
Assisted	Enforced	Negotiated
Balanced	Evaluated	Operated
Built	Guided	Organized
Briefed	Illustrated	Participated in
Cared for	Implemented	Performed
Clarified	Increased	Planned
Coached	Instructed	Prepared
Communicated	Integrated	Promoted
Completed	Facilitated	Proposed
Conducted	Formulated	Provided
Constructed	Generated	Published
Consulted	Justified	Reduced
Controlled	Kept	Reorganized

Repaired	Served	Surveyed
Reported	Simplified	Taught
Researched	Solved	Teamed with
Scheduled	Structured	Trained
Screened	Supervised	Updated
Selected	Supported	Wrote

NOUNS

Many companies are now using computers to search résumés and store the data for later review. Employer computers scan résumés for key words that define the requirements of a particular position. Therefore, you need to include not only action verbs, such as those listed above, but also key words for specific occupations. For example, key words for the medical field may include *referral*, *rehabilitation*, *treatment*, and *patient care*. Make certain you are familiar with key words in your field and use them when appropriate in your résumé, cover letter, application, and interview.

SKILLS

Think through these skill descriptions and choose the ones that you want to demonstrate on your résumé.

Administrative	Listening
Artistic	Managerial
Clerical	Mathematical
Communications	Mechanical
Conflict resolution	Motivational
Coordinating	Musical
Counseling	Negotiation
Critical thinking	Organizational
Debating	Perceptive
Decision making	Persuasive
Delegation	Planning
Design	Presentation
Diplomacy	Problem solving
Editing	Public relations
Evaluation	Public speaking
Fiscal	Sales
Foreign language	Social
Human relations	Supervisory
Innovative	Team building
Inspiring	Training
Interpersonal	Working with people
Investigating	Writing
Leadership	

EXERCISE 3.3   The Benefit Factor

Use action verbs for translating your experiences and showing a benefit to the company, as shown in the example below:

Customer Service Representative
Updated ordering system, established new accounts, trained new employees, assisted with marketing plan. Contracted new wholesalers (increased new contacts by 23 percent).

_____

_____

_____

_____

_____

_____

_____

_____

_____

_____

_____

_____

_____

_____

_____

_____

_____

_____

_____

_____

_____

_____

_____

_____

_____

_____

_____

_____

MILITARY SERVICE

Military experience, such as the examples listed below, will fit into the section under work experience.

- Branch of service or reserve status
- Present rank or rank at discharge
- Duties if applicable
- Dates in the military
- Honors or achievement

If you have military experience, make it work for you by translating your duties and achievements into benefits to the company. Focus on the skills you learned, the services you performed, and your benefit to the military. Translate your duties and skills into the ability to follow orders and work as part of a team. Use civilian terms instead of code military words or jargon whenever possible.

Jargon	Civilian term
Commanded	Directed
Soldiers	Staff
Fighting men	Highly-trained personnel
Long-range patrols	Logistic planning

Look at all your duties and responsibilities. Did you lead field teams, make sound decisions, work effectively as a team member, gather and analyze information, maintain equipment, follow through on difficult assignments, and solve problems? These are experiences and qualities that any company values. Keep this section brief. You can elaborate in the interview or on the application form.

MILITARY SERVICE
1999–2001   U.S. Army
X-Ray Specialist (91P). Operated X-ray equipment, conducted radiographs, and worked as effective team member.

Campus and Community Service

Campus activities and community service and volunteer experiences are important and can indicate leadership abilities and a willingness to make a contribution. Use action verbs to describe your duties. (If you have been out of college for several years, focus on community involvement.) Include the following:

- Dates
- Name of community or campus organization or clubs
- Position held or duties and responsibilities

CAMPUS AND COMMUNITY SERVICE
2003   President of Marketing Club
2002   Co-chaired fund-raising event for American Cancer Society (largest profit in event)
2000   Youth Educational Services (worked on team to develop statewide grant)

Professional Memberships and Activities

List professional memberships, affiliations, and activities. It is never too early to join professional associations. Most have student discounts, and the professional contacts and job leads are worth the time and expense. This is also the place to list speeches you have given or research projects connected with your profession.

PROFESSIONAL MEMBERSHIPS AND ACTIVITIES

2001–present	Board Member, American Marketing Association (student liaison with university).
2000–02	Membership, American Society of Marketing.
2002	Presenter, American Occupational Therapist Association, "Using Play Therapy for Children With Learning Disabilities," Washington Medical Center, Washington, D.C.
	Research, "Study Skills of Undeclared Students."
	Research project for Teaching Institute. Evergreen College, January 2002.

EXERCISE 3.4   The Extras

List campus and community service, professional memberships and activities, and use action words to translate skills. For example:

President of Marketing Club. Demonstrated leadership and good communication skills. Organized a team for fund-raising, increased sales of coffee stand by 25 percent in one year.

Campus service _____

_____

_____

_____

Community service _____

_____

_____

_____

Professional memberships _____

_____

_____

_____

Professional activities _____

_____

_____

_____

References

Like every other aspect of the job-search process, compiling a list of references takes research, planning, rapport with ex-employers and workers, and follow-up. Although some employers might not check references, you must be prepared and have them ready. Avoid writing at the bottom of your résumé "References available upon request." Always have available a separate page of four to six references. Do not send these unless requested. You don't want the interviewer to call your references until you have had an interview. Use the same heading on your reference sheet as you used on your résumé.

These references should be professionals who know your work, skills, and personal qualities and who will give you a good recommendation. Examples of professionals might include the following:

- Supervisor
- Former boss
- Coworker
- Professor or instructor
- Community contacts, e.g.,
  - Rotary president
  - Mayor
  - Local business owner

Review your networking contacts that you compiled in Chapter 2 on pages 54 and 57 for ideas for references. Always **contact your references** and ask permission to use their names, addresses, and phone numbers, and ask what phone number they would like to use or if you can include both work and home phone.

Make certain that the people you ask to be references can give you a good recommendation. Ask directly if they will give you a positive recommendation, and assure them that you will send them a résumé so they can answer questions more knowledgeably.

It is vital that you have a letter of reference from your former supervisor if it's requested. If you left the last position with resentment, or if your relationship with your current boss is cool, try to mend those fences. The only way to handle this situation is for you to take control. Change your perception of the situation and realize that most former bosses probably want you to find another job.

First, write a draft of a reference letter to your supervisor and request that he or she edit it, discuss it with you, and send you a final copy on company stationery. If you are still employed at the company, you can ask for your supervisor's support. Even if you are terminated, your former supervisor can be convinced to write you a letter of support if you attempt to mend the fence and assume at least part of the blame for your termination.

Figure 3.2 on page 88 includes a sample draft of a reference letter that you might provide.

Sample Reference Letter

Figure 3.2
Good References Many prospective employers want to see references. *Can you think of at least three people who would write reference letters for you?*

2930 Apple Lane
Tulip, FL 21192

May 22, 2003

Ms. Jan Tempis
Personnel Director
Avil Corporation
Orlando, FL 28821

Dear Ms. Tempis:

I would like to recommend Jill Burton for an administrative assistant position in your organization.

Jill demonstrated excellent management skills in her position as Human Resource Technician. She is dependable, knowledgeable, and organized. She was responsible for developing a new reference file, organizing marketing lists, and handling all seminar registration details.

Unfortunately, because of restructuring at Sona Company, our new management system required a management trainer with a stronger background and a college degree in management. Ms. Burton is a highly-trained professional. I would recommend her for the new position she seeks with your firm.

Sincerely,

Mark Platton
Sales Director

EXERCISE 3.5   Gathering Your References

Getting a letter of reference from your boss's boss is a big plus, or you can include one from a former supervisor. Then get two or three references from coworkers, professional colleagues, a teacher, or community leader. On the lines provided, write the names of people who would write letters of reference for you.

_____   _____

_____   _____

_____   _____

_____   _____

Career Directions

BusinessWeek

Résumés: Beware of Getting "Creative"

While padding your résumé has never been a good idea, these days it's a particularly bad one. Companies will check; you will in all likelihood get caught; and the damage to your career will be inestimable. "Your name becomes mud," says Kathi Vanyo, a Phoenix-based managing consultant.

But there is hope for the résumé-challenged. While utter fabrications—such as phony academic degrees and made-up jobs—are big no-nos, you can commit some sins of omission with virtual impunity. Few employers care about the number of jobs held [or] bankruptcies that date back more than 15 years.

A far better strategy is to disclose the most damaging information about yourself immediately. Guilty with an explanation, especially one that puts you in a favorable light, is almost always better than guilt compounded by a cover-up.

"There are things you might have been able to get away with a few years ago that you'd be well advised to disclose now," says James Mintz, a New York investigator. Jobs conveniently left unreported represent the most common type of résumé tampering, according to Mintz. Often, the applicant simply stretches the dates for the jobs that came before and after the omitted position. Other misrepresentations include exaggerated accomplishments and salaries.

Knowing that such scrutiny awaits them has made many people overzealous about sanitizing their pasts—when for all but a few, the best strategy is to be up-front about their mistakes.

By Louis Lavelle

Excerpted from October 22, 2001, issue of BusinessWeek Online by special permission, copyright © 2000-2001, by The McGraw-Hill Companies, Inc.

Career Case Study Danielle Stein is ready to change jobs. She has moved up as far as she can within her present company after three years. Her skills and experience are advanced enough that she could find a better job. However, she is unsure whether her résumé gives the best impression to prospective employers because she had been out of work for a year before her present job. She is tempted to cover up that information. ***What advice would you give Danielle to help her write her résumé and why?***

Other Factors for Writing a Perfect Résumé

Now that you have listed essential information and used action words to translate experience into accomplishments, make certain that your résumé is visually attractive and easy to read. Use the following guidelines.

Format

There are two basic résumé formats: *chronological* and *functional.* All other alternatives (such as combination, creative, organizational, marketing letter, or targeted) are simply variations and are generally not as effective.

Examples of all types are shown in this chapter and the chapter appendix. Remember, the purpose of a résumé is to make a good first impression and get you an interview. You do this by presenting yourself in a direct, clear, concise, and honest manner, not by creating illusions, using disguises or gimmicks, or developing a long, detailed, rambling résumé.

CHRONOLOGICAL RESUME

The chronological résumé (like the two shown in **Figure 3.3** puts your most recent experience first and is recommended as the most effective for stating your experience, education, and skills in a direct and traditional manner. Most traditional employers, such as schools, government, and

Figure 3.3
The Traditional Résumé A chronological résumé is one of the most common types of résumés. *What is the main characteristic of this kind of résumé?*

Chronological Résumé
(emphasizing experience)

Chronological Résumés

JASON STOOB

Present Address	**Permanent Address**
1332 Palm Street	21 Pleasant Lane
Amber, OH 57702	Walnut Grove, OH 56343
(313) 273-1928	(313) 822-3283

WORK EXPERIENCE

1999–present **Assistant Manager**
Greenview Apartments, Amber, OH
- Assisted with maintenance of property.
- Collected rent.
- Resolved conflicts.
- Interviewed new renters.
- Reduced turnover rate by 5 percent.

1998–99 **Salesperson**
Johnson's Men's Store, Amber, OH
- Installed software package to improve efficiency of cashier .
- Designed publicity for spring show.

1998 **Intern Salesperson**
Selter's Real Estate Office, Amber, OH
- Assisted with the installation of a new computer office system, answered phones, assisted customers, typed contracts, filed loan applications.
- Organized seminars, two home tours.

EDUCATION

2000 Simpson Business College, Amber, OH
Associate of Science in Business Administration
Major: Real Estate
Minor: Finance

AWARDS, MEMBERSHIPS, AND ACTIVITIES

1999–2000 President, Marketing Club
- Served as chair for Faculty Awards Committee for spring banquet.
- Conducted cave tours to prospective business students.

1999 Outstanding Business Student Award
1999 United Way volunteer

corporations, want to quickly see experience and education listed in a chronological format. They don't want long, detailed paragraphs explaining exactly what job tasks you performed—nor do they want a list of experiences and jobs that lacks dates. **Prepare a chronological résumé** under these circumstances:

- You are a recent college graduate, have advanced degrees and/or specialized training, and want to emphasize your education.
- You want to show career progression.
- You have not changed jobs frequently.
- You are still in the same field.

Gretchen Cash
1883 8th Street
Tacoma, WA 93021
(661) 751-2738

EDUCATION

June 2002	Sequoia Business College Bachelor of Arts Major: Business Administration GPA: 3.6	Tacoma, WA
June 2000	Tacoma Business School Associate of Arts, Computer Science Graduated with honors	Tacoma, WA

ADDITIONAL TRAINING

- Communication seminar, Universal Seminars
- Financial planning, Tacoma Business School
- Computer workshop, Washington State University
- Editing and writing workshop, Washington State University

SPECIAL QUALIFICATIONS

- Fluent in Spanish
- Advanced skills in IBM and Apple computers
- Editing and writing skills

WORK EXPERIENCE

2002   **Management Trainee**

ROCKWAY CORPORATION, Tacoma, WA
- Developed computer-based system for customer service.
- Assisted with staff development program.
- Planned and edited newsletter.

2000–2002   **Office Manager**

ALLSTATE INSURANCE AGENCY, Tacoma, WA
- Answered the phone, assisted in process claims, maintained files.
- Greeted public, assisted with budget, typed and edited letters.
- Worked with team to develop seminars.
- Improved customer service as company grew over 15 percent in one year.

Chronological Résumé
(recent graduate)

Figure 3.4

Skills Count A functional résumé is arranged to emphasize skills. *What skills are emphasized in this résumé, and what is the advantage of doing this?*

Functional Résumé
(reentry)

Vanessa Johnson
2988 Pine Avenue
Fair Oaks, TX 69441
(404) 720-2738

QUALIFICATIONS AND ACCOMPLISHMENTS

Organizational Skills

- Demonstrated ability to organize office information system.
- Maintained accurate and detailed bookkeeping inventory.
- Organized fund-raiser for American Cancer Society (raised $100,000 for Hospice Center).

Computer Skills

- Proven ability to learn new software systems quickly.
- Created computer system for payroll for Sunset Elementary School.
- Trained teachers and staff in computer and word-processing skills.

Communication Skills

- Excellent communication with teachers, staff, and parents.
- Created a newsletter for parents and staff.
- Drafted effective business correspondence.

WORK EXPERIENCE

| 1991–1995 | Secretary, Sunset Elementary School, Fair Oaks, TX |
| 1986–1991 | Caregiver, Rainbow Preschool (self-employed), Fair Oaks, TX |

EDUCATION AND TRAINING

Adult Career Training Center, Fairfield, TX
Secretarial Certificate, 1997

HONORS AND MEMBERSHIPS

Graduated with honors
Outstanding Secretarial Student Award

COMMUNITY SERVICE

Volunteer, American Cancer Society

FUNCTIONAL RESUME

Use a functional résumé or skills résumé (like those shown in **Figure 3.4**) when you want to highlight skills, abilities, and qualifications rather than education or specific dates of work experience. For example, a home-maker may want to use a functional résumé when she or he has had years of experience volunteering, keeping the family budget, paying taxes, traveling, and organizing events but limited formal work experience or education. If you have been out of the job market for a number of years, organize your accomplishments around the major functions you have performed, such as fund-raising, organization, and/or public relations.

Robert L. Ferro
613 Park Avenue
Wales, NY 10992
(914) 621-9882

PHOTOGRAPHY

- Designed setups for and photographed interior displays.
- Photographed numerous nature close-ups.
- Taught basic photography to staff.
- Photographed "how-to" series on gardening.
- Illustrated articles on home and garden.
- Supervised photos, illustrations, and drawings.

GRAPHIC DESIGN

- Designed brochures, business cards, and newsletters.
- Produced paste-ups for weekly magazine.
- Planned displays for major metropolitan art show.
- Produced flyer for SUNY Art Department.
- Designed various outdoor journals.

EDITING

- Home show trade magazine
- *Home and Garden Magazine*
- Articles on interior design
- Videos for college recruiting

AWARDS

Home and Garden Magazine Creative Photography Award

EXPERIENCE

1999–present	Freelance Photographer, Wales, NY 1998–92
1998–99	Graphics Designer and Assistant Editor, Baltimore, MD
1997–98	Intern Staff Photographer, Baltimore, MD

EDUCATION

1998	Maryland Institute of Art, Baltimore, MD
	Bachelor of Arts in Commercial and Graphic Arts

Functional Résumé
(emphasizing skills)

Highlight the skills that will make you stand out. **Prepare a functional résumé** under these circumstances:

- You have little education but years of experience in the job market, and you want to emphasize experience and skills.
- Your work experience doesn't support your job objective.
- You are changing occupations.
- You want to point out specific accomplishments and skills.
- You have had a variety of job experiences.
- You are reentering the job market.

Length

Résumés should be clear and concise. Unless you have years of experience, keep your résumé to one page. Focus on the essentials: experience, skills, and accomplishments. Do not state salary requirements or indicate why you left previous jobs. Employers are not impressed when they see a two- or three-page résumé that has a lot of fluff. Your cover letter can highlight certain accomplishments and skills and how they relate to a specific job. During the interview you can elaborate on duties, explain dates, give examples, and go into detail.

Writing Style

The writing style for your résumé should be professional and formal. Be concise, direct, and clear. Use short statements, action words, and bullets to emphasize skills, accomplishments, and duties. Don't use complete sentences, paragraphs, or the word *I*. For example, write:

> Increased sales by $80,000 in first year.

Instead of:

> I worked very hard in sales, visited outlying areas, and increased the sales in my area by $80,000 in 2000.

State your accomplishments directly and clearly. You want to show confidence. However, you must be honest. You can be fired for misrepresentation. All information should be verifiable.

Make certain your writing is error-free. Check punctuation, grammar, and spelling. Use a spell-check and have a friend or instructor proofread your résumé.

Graphics and Reproduction

Be sure your résumé is visually attractive and professional. Use white space to add balance. Make certain that your résumé is centered.

Don't try to be clever or cute. Unless you are applying to a creative company for a very creative position, use the standard, conservative style for printing and sending your résumé. One person sent his résumé in a shoe with a note that said, "I just want to get my foot in the door." Some companies may appreciate this unusual approach, but in general, your basic résumé should be acceptable to many different companies. Save your creative flair for the interview or your first assignment.

Use the following guidelines:
- Avoid graphics and pictures.
- Use basic, nondecorative typefaces.
- Use a standard font size of 10–12 points.
- Use boldface or underline to highlight.
- Use good-quality paper.
- Use standard colors: off-white, cream, beige, or gray.
- Avoid staples or folds.

Tailoring Your Résumé

There are services that will prepare a résumé for you; however, it will look like many other résumés with identical formats. Write your own résumé and **choose the best format:** functional or chronological. By practicing, you will gain the confidence to write a résumé that reflects you. You will then be able to create different versions to tailor for a variety of jobs.

Try out formats, types, boldface, underlining, and left or right justifications. Choose the combination that best highlights and emphasizes your accomplishments and skills. Clear, concise, traditional résumés are always acceptable. However, if the standard formats seem too conventional and limiting, create your own style and vary your format for different jobs.

Résumé Makeover

EXERCISE 3.6

Correct the following résumé using the format and style that you think would best highlight Jan's experiences. Make up details as needed. Compare it to the annotated résumé on page 96. Then, look at the makeover résumé on page 97 to see a sample result.

Résumé

Jan Winkler
112 Post Street
Ohio Tech College
Lansing, Ohio 49983
724-1058

Sex: Female
Age: 21
Marital Status: Single
Height: 5' 6"
Weight: 142

Job objective

I want to be an engineer.

Education

Ohio Tech. College, BS in Engineering, 2002

Experience

Rockwell Corp. I worked as a receptionist and telephone operator. I answered the phone, typed letters, wrote proposals, and did data processing.
2001-2002

Sunnybrae Animal Clinic. I worked as an assistant to a veterinarian and helped out.

Awards and honors

Dean's List
Awarded a scholarship

Community and campus activities

Presbyterian Food Bank, volunteer Big Sisters, Volunteer

References

Dr. John Hines
Sara McWright
Mr. Joshua Livingston

Before

continued

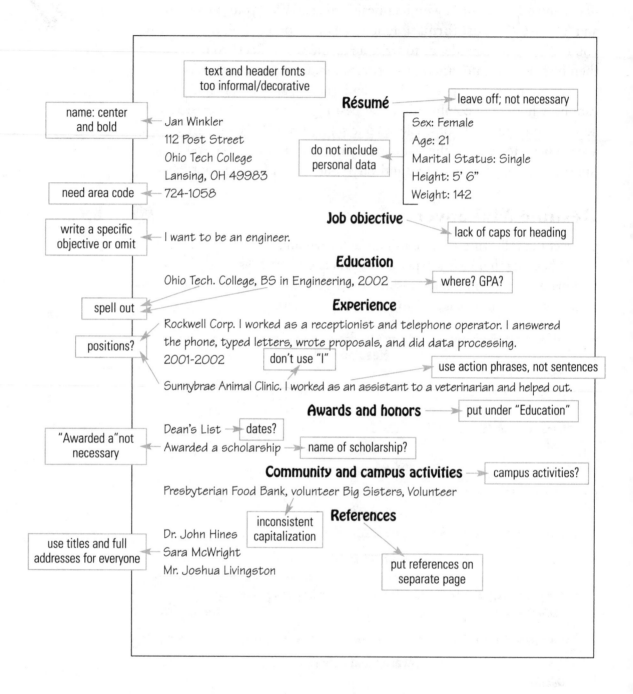

text and header fonts too informal/decorative

name: center and bold

Résumé

leave off; not necessary

Jan Winkler
112 Post Street
Ohio Tech College
Lansing, OH 49983

do not include personal data

Sex: Female
Age: 21
Marital Status: Single
Height: 5' 6"
Weight: 142

need area code — 724-1058

Job objective

lack of caps for heading

write a specific objective or omit — I want to be an engineer.

Education

Ohio Tech. College, BS in Engineering, 2002 — where? GPA?

spell out

Experience

positions? — Rockwell Corp. I worked as a receptionist and telephone operator. I answered the phone, typed letters, wrote proposals, and did data processing. 2001-2002

don't use "I"

use action phrases, not sentences

Sunnybrae Animal Clinic. I worked as an assistant to a veterinarian and helped out.

Awards and honors

put under "Education"

Dean's List — dates?

"Awarded a" not necessary — Awarded a scholarship — name of scholarship?

Community and campus activities

campus activities?

Presbyterian Food Bank, volunteer Big Sisters, Volunteer

inconsistent capitalization

References

use titles and full addresses for everyone

Dr. John Hines
Sara McWright
Mr. Joshua Livingston

put references on separate page

Annotated

continued

Jan A. Winkler

College address	**Permanent address**
112 Post Street	256 Shelter Grove
Lansing, OH 49983	Lakeside, OH 49939
(405) 724-1058	(513) 724-1058

JOB OBJECTIVE:

An entry-level electrical engineering position with a large environmental firm.

EDUCATION

June 2002   Bachelor of Science, Electrical Engineering
Ohio Technical College, Lansing, OH
Overall GPA: 3.89
Senior Project: Creating Software for Customer Service

AWARDS AND HONORS

2001   Business Women's Scholarship
1999–2000   Dean's List at Ohio Technical College

EXPERIENCE

2001–2002   **Internship**
Rockwell Corporation, Lansing, OH
- Created software package for customer
- Answered the phone, typed letters
- Completed data-processing entries

2000–2001   **Veterinary Assistant**
Sunnybrae Animal Clinic, Lansing, OH
- Assisted with animals
- Cleaned cages and fed animals
- Sterilized surgical instruments

CAMPUS AND COMMUNITY SERVICE

2000–2001   Vice Chair of Engineering Club
Ohio Technical College
Summer 2000   Presbyterian Food Bank (served 50 meals, distributed 260 food baskets)
1999–2000   Big Sisters of Lansing

Makeover

Jan A. Winkler
References

Dr. John Hines	Ms. Sara McWright	Mr. Joshua Livingston
Dean of Advising	Director of Marketing	Veterinary Assistant
Ohio Technical College	Rockwell Corporation	Sunnybrae Animal Clinic
112 Post Street	2310 Hopkins Drive	103 12th Street
Lansing, OH 49983	Lansing, OH 49983	Lakeside, OH 49939
(405) 726-4021	(405) 722-3104	(513) 724-1130

References

Write a chronological résumé, using your worksheets as references. Compare it with the sample chronological résumés on pages 90 and 91. Write a functional résumé if you think this format best reflects your skills and accomplishments. See pages 92 and 93 for good models. On the lines below, write out a rough draft of your résumé.

_____

_____

_____

_____

_____

_____

_____

_____

_____

_____

_____

_____

_____

_____

_____

_____

_____

_____

_____

_____

_____

_____

_____

_____

_____

_____

_____

STAYING POWER

*D*o you start with skills, job titles, or past responsibilities? Should you use bulleted lists, short phrases, or paragraphs? Do you limit your résumé to a single sheet or use several? Writing a résumé can be confusing because there's no exact formula for a perfect résumé. However, every résumé should have certain elements.

Grabbing the employer's attention, showcasing your best skills and accomplishments, and having bulletproof grammar and spelling are essential aspects of any effective résumé. However, you should also consider less obvious elements, such as having a consistent style. Do you use complete sentences or phrases? Are all of your verbs in active tense? Be sure your résumé is as succinct as possible, and make sure your strengths jump off the page.

Sometimes it takes fresh eyes to spot mistakes, inconsistencies, and missing information. Ask a friend whose opinion you trust to provide constructive criticism. Reading your résumé out loud will also help you find errors.

Then purchase some good paper, locate a high-quality printer, and prepare your résumé to go to press. Using matching envelopes and new toner in your printer can help you to make a good impression as well. Finally, remember that your résumé isn't worth the paper it's printed on if you don't distribute it.

Try This...

- Instead of giving up on your résumé, refine it. Find the strongest parts of your résumé and develop them.
- If your most recent jobs aren't as impressive as your previous ones, or if you lack experience, organize your résumé according to your skills rather than the order of your jobs.
- Also consider layout. Appearance matters when you're making a first impression. Judge how the résumé looks in print and how it looks in an e-mail.

CHAPTER 3 *Review*

Skill Check Recap

- Organize your database to use in your résumé.
- Write a job objective.
- Translate experiences into job skills.
- Contact your references.
- Prepare a chronological résumé.
- Prepare a functional résumé.
- Choose the best format.

Self-Check List

Keep track of your progress. Read the following and mark *yes* or *no*.

	Yes	No
My résumé is neat, clean, and error-free.	___	___
My résumé is grammatically correct.	___	___
My résumé is printed on quality paper and is visually appealing.	___	___
I have paid attention to organization.	___	___
My résumé includes my address and phone number.	___	___
My chronological résumé includes my most recent experience first.	___	___
My functional résumé includes a list of skills.	___	___
Dates are included for all items.	___	___
All information is clear, concise, and honest.	___	___
The content of my résumé is effective.	___	___
My résumé includes action words, or verbs, and job statements.	___	___
My résumé emphasizes results and accomplishments with measurable benefits.	___	___

Review Questions

1. What four objectives should the résumé achieve?

_____

_____

2. What is the basic purpose of the résumé?

_____

_____

3. What are the seven areas to address in organizing your résumé?

_____

_____

4. What are four useful tips for writing job descriptions?

_____

_____

5. How long should your résumé be?

_____

_____

6. What are three things you should not put on your résumé?

_____

_____

7. What are the two basic formats for résumés? Which are you most likely to use?

_____

_____

8. Why is it better to prepare your own résumé rather than have one prepared by a service?

_____

_____

Critical Thinking

9. Think about the last job you had or currently have. Write a job description that includes four aspects of that job. Be sure to incorporate the four useful tips discussed in question #4.

_____

_____

Cooperative Learning

10. Read Strategies at Work on page 102. Working in pairs, design and create a résumé for Amy. Use a separate sheet of paper for this. Then review and discuss your finished résumés with the class.

The Best Résumé?

Amy has just graduated from a career college with an associate of arts degree. She is eager to begin working as a legal secretary. She was a returning student and has spent most of her adult life raising children and doing volunteer work. She has had little paid work experience.

Amy has always considered a résumé something you write if you've had a "real" job. She is worried about how to explain the years she spent working in volunteer organizations. Should she use a functional or chronological résumé?

Problem Solving The following ten questions are designed to help solve problems and make sound decisions. You can use these questions to find solutions to your own problems. Put yourself in Amy's place and consider these questions from her point of view.

- What is the problem?
- Do I have enough information?
- Can I make the decision by myself?
- Have I brainstormed alternatives?
- Have I looked at likely consequences?
- Have I identified all the resources and tools needed?
- Have I developed and implemented an action plan?
- Have I identified the best solution?
- Have I assessed the results?
- Have I modified the plan, if necessary?

What solution would you suggest to Amy?

_____

_____

_____

_____

_____

_____

_____

_____

_____

_____

_____

Find out more about writing the best résumé by visiting this book's Web site at strategies.glencoe.com

Creating Your Résumé

The following exercise will help you get started. Keep this page and update it regularly. Use it to create an outstanding résumé. Add this page to your career portfolio.

- List your job duties.

  _____

  _____

- List your key responsibilities.

  _____

  _____

- List special projects on which you have worked.

  _____

  _____

- What is your education (include classes and training programs)?

  _____

  _____

- What skills or qualifications do you have?

  _____

  _____

- Have you attended any speaking engagements that might benefit your career? If so, list them.

  _____

  _____

- List any writing projects, community involvement, and honors or awards.

  _____

  _____

- List names of people you can use as references.

  _____

  _____

CHAPTER 4

Cover Letters
and Applications

Winning Points

- Make your cover letter look professional and neat.
- Write a clear, direct, and grammatically correct cover letter.
- Indicate how your education and accomplishments fit the requirements for the job opening.
- Engage the reader's attention.
- State your specific job objective and purpose.
- State when you will call for an interview.

Introduction

Many serious job hunters put a great deal of time into writing an outstanding résumé and preparing for the interview but then write a quick and general cover letter as an afterthought—if they send one at all. Companies are often bombarded with hundreds of unsolicited résumés. A large corporation such as IBM receives over a million résumés a year. However, few résumés are accompanied by well-written, specific cover letters. For many people, writing a cover letter can be intimidating. Keep in mind that writing a simple, specific, targeted, and personalized letter is a job-search strategy that produces results.

When you do get a response as a result of a great cover letter and résumé, the application process begins. Often the next step before the interview is testing. A basic skills test is another opportunity to display your abilities. Make sure to:

- Ask for any special instructions.
- Skim the test quickly.
- Read each question carefully.
- Finish in the time allotted.

Chapter 4 Objectives

After you have completed this chapter, you will be able to:

- Explain the importance of the cover letter
- Write an effective cover letter
- Complete a job application form
- Explain how to prepare for employment tests

The Importance of the Cover Letter

An effective cover letter increases your chances of being asked for an interview. Your résumé should be general enough so that you can use it to apply for a number of jobs, but your cover letter should be specific to each job. The purpose of the cover letter is to entice your reader to take a closer look at your résumé. It should also communicate your purpose, enthusiasm, intelligence, energy, drive, and your unique abilities and personal qualities.

A cover letter is written to introduce your résumé, focus your skills, identify your job objective, indicate your enthusiasm, illustrate that you've done your homework, and add a personal touch. In addition, as with any business letter, it serves as a record. Always keep a copy for your files.

An effective cover letter can be one of the most important factors in getting a job interview. **Send a cover letter with every résumé.** If the cover letter is dull or sloppy, it can ruin your chances for an interview. Since communication skills are among the most important skills you can bring to a job, a cover letter is your opportunity to demonstrate that you can write in a clear, concise, and direct manner.

An effective cover letter highlights your positive characteristics:

1. **Create a positive first impression.** Begin by telling the employer why you are applying for the position. You want to make an immediate good impression. You can make your personality and a sense of warmth shine through.
2. **State your accomplishments.** You want to list one or two main accomplishments that have made a difference.
3. **State the benefit factor.** State how your skills can meet the company's needs. This indicates that you have done your research on both the organization and the specific office in which you are interested and that you know what the employer is looking for in ian employee. You want to show how you can contribute to the company's success.
4. **Indicate that you are a problem solver.** Describe how you have used creativity or critical thinking to solve problems and make sound decisions. Employers value creative problem solvers.
5. **Show initiative and confidence.** The letter should state when you will call to set up an interview. This shows that you have initiative and will follow up on details.

Elements of a Successful Cover Letter

A successful cover letter has the following characteristics:

- Necessary structural elements: date, inside address, salutation, body, closing, and signature

"There is nothing wrong with having nothing to say, unless you insist on saying it."
—Anonymous

- Two to four paragraphs
- Short, action-oriented, concise paragraphs
- Complete name and title of the person who will receive your cover letter
- Reasons you are attracted to the company and an indication of your personal qualities and warmth
- Demonstration that you've done your homework
- Evidence of how you can benefit the company
- Your skills that match the company's needs point-by-point
- Evidence of your enthusiasm and an indication that you are willing to strive to be successful
- Specific aspects of your résumé

Guidelines for Better Cover Letters

Job-search letters should not be written as an isolated event. Effective letters are only one component of a group of interrelated tasks that work together in the job-search process. It is difficult to write an effective letter if you have not researched a prospective company. Your research should also identify the person who is doing the hiring for the position. Networking with friends and professionals that you have met at trade associations, friends of friends, and contacts in the business community will help you find out more about a particular company and the names and titles of key people.

By now you may be aware of how the job-search steps are interconnected. Time spent assessing your skills, interests, values, and achievements; researching occupations, jobs, and companies; identifying your career goals and objectives; networking; and writing a professional résumé will pay big dividends at this stage of the job search. Your cover letters should flow from and be linked to all of these steps as you navigate the career path. If you are having difficulty writing a cover letter, you may want to go back to earlier self-assessment steps and clarify and identify your values, interests, accomplishments, and goals, and how you would benefit potential employers.

Remember that your cover letter is also a business letter and creates an image that reflects who you are. The following guidelines can help you create a professional image as you **write a standard cover letter.**

Research

All good writing starts by deciding on your purpose and analyzing the audience. Research the company and decide what needs exist. You can then show how your background can meet these needs. **Write a tailored cover letter** for each specific job.

Complete Elements

As illustrated in the sample letters on pages 110 and 111, a business letter essentially contains seven parts:

1. Letterhead or return address
2. Date
3. Inside address
4. Salutation
5. Body
6. Complimentary close
7. Signature

Interest

The letter should get the reader's attention, create interest, and be action oriented. Keep the reader's interest by varying sentence length and structure. Keep your tone warm, yet professional. This is a formal business letter.

Career Directions

BusinessWeek

How to Answer an Online Job Posting

You're wise to clarify the etiquette of electronic applications. The experts we talked to say you don't need to address your [cover] letter to anyone. Companies often don't name a contact person in job postings because the materials are headed to human resources, where a computer or some HR staffer will do the initial screening.

Online ads can get thousands of responses. Answer exactly as instructed. If the company requests résumés by e-mail, don't send another copy by regular mail because the corporate machinery will register that as a goof. Job-search consultant Margaret Riley Dikel also suggests that you copy and paste your electronic résumé in basic ASCII format.

Arrange your cover letter and résumé to impress the search engine that's likely to handle the first screening. Not only is the software programmed to reject unqualified résumés, it's often set to look for keywords that you spot in the ad, such as "e-commerce experience." It can even be programmed to favor résumés that contain such words more often or higher in the text.

Kate Wendleton, founder of national career-counseling network The Five O'Clock Club, says one crucial job-search strategy is to think of the online job listing as just the first step. And remember: Some 20% of jobs aren't even advertised, so don't neglect good old-fashioned networking.

By H. J. Cummins

Excerpted from June 26, 2000, issue of BusinessWeek Online by special permission, copyright © 2000, by The McGraw-Hill Companies, Inc.

Career Case Study Tyree Price just completed a five-year program in nursing while working as a cosmetics salesperson. She is now ready to begin her job search and plans to use the Internet as one of her resources. When Tyree looked for a job four years ago, she used the same cover letter for every response. She wants to update her letter but is unsure of what to write. *Should she use the same letter for all job responses? What key features should she include in her letter? Why?*

Brief Length

Keep letters to one page. Concentrate on the jobs that best demonstrate your accomplishments and skills. Brevity is important. It shows that you respect how busy the reader is and that you are capable of writing in a clear, simple, and concise manner.

Address to a Specific Person

Always address your letter to a specific person whenever possible. Generally, a phone call to the targeted company will give you the name, title, and correct spelling of the person hiring.

Focus on Your Benefit to the Company

Your letter should be employer-centered, not self-centered. Highlight your accomplishments and skills and relate them to how you will benefit the company through this specific job.

Remember, one of your best resources is **strategies.glencoe.com**

Confidence

Your tone, choice of words, and content should suggest that you are a positive, productive, and optimistic person who has skills and qualities to offer the employer. Avoid conveying doubt or uncertainty with words such as *sort of*, *hope*, *guess*, *think*, and *wish*. Use affirmative, direct statements that communicate confidence without arrogance.

Action Words

Action words, or action verbs, such as the ones used in your résumé, create a powerful letter. Also indicate that you will call to follow up.

Honesty

Make certain that you can back up, give specific examples of, and demonstrate all your accomplishments.

No Errors

Proofread each letter for spelling and other errors. Your letter should be flawless.

Professional Appearance

Just as your personal appearance gives an immediate impression of who you are and your possible work habits, the appearance of your cover letter suggests your professional level. Invest in good-quality paper with matching envelopes. Use off-white, beige, or gray. A word processor or computer will give your letter a professional look, and you will be able to change or edit your letter to specifically fit each job. If sending your cover letter and résumé via e-mail, be sure to follow e-mail format. Proofread and correct any errors as you would do for a hard-copy letter to make the best impression.

Elements of Good Cover Letters

1 Letterhead or return address

2 Date

3 Inside address

4 Salutation

5 Body

6 Complimentary close

7 Signature

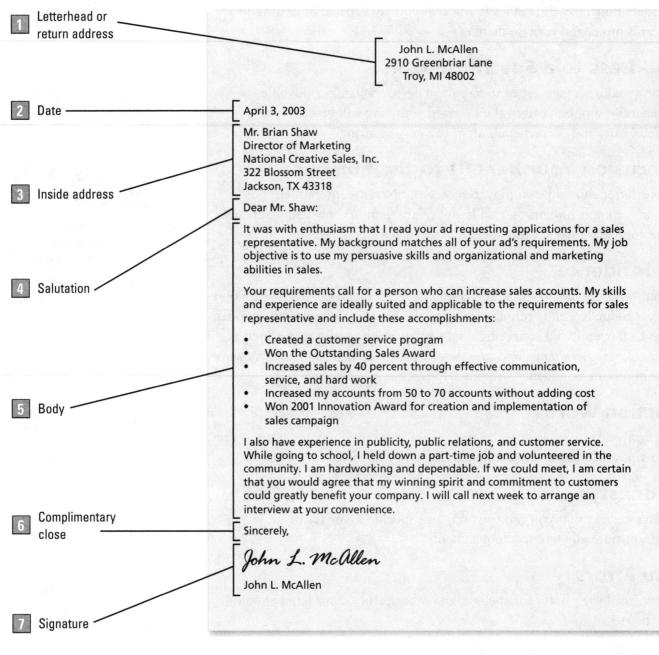

John L. McAllen
2910 Greenbriar Lane
Troy, MI 48002

April 3, 2003

Mr. Brian Shaw
Director of Marketing
National Creative Sales, Inc.
322 Blossom Street
Jackson, TX 43318

Dear Mr. Shaw:

It was with enthusiasm that I read your ad requesting applications for a sales representative. My background matches all of your ad's requirements. My job objective is to use my persuasive skills and organizational and marketing abilities in sales.

Your requirements call for a person who can increase sales accounts. My skills and experience are ideally suited and applicable to the requirements for sales representative and include these accomplishments:

- Created a customer service program
- Won the Outstanding Sales Award
- Increased sales by 40 percent through effective communication, service, and hard work
- Increased my accounts from 50 to 70 accounts without adding cost
- Won 2001 Innovation Award for creation and implementation of sales campaign

I also have experience in publicity, public relations, and customer service. While going to school, I held down a part-time job and volunteered in the community. I am hardworking and dependable. If we could meet, I am certain that you would agree that my winning spirit and commitment to customers could greatly benefit your company. I will call next week to arrange an interview at your convenience.

Sincerely,

John L. McAllen

John L. McAllen

190 Rose Lane
Kalamazoo, MI 49007

March 26, 2003

Mr. Arthur Shaw
Director of Sales
National Creative Sales Company
992 Timmons Street
Petersburg, ND

Dear Mr. Shaw:

I have read the annual report for the National Creative Sales Company. You have developed and marketed fine products, and I am pleased to know that your new sports line is also doing well. I am interested in contributing my marketing, organizational, and persuasive skills to a progressive company in a sales position that offers substantial challenge. National Creative Sales is a growing company with an excellent reputation. I would like to contribute to its success.

Throughout college and during the summers, I have worked in the area of sales and have progressively increased my sales and marketing skills. In June, I will graduate with an Associate's Degree in Marketing and want to continue in the area of sales. I have accomplished the following:

- Demonstrated excellent communication, organizational, and team skills
- Handled customer complaints and solved concerns of major customers
- Developed a program to spot and solve company's customer-service complaints

For an internship project, I developed some marketing materials that I think would fit in perfectly with your latest campaign. I have earned the reputation of being a team player and spreading goodwill where I have worked. I will call you next Tuesday to see if a meeting could be arranged to discuss these exciting ideas. In the meantime, if you would like to contact me, my number is (408) 521-2370.

Sincerely,

Mary Gearly

Mary Gearly

Figure 4.1
Well-Written Cover Letters A great cover letter with the correct elements will help your résumé stand out in the crowd of other résumés. *Do you think a good cover letter is more important than a good résumé? Why?*

Seven Steps to a Successful Cover Letter

Like a résumé, a cover letter can be broken down into steps, or sections, each one with its own purpose. There are seven sections in a successful cover letter. The following guidelines cover each part of a successful cover letter and give you an opportunity to practice. The section numbers correspond to the numbers shown on the preceding cover letter on page 110.

Section 1 Letterhead or Return Address

When you are preparing a cover letter on plain paper (using the block format), type the return address approximately two inches from the top of the page, single-spaced, and flush left. Don't use abbreviations.

You can have your stationery printed with your letterhead at the top or type it yourself. Make certain it is centered. This will make your cover letter look professional. You can also type your address immediately below your name as part of the signature block.

> 2910 Greenbriar
> Lane Troy, MI 48002

Section 2 Date

The date is typed directly below the return address. If you use letterhead paper, type the date three to five spaces below the last line of the printed or typed letterhead. If you used plain paper and you type the return address as part of the signature block, type the date six spaces (two inches) from the top of the page.

> 2910 Greenbriar Lane
> Troy, MI 48002
>
>
> April 19, 2003

Section 3 Inside Address

An inside address is essential for business correspondence. Make certain you have the correct title, address, and spelling. If you are unsure of the person's correct name and address, call the place of business and ask the operator or receptionist. Type the inside address on the left, four to six spaces below the date. For example:

> Dr. Albert L. Ferraro
> Dean of Graduate Studies
> Alberta Career School
> 1324 Elmwood Avenue
> Alberta, MI 48821

Section 4 Salutation

The salutation begins with *Dear;* includes titles such as *Mr., Mrs., Ms., Miss,* and *Dr.;* and ends with a colon (:). (For the appropriate forms of address for government or church officials, see the appendix of *Webster's New World Dictionary.*) You should call first and find out to whom you should address the cover letter and his or her correct title. Occasionally, you may not know a person's name. If you don't know and cannot get a name, it is recommended that you omit a salutation and refer to the position you are applying for.

Dear Dr. Ferraro:

or

Re: Account Executive position

Dear Ms. Banks:

or

Re: Instructor position

Starting Your Cover Letter

EXERCISE 4.1

Write out your letterhead, date, return address, and salutation.

_____

_____

_____

_____

_____

_____

_____

_____

_____

_____

_____

_____

_____

_____

_____

_____

_____

_____

_____

Section 5 Body

The body of your cover letter will consist of several paragraphs that will accomplish the following goals:

- Capture attention.
- Create interest.
- Indicate action.

To lay a foundation for your cover letter before you begin writing, ask yourself a few pertinent questions listed in **Figure 4.2.**

FIRST PARAGRAPH: CAPTURE ATTENTION

Single-space the body of the letter and use double spaces between paragraphs. Use the block format so that every paragraph starts at the left margin, as shown in the sample letters in **Figure 4.1** on pages 110 and 111.

The first paragraph should introduce you and your purpose for writing. This is the place to clearly **state your job objective.** Capture the employer's attention by describing why you are interested in the job.

Demonstrate that you have done your homework and be sure to **indicate that you know about the company.**

SECOND PARAGRAPH: CREATE INTEREST

The second paragraph of your letter should get the reader interested in meeting you. It should briefly highlight your skills and accomplishments

and relate them point-by-point to the prospective job. **Relate the needs of the employer to your skills.** Use action words to highlight your skills and abilities without appearing self-centered. Use the word *you* whenever possible. For example:

> Your annual report indicates you are expanding in the area of sales. You may find that my expertise in sales and customer relations is just what you need.

Don't state a salary requirement even if the ad requests it. You can simply say that the salary should be comparable to other professionals in your field with your experience and education. Remember, you do not want anything to keep you from the all-important interview. Too high a salary requirement may cause employers to reject you; too low and they may wonder about your worth.

FINAL PARAGRAPH: INDICATE ACTION

In the final paragraph, indicate what the next step will be. Never be vague or put the action in the employer's court. Close by saying that you will call in a few days. Don't request an interview or ask them to call you. You want to show initiative and drive. Tell the person that you will be calling on a certain date to discuss an interview. Make certain you follow up.

Section 6 Complimentary Close

The complimentary close is the formal end of the letter and is typed two spaces below the last line of your final paragraph. It should be capitalized and followed by a comma. Complimentary closings used in business include *Sincerely, Cordially, Yours Truly,* and *Respectfully.*

Questions to Consider

1. What does the prospective employer need?
Which skills, knowledge, and experience would be an asset for the job you are targeting?

2. What are your objectives?
Are you applying for a specific job, trying to get an interview, or simply hoping to speak with someone about general opportunities at that organization.

3. What are three to five qualities that you would bring to this employer or this job?
If you're responding to a job listing, then your qualities should be those mentioned in the ad. If you're not applying for a specific job, mention skills and experience that are usually valued.

4. How can you match your experience to the job?
What are at least two accomplishments you can mention that support the qualities you identified in question #3?

5. Why do you want to work for this particular organization or person?
What do you know about the company (i.e., products, services, mission, and needs) that relates to your own background, values, and objectives?

Figure 4.2
Think Before Writing Prospective employers are most interested in knowing how your skills and experience will fill their needs. Knowing this information in advance will help you compose an effective cover letter. *What other important information can you provide in a cover letter?*

SOURCE: From *Job Notes: Cover Letters* by L. Michelle Tullier, copyright © 1997 by The Princeton Review LLC. Used by persmission of Princeton Review, a division of Random House, Inc.

Section 7 Signature

Leave four spaces for your signature after the closing. Type your full name. Professional titles or degrees may be typed after your name but are not included in your signature. Write your signature in a legible, careful manner, using a good pen. Take care not to scrawl your name. Two spaces below your name, type *Enclosure* if you are also including your résumé.

Sincerely,

John L. McAllen

John L. McAllen

Enclosure

Jot down the outline of a typical cover letter. Use a separate sheet of paper to write a complete draft of a standard cover letter showing all seven parts.

_____

_____

_____

_____

_____

_____

_____

_____

_____

_____

_____

_____

_____

_____

_____

Helpful Hints

Margins and Spacing

Margins vary depending on the length of the letter. Letters should be centered with at least a one-inch margin on all sides. If typing a short letter (under 100 words), insert extra line spaces at the top of the page so that your letter looks centered. When using the block format, single-space your text and double-space between paragraphs and when introducing a list. If you want to use a modified block format, indent each new line of a paragraph five spaces.

Word Processing

Use a word processing program so that you can easily make corrections and update your cover letter for each job. Your letter should not have any errors. (See **Figure 4.3** on page 118 for common mistakes.) Your cover letter reflects you, and it should look neat, clean, and professional. Be sure to save your résumé and cover letters on a disk.

Accuracy Is Important

Make sure your cover letter is accurate. When in doubt about grammar, usage, and spelling, double-check a dictionary or grammar handbook. Here are a few useful rules:

CAPITALIZATION

Capitalize proper nouns (people, places, and things):

- Senator Jones
- Eureka, California
- Red Cross
- The Southwest (specific geographical location)
- *How to Start Your Own Business* (Capitalize and either italicize or underline titles of books and magazines.)
- Jello® (Capitalize trademarks.)
- Dr. Jones, Vice President of Academic Affairs (specific title)

Don't capitalize:

- Titles unless they are specific (e.g., Dr. Jones is a competent vice president of academic affairs.)
- Seasons (e.g., spring, fall)
- Points on the compass (e.g., Drive south and then north.)

ABBREVIATIONS

Limit the use of abbreviations in your cover letter and résumé:

- College degrees: Instead of B.A., use Bachelor of Arts; B.S., use Bachelor of Science; M.A., use Master of Arts; M.B.A., use Master of Business Administration; and Ph.D., J.D., C.P.A., etc., should always be abbreviated.
- Most abbreviated words are followed by a period: Jr.
- When states are abbreviated, do not use periods: WA
- The abbreviation of *etcetera*, (etc.) is always preceded and followed by a comma, unless it ends a sentence. *I have experience using office equipment, such as copy machines, fax machines, computers, printers, scanners, etc.*

APOSTROPHES

In general, it is best to limit the use of apostrophes since the cover letter is a formal business letter.

Use an apostrophe to indicate one or more omitted letters in a contraction:

- It's (It is) time to follow up on phone calls.
- Don't (Do not) wear inappropriate clothes to a job interview.
- They're (They are) interested in good manners.

Use an apostrophe to indicate possession:

- The company's profits rose by 23 percent.
- I had the honor of being a President's Scholar.
- The employees' pension plan is part of the benefits package.

USAGE

They're, their, and *there* are spelled and used differently:

- They're (They are) going to set up an interview for Friday.
- Their offices are in Sieman's Hall.
- There are many job opportunities available.

Lay and *lie* are used differently:

- Lay the book down.
- Lie down and rest.

Principal and *principle* are used differently:

- The principal gave me a letter of reference. The principal is a pal.
- His principles reflect the highest integrity.

Figure 4.3
Avoiding Common Mistakes
By creating a flawless cover letter, you present yourself in the best light. *Should you repeat what you include in your résumé in your cover letter?*

Common Mistakes Found in Cover Letters
✘ **Misspelled words** Make certain that your letter has correct spelling. Errors are unforgivable and reveal you as being incompetent and sloppy. Besides using a spell checker, ask someone else to check your letter.
✘ **Excessive length** Your letter should be concise, crisp, and to the point. Don't waste the employer's time.
✘ **Too general** Your letter should be written for a certain position and addressed to a specific individual, and it should summarize outstanding skills and accomplishments. Don't address a letter *To whom it may concern.* Make certain you have the person's correct title, name, and address.
✘ **Too many duties** Don't summarize your résumé, use dates, or try to cover all of your previous duties. Explain one or two of your most outstanding accomplishments.
✘ **Too much focus on your needs** You should focus on the needs of the company, not on your needs or wishes. What can you do to benefit the company?
✘ **Gimmicks** Don't try to be cute or resort to gimmicks. Respect the intelligence and dignity of your reader.
✘ **Weak, insecure, and boring tone** Don't be unduly modest. You want to show confidence and self-assurance and allow your personality to come across. Don't sound as if you are so desperate or needy for a job that you will take anything. Use a strong ending. Don't wait for the employer to call you. Set a time to call.
✘ **Passive tone** Choose your words carefully to show action and energy.
✘ **Disjointed and aimless** Your words and style should indicate that you are organized, have a purpose, and can write logically. State the purpose of the letter and your career goal.
✘ **Messy, unprofessional appearance** Make certain your letter is flawless and produced on quality paper. Your envelope should match. You want to make a good impression.

Responding to Job Ads

Respond to one of the following job advertisements. Create an accurate, complete, and focused cover letter in the space provided. Don't forget the seven sections.

HELP WANTED
Chiropractic Assistant
Full-time position available. Must be good with people and paperwork, and have a positive mental attitude and good communication skills. Will provide training. Send résumé and references to **Dr. John Fullerton, Box 349, Riverton, Ohio 43998**

HELP WANTED
Accounting Technician
Fortuna Union High School District is accepting applications for a full-time Accounting Technician. Payroll, accounts payable, and benefits experience required. Salary: $2,028/mo. Applications and job descriptions available from business office at **14th St., Fortuna, Maine 01276**

_____
_____
_____
_____
_____
_____
_____
_____
_____
_____
_____
_____
_____
_____
_____
_____
_____
_____
_____
_____

No Specific Job in Mind?

In many cases, you may not be applying for a specific job, but you want to write to companies where you would like to work, or you want to follow up on contacts you have met through networking. The "blind" cover letter in **Figure 4.4** is a response to a networking contact.

"Blind" Cover Letter

October 29, 2003

Mr. John Tempis
231 Brook Street
John's Texaco Station
Bennet, ME 01223

Dear Mr. Tempis:

It was a pleasure to talk with you yesterday. I appreciate your taking the time to discuss the field of auto mechanics and have enclosed a résumé for your review and evaluation. As we discussed, auto mechanics is my chosen occupation and my passion. I have worked on cars since I was 11 years old and have developed a reputation for customer satisfaction. I recently earned a certificate in foreign car engine repair.

Your station has grown in the last two years and has a reputation for being customer-service oriented. In addition to excellent technical skills, I have demonstrated a willingness to help customers and build good relationships. My accomplishments include:

- Designing a customer satisfaction form.
- Increasing sales by 25 percent.
- Never being late for work in two years.
- Earning a reputation for being dependable and hardworking.

I have hands-on experience with solving problems in the automobile business and with increasing sales. If you know of openings at your company or other opportunities that may exist for a self-starter, please let me know. Thanks again for taking time to meet with me.

Sincerely,

Thomas R. Kason

Thomas R. Kason

Enclosure

Figure 4.4
Contacting Your Network
Networking can provide great sources for job opportunities. You can use a blind cover letter to follow up your initial contact. *What are the differences between a blind cover letter and a standard cover letter?*

Cover-Letter Makeover

Review all the mistakes made in this cover letter and correct them by writing on this page. Write any additional comments on the lines below.

```
May 19, 2003


Global Service Industry
South Street
Boston, MA

Dear Sir,

Don't read another résumé! You have found yourself
the perfect employee for a job as automotive tech-
nician or in sales.
    I have had the pleasure of many years of exper-
ience working in the automotiv field as a technician,
mechanic, and salesman. I have a real interest in
living in the Boston area. I love the ocean and
cultural events, too. I have a strong background in
electronics, mechanics, and Pro.
    I would like a position of authority where I can
learn more about sales and public relations. I have
worked for Bob Knells of Shell station for 3 years
(from 1998 to 2001). Bob and I were frends and he
allowed me to deal with customers, put out fires,
work on various cars and trucks, and I had input on
advertisement. Unfortunately Bob  was hard to work
for so I quit. Now I work for my uncle.
    I am sorry that this letter does not reflect my
best effort. My typewriter is worn and I didn't have
time to have it typed professionally or even to buy
better paper.
    Here is my adress and you can call me at work any
time: 738-9937.


Hoping for a interview,


Jeff Meyers
```

_____

_____

_____

_____

_____

_____

Compare this direct contact letter to the previous letter written by Jeff. Do you have any more suggestions? Write them directly on this page.

May 19, 2003

Ms. Gloria Webb
Vice President of Sales
Global Service Industry
221 South Street
Boston, MA 08771

Dear Ms. Webb:

I read in the March issue of *Auto Journal* that Global Service has a wonderful new line of automobiles. The following achievements demonstrate my commitment to sales:

- Possess technical plus sales experience
- Exceeded my quoted by 68 percent for last year
- Named salesperson of the year 2001
- Developed a follow-up plan to ensure customer satisfaction
- Persuaded company to start training program for sales
- Paid 100 percent of my business school cost

My background as a skilled automotive technician and mechanic has made me a better salesman. I love selling and have demonstrated excellent human relations and communication skills. I want to set new records in sales. I feel confident that I could really excel and make a contribution to the company.

I have the skills, the passion, and the talent to produce results. I can be reached at (555) 445-2365. I will call you next week to request a meeting at your convenience.

Sincerely,

Michael Kramer

Michael Kramer

Enclosure

_____

_____

_____

_____

_____

_____

Job Applications

Some employers consider a cover letter with a résumé equivalent to an application. However, others do not, and they will ask you to fill out an application. Once you have a good working sample, it will be easy for you to complete other applications and to update them. **Organize a database to use for job applications.** Your database (Chapter 1) includes information that is required on most applications.

When you are asked to complete a job application, request to take it home. It will be easier for you to concentrate. You'll have the information you need at your fingertips. Practice first in pencil or on a copy of the application. However, if you can't take a job application home, be sure to bring your database of personal facts with you.

An application is similar to a résumé: It won't necessarily get you the job, but it can keep you from getting an interview. The application can be the employer's first glimpse of you if you haven't already submitted a résumé. Therefore, it should create a positive and professional image. **Make your job application neat and correct, and follow directions carefully.** The most common mistake is to fill out an application in a hurry, guessing at dates, addresses, or work-history information. However, if you carry your database with you, you know that the information you put on an application will be accurate. Make certain to double-check dates. Both the application and your résumé will usually become part of your permanent file if you are hired.

Follow these guidelines for completing a job application:

1. **Read carefully.** Read through the application and follow directions. Some applications instruct you to print in ink; others will ask you to type. Some applications ask for last name first. Applications vary, so don't assume and start writing before you read the directions. Read every question before you answer.

2. **Be accurate.** Don't guess. Have your database and résumé on hand to check dates so you can answer questions easily and accurately.

3. **Be neat.** Buy a couple of fine-point blue or black pens to prevent blots and smears. Fill in blanks carefully. Check to see the amount of space available so you don't run over into the next blank space.

4. **Be complete.** Answer all questions that are applicable. However, if the question does not apply to you, use a dash (—) or print *N/A* (not applicable). This will indicate that you have read the question but that it does not apply to you. You can also write in a blank space, "See attached," and then attach appropriate material; or write, "Will explain in interview."

5. **Use your full name.** Don't use a nickname.

6. **Include job title.** Write the title of the job you are applying for or your job objective.

7. **Be selective.** List only full-time jobs unless you have little work experience. If the company requests all jobs, list part-time jobs as well.

8. **List volunteer work.** List volunteer work, internships, and co-op programs (educational/work programs in cooperation with business). Having this type of experience indicates a willingness to contribute and get involved.

9. **Be flexible.** Indicate that you are willing to travel, relocate, or work various shifts.

10. **Include references.** Make certain you have names, titles, addresses, and phone numbers of references and that you have asked their permission before you include them on the application. Choose your references carefully. Bring your list of references with you if you cannot take home the application.

11. **Be honest.** Always tell the truth, but don't list disabilities unless employers specifically ask for details. In many cases, employers are prohibited legally from requesting this information.

12. **Be positive.** Never be negative about former employers.

13. **Check carefully.** After completing the application, read through it carefully to make certain the information is correct and neat. Check for spelling, grammar, and punctuation. Enter the correct date and sign, using your best handwriting.

14. **Make a copy.** If possible, before filling out the application, make a copy in case you make a mistake. Make a copy of the completed application to use as a guide for other applications.

Application Practice

Practice applying for a job. Use the information from your database and fill in the following job application.

SAMPLE APPLICATION FOR EMPLOYMENT

LAST NAME	FIRST	MIDDLE	SOCIAL SECURITY NO.

PRESENT ADDRESS		TELEPHONE
CITY	STATE	ZIP

PERMANENT ADDRESS		TELEPHONE
CITY	STATE	ZIP	U.S. CITIZEN? YES ☐ NO ☐

REFERRED BY

RELATIVE EMPLOYED BY COMPANY? NAME/DEPT.

IN EMERGENCY: NAME/ADDRESS	TELEPHONE
PERSONAL PHYSICIAN: NAME/ADDRESS	TELEPHONE

EDUCATION

MIDDLE	HIGH SCHOOL—NAME/LOCATION	YEARS ATTENDED	GRADUATE? YES ☐ NO ☐	WHEN
		MAJOR SUBJECT AREA		
	COLLEGE/TECHNICAL	YEARS ATTENDED	DATE GRADUATED	
		MAJOR	DEGREE RECEIVED	
FIRST	COLLEGE/TECHNICAL	YEARS ATTENDED	DATE GRADUATED	
		MAJOR	DEGREE RECEIVED	
	MEMBER PROFESSIONAL ORGANIZATION	REGISTRATION NUMBER		
	MEMBER PROFESSIONAL ORGANIZATION	REGISTRATION NUMBER		
	SUBJECTS OF SPECIAL STUDY/RESEARCH			
LAST NAME	BUSINESS MACHINES YOU CAN OPERATE			

continued

EMPLOYMENT RECORD

EMPLOYER—NAME/ADDRESS	JOB TITLE	REF. CHK'D OFF. USE ONLY
	NAME OF SUPERVISOR	
	EMPLOYED FROM TO	SALARY
	NAME WORKED UNDER	
	REASON FOR LEAVING	
EMPLOYER—NAME/ADDRESS	JOB TITLE	REF. CHK'D OFF. USE ONLY
	NAME OF SUPERVISOR	
	EMPLOYED FROM TO	SALARY
	NAME WORKED UNDER	
	REASON FOR LEAVING	
EMPLOYER—NAME/ADDRESS	JOB TITLE	REF. CHK'D OFF. USE ONLY
	NAME OF SUPERVISOR	
	EMPLOYED FROM TO	SALARY
	NAME WORKED UNDER	
	REASON FOR LEAVING	
EMPLOYER—NAME/ADDRESS	JOB TITLE	REF. CHK'D OFF. USE ONLY
	NAME OF SUPERVISOR	
	EMPLOYED FROM TO	SALARY
	NAME WORKED UNDER	
	REASON FOR LEAVING	

REFERENCES

NAME	BUSINESS	REF CHK'D OFF. USE ONLY
ADDRESS	YEARS KNOWN FROM TO	
CITY STATE		ZIP
NAME	BUSINESS	REF CHK'D OFF. USE ONLY
ADDRESS	YEARS KNOWN FROM TO	
CITY STATE		ZIP
NAME	BUSINESS	REF CHK'D OFF. USE ONLY
ADDRESS	YEARS KNOWN FROM TO	
CITY STATE		ZIP

HIRING INFORMATION

Position Wanted		If Employed, May We Contact Present Employer?	How Much Notice Given to Last Employer?
Date Able to Start	Indicate Shifts You Can Work	Can You Work Weekends?	Method of Transportation
Salary Desired	Ever Apply to This Company Before? Where?	When?	Ever Convicted of a Felony or Misdemeanor?

I authorize investigation of all statements contained in this application. I understand that misrepresentation or omission of facts called for is cause for dismissal. Further, I understand and agree that my employment is for no definite period and may, regardless of payment of my wages and salary, be terminated at any time without previous notice.

Date	Applicant's Signature

DO NOT WRITE BELOW THIS LINE!

TELEPHONE REFERENCES CHECKED

	REFERENCE 1						REFERENCE 2						REFERENCE 3				
	EXCELLENT	GOOD	AVERAGE	FAIR	POOR		EXCELLENT	GOOD	AVERAGE	FAIR	POOR		EXCELLENT	GOOD	AVERAGE	FAIR	POOR
INTEGRITY	☐	☐	☐	☐	☐	INTEGRITY	☐	☐	☐	☐	☐	INTEGRITY	☐	☐	☐	☐	☐
NEATNESS	☐	☐	☐	☐	☐	NEATNESS	☐	☐	☐	☐	☐	NEATNESS	☐	☐	☐	☐	☐
CONSCIENTIOUS	☐	☐	☐	☐	☐	CONSCIENTIOUS	☐	☐	☐	☐	☐	CONSCIENTIOUS	☐	☐	☐	☐	☐
INTELLIGENCE	☐	☐	☐	☐	☐	INTELLIGENCE	☐	☐	☐	☐	☐	INTELLIGENCE	☐	☐	☐	☐	☐
SKILL IN POSITION	☐	☐	☐	☐	☐	SKILL IN POSITION	☐	☐	☐	☐	☐	SKILL IN POSITION	☐	☐	☐	☐	☐
COOPERATION	☐	☐	☐	☐	☐	COOPERATION	☐	☐	☐	☐	☐	COOPERATION	☐	☐	☐	☐	☐
ABSENTEEISM	☐	☐	☐	☐	☐	ABSENTEEISM	☐	☐	☐	☐	☐	ABSENTEEISM	☐	☐	☐	☐	☐

REASON FOR SEPARATION	REASON FOR SEPARATION	REASON FOR SEPARATION
WOULD YOU RECOMMEND APPLICANT?	WOULD YOU RECOMMEND APPLICANT?	WOULD YOU RECOMMEND APPLICANT?
WOULD YOU RE-EMPLOY?	WOULD YOU RE-EMPLOY?	WOULD YOU RE-EMPLOY?

REMARKS

INTERVIEWED BY			DATE
REPORT FOR DUTY (DATE)	DEPARTMENT	POSITION	SALARY

Job Testing

Throughout this book, preparedness has been stressed, both for finding a job and for job success. You will want to be ready to fulfill any necessary requirements to be hired. For example, when you apply for a job, you may have to take one or more tests:

- A performance test, such as a typing test, evaluates how well you can perform a particular task.
- A drug test, such as a blood or urine test for illegal drugs, may be required for companies in nuclear power and transportation industries.
- A polygraph test or a lie detector test may be required if you apply for a job in law enforcement or government.

Certain office or retail positions may include tests in basic math or calculations, typing, shorthand, data entry, word processing, punctuation, spelling, composition, or problem solving. Some jobs also require a physical examination that may include both drug and alcohol testing. You can find this out by calling personnel offices of interested companies, calling job placement agencies, and asking your instructors in the field you are studying.

Before the Test

Be prepared for skill tests that are part of certain jobs. If you are in a secretarial or business course, save your key books and ask your instructor for additional testing materials that may be required before you are interviewed for a position. When you inquire about the job, ask if there are required tests and practice before you take them. Employment agencies often have sample tests that can help you prepare. Knowing what to expect and spending time reviewing will help you to relax, and you will do better on the test.

During the Test

Ask the person in charge for special instructions. For example, if you make a mistake, can you repeat a portion of the test? Can you repeat the entire test and, if so, how many times?

Read through the entire test quickly before you begin answering questions to get an idea about the content and how much weight is given to each section. Read each question carefully. Ask questions and make certain you know what is being expected.

STAYING POWER

Keep Writing

*C*omposing an excellent cover letter is an art, like any form of composition, that requires thought, time, and practice. You may find that perhaps the most difficult task in writing an effective cover letter is getting started and staying focused on its purpose. Your goal is to persuade a potential employer that you are the right person for the job. You must also highlight some of your skills that relate to the specfic job. This requires not only the right words and information, but also the proper style, angle, and tone.

You might feel overwhelmed by having to send more than one type of cover letter to a single prospective employer, using e-mail, facsimile, or "snail mail." Each of these cover letters will be different, and they may refer to each other.

You may also think that you have difficulty with poor grammar, misspellings, and other errors, which can be the kiss of death for a cover letter. Always ask for help in proofreading your letter if you feel unsure. Practice and you will improve, especially if you are uncomfortable with writing.

Try This...

Use these strategies to deal with difficulties writing your cover letter:
- Getting started on your letter can be difficult—even great authors sometimes get writer's block. It's important to begin a draft, even if it's not perfect. Set a ten-minute time limit to finish an introductory paragraph. Then go back and make changes.
- Become adept at researching companies. Match your qualifications to a specific job description and explain why you are a great fit for the job.
- When you write your cover letters, check grammar and spelling.
- When you feel comfortable with your complete draft, read the letter aloud or ask a friend to give feedback.

Skill Check Recap

- Send a cover letter with every résumé.
- Write a standard cover letter.
- Write a tailored cover letter.
- State your job objective.
- Indicate that you know about the company.
- Relate the needs of the employer to your skills.
- Organize a database to use for job applications.
- Make your job application neat and correct, and follow directions carefully.

Self-Check List

Keep track of your progress. Read the following and mark *yes* or *no*.

	Yes	No
• I have effectively organized my cover letter.	_____	_____
• My cover letter is tailored for each job.	_____	_____
• My cover letter is grammatically correct and error-free.	_____	_____
• My cover letter is concise.	_____	_____
• My cover letter is written in the correct format.	_____	_____
• I have paid close attention to content.	_____	_____
• I have carefully completed the job application.	_____	_____
• I am prepared for job testing.	_____	_____

Review Questions

1. What are the five benefits of an effective cover letter?

   _____

   _____

2. What are the seven sections of a successful cover letter?

   _____

   _____

3. How should the body of the cover letter be set up?

   _____

   _____

4. What is a "blind" cover letter?

   _____

   _____

5. Why are basic grammar and spelling important in a cover letter?

   _____

   _____

6. What are the first four guidelines in completing job applications?

   _____

   _____

7. What is the advantage of listing volunteer work?

   _____

   _____

8. Why should you write a new cover letter for each résumé you send?

   _____

   _____

Critical Thinking

9. Select three of the common mistakes in cover letters that you recognize as problems that you have. Consider why these are problems for you and how you can solve them.

   _____

   _____

   _____

   _____

Cooperative Learning

10. With a partner, write one cover letter for a prospective job—a real job or an invented one. Then join with another pair in the class and exchange letters. Constructively discuss and critique each other's letters.

Writing the Right Cover Letter

James is recent graduate with a certificate and associate of science degree in computer technology. He has sent out hundreds of résumés but has received only a few interview appointments. Most companies have not even acknowledged receiving his résumé. He hasn't developed a cover letter because he hates writing and thinks that, in technical fields, a résumé should provide enough information.

James has listed his career objective as a computer programmer at a large corporation. He thought he would be able to get a job more easily at a large company than at a small one. He is now wondering if his objective is too narrow.

Should he write a specific cover letter for each job? Help James explore ways to write a cover letter that is specific, interesting, and attention getting for working in a large company.

Problem Solving The following ten questions are designed to help solve problems and make sound decisions. You can use these questions to find solutions to your own problems. Put yourself in James's place and consider the questions.

- What is the problem?
- Do I have enough information?
- Can I make the decision by myself?
- Have I brainstormed alternatives?
- Have I looked at likely consequences?
- Have I identified all the resources and tools needed?
- Have I developed and implemented an action plan?
- Have I identified the best solution?
- Have I assessed the results?
- Have I modified the plan, if necessary?

What solution would you suggest to James?

_____

_____

_____

_____

_____

_____

_____

_____

STRATEGIES Online

Find out more about tailoring your cover letter to the job by visiting this book's Web site at strategies.glencoe.com.

Your Career Portfolio

Cover Letters

Go to your school's career center to review and collect samples of effective cover letters for specific jobs. Then write a cover letter to a specific company. Make certain you have researched the company before you write the letter.

Answer the following questions to help you focus when writing your cover letters. Then rewrite your cover letter as necessary.

- Am I focusing on the needs of the company and how I can meet these needs?

  _____
  _____

- Am I making my cover letter address specific needs of this company?

  _____
  _____

- How can I add value to this company?

  _____
  _____

- Am I being totally honest about my education and accomplishments?

  _____
  _____

- Is my cover letter brief, interesting, and addressed to a specific person?

  _____
  _____

- Have I double-checked for accuracy and errors?

  _____
  _____

- Does my letter look professional?

  _____
  _____

- Have I had a career counselor review my résumé and cover letter?

  _____
  _____

CHAPTER 5

Winning Points

- Do your homework and be prepared.
- Research yourself.
- Research the company.
- Research the industry.
- Research interview questions.
- Research all details of the interview.
- Dress professionally and appropriately.
- Rehearse your interview until you are comfortable.

Introduction

The moment of truth in the job-search process is the all-important interview. This chapter will help you prepare for it as you look at the planning process for the interview within the larger context of the job-search process. Remember, your résumé and cover letter got the potential employer's attention; your job interview will get you the job. Strategies and techniques will help you to market your work experience, education, personal qualities, and skills, and create an overall positive image.

Chapter 5 also highlights creative problem solving and critical thinking as important abilities you will want to demonstrate during the interview. By preparing, getting organized, and learning verbal and nonverbal communication skills, you will stand out from the crowd.

If you follow the strategies in this book, you can turn an interview into a job offer. Mastering the art of interviewing may also help you get promoted faster, make great presentations, and have high self-esteem.

Chapter 5 Objectives

After you have completed this chapter, you will be able to:

- Explain the purpose and importance of the interview
- Explain the importance of preparation as a key to success
- Describe essential factors of the interview process
- Research likely questions and prepare good answers
- Describe how to plan a professional image
- Explain the importance of rehearsing the interview

Your Chance to Shine

<blockquote>
"Those who are prepared for all the emergencies of life beforehand may equip themselves at the expense of joy."

—E.M. Forster
Writer
</blockquote>

After all the time and effort you've spent, you've landed an interview! You feel a surge of excitement and relief. You've been very busy, and everything you have done up to this point has been preparation for the interview. Planning, networking, researching, writing your résumé, composing specific cover letters, filling out an application, contacting references, and making telephone calls have all been done to get an interview. You have been "sharpening your saw," and your preparation will pay off.

Throughout the book, we have stressed that all job-search steps are interrelated and involve preparation, planning, and communication. The steps in the interview process are also linked to each other, with planning and communication as a foundation. Just as you have taken control of your job search so far, you can learn the strategies that will make you shine during each step of the job interview.

An effective interview is a combination of several factors and ten steps. We'll cover the first three steps in this chapter—before the interview—and the remaining steps in Chapters 6 and 7.

The Importance and Purpose of the Interview

The first step in preparing for the interview is to realize its importance. In fact, it is the face-to-face interview that is most critical in getting the job you want. The best résumé, the most competent skills, and the most persuasive cover letter will not get you a job without an interview. The interview also creates a lasting impression that will influence your success on the job. A successful interview can help you command a higher salary, create higher expectations, and determine how well you will fit into the organization.

The purpose of the interview from the employer's point of view is to determine what skills you have and if these skills will match the needs of the company. The interviewer also wants to find out what kind of person you are, if you are a team player, and if you will benefit the company. The purpose of the interview from your point of view is to sell yourself. To do that, you need to show that your skills match the needs of the company, that you can make a contribution, and that you will fit into the company. In other words, you must convince the employer that you are the solution to the company's need or problem. In order to sell yourself, you must be well prepared and communicate your strengths and value.

An equally important purpose of the interview is to determine if the job is right for you. Through research, preparation, and asking questions, you will be able to make a sound decision that fits with both your immediate and long-term career goals.

The Ten Steps of Interviewing

For an overview of the interview process, review these ten steps, or ten "Rs," of interviewing. Then read this chapter for a discussion of the first three steps.

Before the Interview:

1. Research.
2. Remember image.
3. Rehearse.

During the Interview:

4. Relax.
5. Build rapport.
6. Review basic questions and answers.
7. Reinforce your skills and strengths.
8. Respond with questions.
9. Readjust, correct, and close.

After the Interview:

10. Reassess and follow up.

Step 1. Research

Research the Company

It is amazing that so few people investigate a company before an interview. Do your homework. **Research companies before your interview.** You can't ask good questions or give really good answers if you don't have the necessary information. This is where your networking will pay off. Talk with your professional contacts. Someone may know an employee at the company where you're interviewing. Talk with anyone currently employed with the company or anyone who has previously worked with the company. Ask about problems, such as:

- Turnover rate of personnel
- Working environment
- Management style

Preparation is the key to success. You should be aware of the company's products, services, size, divisions, age, recent activities, reputation, concerns or problems, new directions, and growth potential. Read as much as you can and get a corporate profile. Your local library can help you with this as well as with your search for articles about the company. Also check with your local chamber of commerce, or call the company directly and ask a receptionist to send information. Company Web sites are also excellent sources of information.

Remember, one of your best resources is **strategies.glencoe.com**

Other resources might include:
- Annual reports
- Catalogs, flyers, and newsletters
- Business Periodicals Index
- Standard and Poor's

For each interview, create a company profile that includes the following information:
- Company name
- Job position
- Plant size and location
- Number of employees
- Products
- Sales
- Profits
- Concerns
- Future plans
- Job description of positions in question

This information can be used in the interview to demonstrate you have done your homework. This degree of preparation indicates career maturity and ambition. For example:

> I was interested to read an article in *The Wall Street Journal* about your employee incentive program.
>
> *or*
>
> Your annual report describes your impressive management training programs.

Research the Industry

Stay current on industry trends. You should be well versed about the industry in which you want to work. **Research the industry before your interview.** Let's say you have just received your certificate as a medical technician. As a professional, you should know about key medical issues, new products, preventive treatment, and new trends in your field. Be prepared to talk about the industry. Put your network to use and talk with people in the field. Ask about the special problems, concerns, challenges, opportunities, and rewards involved. What is new in the field?

Your preparation will pay off when you are asked, "Why do you think you will like being a medical technician?" You will be able to give an informed and sensible answer. You have done your homework, shown interest, and taken the initiative.

Research the latest industry buzzwords—words that are used specifically in the field. Take time to find out what they are in your area. You don't want to sound false and overprepared, but you should know the trends and language of your industry. See **Figure 5.1** for examples of typical words used in certain industries.

Common Words in Industry

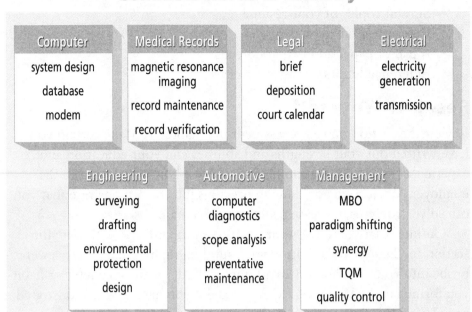

Computer	Medical Records	Legal	Electrical
system design	magnetic resonance imaging	brief	electricity generation
database	record maintenance	deposition	transmission
modem	record verification	court calendar	

Engineering	Automotive	Management
surveying	computer diagnostics	MBO
drafting	scope analysis	paradigm shifting
environmental protection	preventative maintenance	synergy
design		TQM
		quality control

Figure 5.1
Knowing the Lingo If you do your research for your career area, you'll be up-to-date on the terminology in current use. *Why do you need to know these "buzzwords" when you prepare for an interview?*

Research Details

Get organized and write down every detail. Begin by finding out the format for the interview. Write down the data on a sheet, leaving nothing to memory:

- Time of interview
- Place of interview (Find out exactly where it is: building and office.)
- Most convenient parking
- People who will be present (Check spelling, titles, and pronunciation.)

  Mr. John Ryan, Director of Marketing
  Ms. Roberta Bess, Director of Public Affairs
  Mr. Brian Weiss, Sales Director

  (Remember, a receptionist or secretary may play the role of an unofficial screener. Everyone you meet may be asked his or her opinion of you.)
- Phone numbers of the main office and each of the contacts (in case you are delayed)
- Directions to the company and the offices (Ask the best way to get to the interview. If the company is close, do a trial run and find out where the company and specific offices are, and how long it takes to get there.)
- Length of the interview and plan for the day
- Material or information needed (samples of work applications, artwork, etc.)
- List of questions that may be asked
- List of questions to ask

Pack your briefcase with the previous information, plus the following:
- Several copies of your résumé
- Research on the company
- A pad of paper and two good pens
- Reference letters

Research Yourself

Review the section on self-assessment in Chapter 1. Make certain you have written out your strengths and abilities and your education and experiences, and then determine their value—both to you and to the employer. What have you done in previous jobs to demonstrate that you can solve problems, increase profits, and decrease costs?

Outline what you most want to stress in the interview. Review the section in Chapter 1 on writing your autobiography. Many interviewers probe into your early life in an attempt to find out the character or habits you formed early. What life experiences did you have that demonstrated positive qualities? Later in this chapter, you will learn how to connect your skills and accomplishments with the needs of the job. In the next chapter, you will learn how to build rapport. Researching yourself is good preparation for both of these important areas.

Take some time to review your résumé again, too. Remind yourself of the skills you've demonstrated.

Research Questions

Prepare questions that you think the interviewer will ask based on the job description and your research about the company. Collect other questions from people in your network. Your contacts in the same field or at similar companies will be able to provide you with questions you are likely to be asked. You can expect questions concerning your education, job skills, work experience, personality, whether you are a team player, and how you deal with stress. The most common questions fall into the categories below:

WORK EXPERIENCE
- What do you enjoy most (or least) about your present job?
- What were your major accomplishments in each of your jobs?
- Describe your technical skills.
- Explain specific duties or a typical day on the job.
- Describe the best supervisor you ever had. Describe the worst.
- What have been the biggest failures or frustrations in your professional life?
- Why do you want to leave your current job?

EDUCATIONAL BACKGROUND AND TRAINING
- Why did you decide to go to college?
- How well did you do?

- What did your major courses prepare you to do?
- What computer skills did you learn?
- Did you work while going to school?
- What leadership role did you demonstrate in school activities?
- Are you willing to get advanced training?

CHARACTER AND PERSONALITY TRAITS

- Tell me about yourself.
- What are your major strengths? Your major weaknesses?
- What causes you to lose your temper?
- Have you ever had to deal with an angry customer? How did you handle that person?
- How do you deal with stress?

DECISION-MAKING AND PROBLEM-SOLVING ABILITIES

- Describe a problem that you solved, which made you proud.
- What decision do you most regret making?
- What problems do you think you could help us solve?
- Here's a typical work problem. How would you solve it?
- Here's a typical decision that you may make on this job. What process would you go through to make a sound decision?
- In this job, there are a lot of pressures to meet deadlines. If you were given three top priorities, how would you determine which to accomplish first? (They may give you examples such as: The computer is down; a colleague wants to talk about personal problems; and a disgruntled customer is waiting to see you.)
- What process do you go through to make important decisions?
- What is the worst problem you ever had to solve?

CAREER GOALS

- Where do you want to be professionally five years from now?
- What do you see yourself doing to make yourself more effective?
- What are your long-term career goals?
- Why do you want this job?
- Why do you think you're the best person for this job?
- How do you feel about traveling, relocating, or learning new skills?
- What attracted you to this company?
- Why should we hire you? What can you do that will benefit the company most?
- If you could create your ideal job, what would it be?

TEAMWORK

- What types of people do you like to work with?
- What types of people do you find difficult?
- Describe a team project in which you were involved.
- Do you tend to take a leadership role in a group?
- Do you tend to work as an equal team member in a group?

Confident Answers to Tough Questions

Once you have researched likely interview questions, you can begin to **prepare your answers for standard interview questions.** Preparation will help you answer even tough questions. You will want to use your own style and give appropriate examples and personal accomplishments. You want to be prepared, rehearsed, and confident, but your answers shouldn't sound glib or pat. Use the answers below only as a guide. Sincerity is important in an interview.

Keep in mind that you want to listen for the *intent* of the question. Sometimes there is a hidden meaning beneath the surface of a question.

Tell me about yourself.

This question is often designed to help break the ice, to get you talking freely about yourself, to determine what you consider to be important about your life, and to see if you ramble at such an open-ended question.

Be prepared. Outline the main areas of your life that are most relevant to the job. Choose one personality characteristic on which you want to focus. You may want to highlight your hardworking nature and include an example:

> I started working when I was 12. I had a paper route and also worked in my parent's business after school and on weekends. I put my heart into what I do and am not concerned about quitting at 5 p.m. I have worked late many evenings and weekends to complete a project that I am proud of.

Talking About Yourself

"Tell me about yourself" is one of the most common interview questions. Take some time to outline your response in the space below.

_____

_____

_____

_____

_____

_____

_____

_____

_____

_____

Why do you want to leave your current job?

The standard answer is that you are ready for a new challenge, or you want to develop your skills and use all your capabilities. You may want to expand your answer to include your present situation. Say, for example, that your company has cut back on promotions due to tough times. You might respond:

> When I accepted this position last year, I understood that I would be promoted within a year if my performance reviews were acceptable. I have received outstanding reviews, demonstrated my abilities, and have a solid track record of producing results. However, because of cutbacks and reorganization, the company has decided not to expand our department, and a promotion will not be possible for at least another year. It has been a difficult decision, but I believe it is time to find a company where I can make a real contribution in a position for which I am qualified.

What can you contribute to this company?

This type of question is designed to see if you have done your homework on the company and to determine if you are just after any job, or if you have specific skills that you think can benefit the company. You will want to take one point in the job description and highlight how your skills would meet these current needs. For example:

> You have mentioned that you want to improve customer relations in this office. I have a real interest in and have excelled in this area. I developed the first guidelines for customer relations while I was an intern at Bancroft. I also have received several letters from satisfied customers for putting extra effort into solving their concerns. I have called customers on my own time if I cannot reach them during business hours. I believe that customer service is the heart of a business. A little extra time and concern really pays off.

What kind of people annoy you most?

Questions like this one or "What makes you angry? or "What do you worry about?" can give you the impression that the interviewer wants to chat. Actually, these types of questions are designed to determine if you are a team player, appreciate diversity, and can handle stress. Don't reveal your personal life or make a confession. Maintain a professional demeanor at all times. It is best to keep your answer focused on how you handle difficult people, tension, conflict, or pet peeves on the job. For example:

> I am a professional and am responsible for my behavior. I respond in a calm manner even to angry people. I focus on the problem and don't let people cause me to lose sight of finding a solution. I work well with a variety of people and see diversity as an important element in working teams. My ability to work well with a variety of people is one strength that has helped me in my career.

I see you have worked with Tom Smith. Did you enjoy this experience?

Be careful about giving a negative response even if the interviewer implies that a person is difficult to work with. Standard advice is to never criticize anyone during an interview. You might say, "Oh, so you know Tom. I learned a lot working with him. Did you work with him too?"

What are your greatest strengths or personal qualities?

Avoid rattling off a list of virtues. Select key strengths and explain how you have demonstrated them. For example:

> I am persistent and take initiative. I worked full-time and finished my degree by going to school three or four nights a week. In addition, I organized a leadership conference for the marketing club.

Review your list of most desirable personal characteristics and determine what experiences you want to highlight.

What are your greatest weaknesses or shortcomings?

Almost everyone has weaknesses. An interviewer may not voice concern but may wonder if a factor would affect your ability to perform or fit into the company. (See **Figure 5.2** for a list of common liabilities according to most employers.) It's best to face a liability and turn it into an asset. For example:

> Some people call me a perfectionist. I am a stickler for details and must admit I have worked nights to make sure projects were completed. I have learned, however, to pace myself and delegate tasks to get the job done.

Common Liabilities
✗   Too young
✗   Too old
✗   Change of jobs too frequent
✗   Change of careers
✗   No work experience
✗   Unemployed
✗   Applying in a gender-traditional field
✗   Physical disability

Figure 5.2

Employer's Point of View An employer may not necessarily mention these liabilities in a job interview. *How could an interviewee address each of these listed liabilities and present them as assets to a prospective employer?*

Turning a Weakness Into an Asset

EXERCISE 5.2

Review the perceived list of liabilities in **Figure 5.2** and turn each into an asset.

Perceived Liability	**Positive Asset**
Too young	Ability to learn quickly, flexibility, enthusiasm, high energy
Too old	Maturity, good judgment, experience, good work ethic
_____	_____
_____	_____
_____	_____
_____	_____
_____	_____
_____	_____
_____	_____
_____	_____
_____	_____
_____	_____

How have you handled a major disappointment in your life?

You can use the same pattern for questions that ask about an important decision that you have made, how you handled a major challenge in your job, or how you have handled a major disappointment. Always look at these as two-part questions. First tell the process and then give an example. Look over your list of personal qualities and decide how to build an example around one of the qualities you possess. For example:

> I was very disappointed that I was turned down for college football. I had excelled in high school and spent the summer in training, but I view disappointments as stepping-stones, not barriers. I always ask myself what I can learn from a situation and how I can benefit from it. I looked for other doors to open. After getting over my disappointment, I joined the swimming team and, as a result, earned a scholarship and made wonderful friends. Resiliency and a positive attitude have seen me through many disappointments.

When was the last time you worked on a team project? What did you accomplish?

The purpose of this type of question is to determine if you are a team player and can work well with others to achieve the mission of the organization. (During your research of the company, you can call and obtain a copy of the organization's mission statement.) In the new workplace, employees increasingly work in self-managed teams. Since there is a greater emphasis on teamwork, employers want to hire self-starters who are team players with effective interpersonal communication skills. Your answer should include knowledge of other departments and examples of how you have worked as a team member to accomplish results. Give examples of how you have demonstrated creative problem-solving, critical-thinking, and listening skills.

What is the worst job you've ever had?

The interviewer is trying to discover your sense of values, what you consider menial, your appreciation of the whole process, and if you have failed to omit a job on your résumé. (Some people leave out jobs they consider unpleasant or irrelevant.) You will want to assure the interviewer that even part-time, low-level jobs have been valuable. You have learned the importance of hard work, time management, working with others, and so forth. You know the importance of the entire job process; have empathy for workers who perform all types of tasks; and see the value of each component in the completed product.

Describe a difficult problem you have solved.

Don't focus so much on the problem as on the process. Employers are interested in problem-solving ability and whether you can use critical-thinking skills and creativity to solve problems and make decisions. You might say:

I take a step-by-step approach. First, I state the problem clearly and in writing. I look for the real issues involved and who is affected, and determine if I can solve the problem by myself. Next, I gather information on the problem, talk to others about similar situations, and brainstorm a list of possible solutions. Third, I weigh and project the probable consequences for the top solutions.

Continue with this process and give an example:

When I was hired as a new sales rep, sales were down and morale was poor. I had a problem with customers' perception of service. I increased my service line, installed a hotline where complaints could be handled, and increased my contacts with each contractor. The results were amazing. We increased our sales by 25 percent and, just as important, evaluations showed that our customers were delighted by our new service.

Describe the worst boss you ever had.

Questions regarding your previous bosses, how you handle criticism, or what your boss or references would say about you are designed to catch you off guard and see if you blame others or are a negative person. Always be positive, and keep this answer short. You might say that one boss was a perfectionist and was outspoken. Another had personality problems, but you worked with her very well and appreciated knowing where you stood at all times. You learned to follow through on even tiny details, and as a result you take enormous pride in your work. This is one of those "Will this person fit in?" questions. Variations include: "What don't you like about your boss?" "How do you handle disagreements with your boss?" "Can we call your references?" The same rule applies. Stay positive. No one wants a troublemaker, someone who is thin-skinned, or someone who has something to hide. Always be honest, but don't volunteer information that hasn't been asked. Stay focused on the positive.

Don't send reference letters unless they are asked for, then say, "Please feel free to contact my references. I've alerted them that you may be calling."

How do you handle stress?

You want to demonstrate that you can deal with stress effectively. Rather than react to stress, you work to eliminate the causes of stress, and you plan and solve problems before they become crises. No employer wants to hire a hothead or someone who blows up or is petty with customers or coworkers. Nor do employers want employees who consistently ignore problems until they become serious, stressful matters. You might say:

I transform stress into positive energy. I like the excitement of a busy day, but I don't let tensions build. I find that if I am well organized, break tasks down, set priorities, and have a vision of the final project that I can stay on track and not feel overwhelmed. I plan my work and solve problems as they arise so that crises don't occur. I also jog or walk every day to get rid of stress. It helps me to keep from overreacting or panicking about deadlines.

Stress Savers

Plan Ahead and Relax

A little preparation goes a long way toward reducing your stress level on the day of your interview. Take these few steps so you can focus during your interview:

- Drive by the office the day before and time your arrival 15 minutes before your appointment.
- Find out the name (and pronunciation) of the interviewer by calling the receptionist or the human relations department.
- Plan your wardrobe in advance with traditional business attire.
- Check the company's Web site or local library for background information.
- Have 2–3 questions prepared in advance.

Figure 5.3
Appearance Matters Styles change, and fads come and go, but 92 percent of employers surveyed still say appearance affects their opinions about job candidates at interviews. *What employer attitude about appearance do you think has changed over the past decade?*

Employee Appearance Survey

Job Candidate Appearance	Employer Negatively Influenced	Employer Not Influenced
Nontraditional attire	82%	
Unusual hair colors	73%	
Body piercing (e.g., nose rings, studs)	72%	
Obvious tattoos	69%	
Unusual hairstyles (e.g., spikes)	64%	
Beards		83%
Mustaches		90%

SOURCE: Job Outlook 2002 Survey, National Association of Colleges and Employers, Bethlehem, PA.

Step 2. Remember Image

Creating a Polished, Professional Image

Prepare for the interview by giving thought to the professional image you want to project. (See **Figure 5.3.**) Your clothes, hair, and body language make a statement about you. (Tips for creating a positive first impression will be discussed further in Chapter 6.)

You should project the image of being neat, conservative, and clean. **Prepare your interview wardrobe.** Dressing for a job interview is not just a matter of personal opinion or style. It is actually a science, based on research involving thousands of professionals. Dressing for an interview is essentially wearing an appropriate uniform. You do not want to detract from your message, but rather use clothing to enhance your professional image. John Molloy, in his book *Dress for Success*, stresses the importance of looking professional. Of course, there are exceptions to the rules, such as jobs in art fields or in entertainment, but you should only dress differently if you know your supervisor and interviewers will be dressed in a similar manner.

Projecting a professional, businesslike appearance is very important. Remember that a job interview is not a social event. Underdressing tends to be more of a problem. Short-sleeved dresses and shirts or casual and sloppy clothes are unacceptable. In general, dressing for the job higher than the one you are applying for is a good rule of thumb. Even if you are interviewing for a job that allows casual dress, you should wear a suit for the interview.

The guidelines in **Figure 5.4** are appropriate for men and women who want to project a positive and professional image.

Guidelines for Success

Men	Women
✔ **Suit:** Dress in a conservative, tailored, good-quality, dark blue, gray, or muted pin-striped suit. Don't wear bold plaids or stripes.	✔ **Suit:** Wear a good-quality, conservative, dark suit that is at or just below the knee. A conservative dress with a jacket is the next best choice, or a pantsuit, but a suit is preferred. Blue, gray, beige, or tan are preferred colors. Avoid faddish styles.
✔ **Shirt:** Wear a good-quality, white or pale blue, button-down shirt that is clean and pressed. Cuffs should show no more than $1/2$ inch. Make certain the shirt fits. A tight collar is very uncomfortable. Don't wear faddish styles or cheap fabrics.	✔ **Blouse:** Wear a good-quality, simple blouse. Avoid tight or low-cut blouses. Wear a color that complements you.
✔ **Tie:** Wear a conservative, good quality tie that complements your suit. Avoid faddish prints, loud colors, bold patterns, clip-ons, or bow ties.	✔ **Stockings:** Wear beige, tan, or neutral hose. (Keep an extra pair in your briefcase.)
✔ **Socks:** Socks should be calf-length and match your suit and shoes.	✔ **Shoes:** Wear dark, two-inch or less, closed-toe heels. Shoes should be polished.
✔ **Shoes:** Wear polished, laced, dress, or slip-on shoes in black or brown. Don't wear loafers, faddish styles, scuffed heals, or light colors.	✔ **Watch and jewelry:** Wear a conservative watch. Wear small earrings and no more than two simple rings. Don't wear dangling earrings or evening jewelry. Less is best.
✔ **Watch and jewelry:** Wear a conservative watch. Don't wear jewelry except for a wedding band or a class ring. Don't wear pins or jewelry that are religious or affiliated with societies or organizations.	✔ **Hair:** Wear a simple and becoming style that is clean and neat. Avoid fads and extreme styles.
✔ **Hair:** Hair should be neatly styled.	✔ **Grooming:** You want to project a clean, neat, and professional image. Eyeglasses should be spotless. Avoid heavy makeup. Don't use perfume, or use only a tiny amount. Nail polish should be clear or light, and nails should be trimmed neatly.
✔ **Grooming:** Grooming should be impeccable. Eyeglasses should be spotless; fingernails should be clean and trimmed. Avoid heavy aftershave or cologne.	

✔ **Briefcase:** Both men and women can carry a good attaché case or portfolio. This can contain a good pen, backup pens and pencils, a legal pad, breath mints, a comb or brush, extra copies of your résumé, and other important material. The case can also double as a purse for a woman, or a small purse can fit inside the attaché case. Keep the essentials together. You don't want to fumble when you are shaking hands. You want to look professional, simple, neat, and confident.

Figure 5.4
A Positive Image An employer will get an impression of you and how you might perform your job from your overall appearance at an interview. *Why do you think you should dress conservatively for an interview at any company, even if the workplace is generally casual?*

Dress for Career Success

You may be thinking that these guidelines are too rigid and confining. After all, shouldn't a company be more concerned with your skills and accomplishments? Yes, but your clothes and style make a statement, and image is important to all companies. Few employers want to hire someone who is sloppy and poorly groomed, or who looks as if he or she were going out for the evening. The above guidelines will help you project a professional image in almost all business interviewing situations. It is often the little things that make a difference in a successful interview. This is not the time to have a chip on your shoulder that says, "I'll dress any way I like." You will have the competitive edge if you present yourself in a neat, conservative, and professional way. Dress any way you want on your own time. Dress professionally and appropriately when at work.

EXERCISE 5.3   ![] **Putting It Together**

Pull together one great-looking outfit. Look through your closet for clothes that you can use to build an outfit around. Do you have a great blouse or shirt, tie, scarf, or shoes? You probably know at least one friend who likes to shop and is aware of how important a professional look is. Ask this friend for advice or if you can borrow clothes if necessary. This is not the time to go for fads or far-out costumes. You want to pull together one or two good business outfits. Consignment shops or secondhand stores can be good sources. Often they have expensive, timeless suits, silk shirts, and classic accessories at a fraction of the original prices. Be careful to avoid clothes that are too worn or out of style, however.

Describe your ideal professional outfit on the lines provided.

_____

_____

_____

_____

_____

_____

_____

_____

_____

_____

_____

_____

_____

Step 3. Rehearse

Any new skill requires practice. **Rehearse an interview** on a tape recorder or on videotape, and with one of your networking contacts. Critique yourself and request feedback from others. How do you come across? Feeling prepared helps you relax and be yourself. The more you practice, adjust, and rehearse, the more comfortable and easy it will be to interview. You don't want to sound forced but relaxed, natural, and confident. Role-playing will help you practice and will also help you reduce fear and anxiety.

Career Directions — BusinessWeek

Interview or Interrogation?

A job application turns unexpectedly hostile, and the candidate naturally wonders why. Our experts offer several possible interpretations.

If you were applying to be a customer-service worker for Bridgestone/Firestone during its tire recall—and the company really needed to know how you react to hostility—the "interrogation-style" interview might make sense, says Rebecca Hastings, a senior professional in human resources at the Society for Human Resource Management. In fact, she notes, there's such a thing as a "stress interview," where prospective employers try to provoke candidates to see if they keep their cool.

Hastings isn't a fan of the technique, however, because it starts things off on such a sour note. She also believes that employers can gauge your equanimity via more civil means—such as asking you to describe the tensest incident of your career and how you got through it. But the bully style is perfectly legal, she says, unless you've been singled out for such abuse because of your race, age, gender, or other characteristics that have special legal protection.

One lesson is already clear:

As a job applicant you need to be prepared for anything—hostile interviews, panels of interviewers, daylong interviews, anything a company can throw at you. Therefore, you might want to consult a career counselor or professional recruiter to hone your interviewing skills. One small error—like rushing into vacation requests—can torpedo an interview in seconds.

By H. J. Cummins

Excerpted from May 4, 2001, issue of BusinessWeek Online by special permission, copyright © 2001, by The McGraw-Hill Companies, Inc.

Career Case Study When Kent Cheng got a call to come in for an interview for a job at a prominent advertising firm, he immediately contacted his friend who used to work there. His friend told Kent to expect to be grilled extensively about why he wants to leave his present job. This is a touchy subject because Kent believes his current boss employs incompetent and unethical methods of management. *If Kent is asked about his reasons for wanting a different job, what should he say?*

EXERCISE 5.4 ▦ Practicing Your Interviewing Skills

You become better at any skill by practicing. Your interviewing skills will improve through practice and role-playing. Review the suggested interview questions and answers in this chapter on pages 140–147. Add to the list and modify the answers to fit your particular style and experience.

Task 1: Form a group of three students: Person *A* is the interviewer; person *B* is the interviewee; and person *C* is the observer. Form three or more questions to use for your mock interview. The observer takes notes on the answers.

Questions:

_____

_____

_____

_____

_____

_____

_____

Observations on answers:

_____

_____

_____

_____

_____

_____

_____

Task 2: Take turns playing each role and repeat the interview. Write out your observations. Use a separate sheet of paper if needed.

▦ The Next Step

In Chapter 6, you will learn how to channel fear into focused energy, build rapport, and readjust and close an interview. Both Chapters 5 and 6 stress the importance of connecting your skills and strengths to the needs of the company.

Though every interview is different, the positive habits and techniques you've learned in this chapter will prepare you for almost any interview situation. By researching the company, the field, and yourself; preparing questions and answers; learning verbal and nonverbal communication; creating a professional image; and practicing, you are now ready to shine during the actual interview.

STAYING POWER

The Extra Steps

*I*s there such thing as being too prepared? Researching the company where you're interviewing, being able to describe your goals and strengths articulately and honestly, and making a good impression are a good start. However, steps can you take after your initial preparation?

When research becomes redundant and practice becomes routine, your preparations for interviewing may seem finished. You might even feel some apathy about the interview to come. Keep in mind that it's important to make sure your approach is effective, attitude is positive, and energy is fresh. Ask friends about their job interview experiences and what they have found to be successful. Also talk to people who have experience in giving job interviews or hiring people. Ask them what they look for in an applicant.

Some job hunters may have difficulty viewing the interview in a positive light and may focus on their fears once they've prepared. If you have this problem, think about your past accomplishments and build on them. Take the extra step of seeing your interview not as something to fear but as something to look forward to—your chance to shine.

Try This...

- Look at the job interviewing process in a new way by taking the interviewer's point of view. Select a job that you want and write down questions that an interviewer might ask. What skills and experience would the interviewer look for in an applicant? What type of dress and mannerisms would give an interviewer the right impression?
- Ask a friend to role-play the interviewee while you play the interviewer. You may be surprised by what it's like being on the other side.
- Afterwards, revise the answers you would give and the questions you would ask in a job interview.

CHAPTER 5 *Review*

Skill Check Recap

- Research companies before your interview.
- Research the industry before your interview.
- Prepare your answers for standard interview questions.
- Prepare your interview wardrobe.
- Rehearse an interview.

Self-Check List

Keep track of your progress. Read the following and mark *yes* or *no*.

	Yes	No
• I have reviewed the preinterview process.	____	____
• I have completed the necessary research involving:		
• The company	____	____
• The industry	____	____
• Myself	____	____
• I have considered the importance of my overall appearance.	____	____
• I have prepared anticipated questions from the employer.	____	____
• I have rehearsed the interview.	____	____

Review Questions

1. Why is the job interview important?

2. What is the purpose of the interview from the employer's perspective?

3. What is the purpose of the interview from your point of view?

4. What are the three steps to consider before the interview?

5. Research should ideally focus on at least three areas. What are they?

6. What are the six steps to use during the interview?

7. Name an important issue to discuss if you are asked what you can contribute to the company.

8. What is the importance of dressing for career success?

Critical Thinking

9. Imagine you are in an interview and are asked to name your greatest weakness. How would you respond and turn the answer to your advantage?

Cooperative Learning

10. Form groups of three students. One student should ask two difficult questions to a designated student. The third student takes notes and rates the answer. Rotate the tasks so that each of you can role-play the interviewee. Then discuss the ratings.

CHAPTER 5 Strategies AT WORK

Skills vs. Image?

Jocelyn graduated with an associate of arts degree from a well-known community college. She has an impressive array of computer and office skills and has developed good work habits and a positive attitude.

Jocelyn very much wants a career as an executive assistant. She will be interviewing for a top administrative position at a large conservative corporatio, and she has prepared for the interview. She researched the company and the industry. She has written down all the details concerning the interview and knows the name and title of the people who will be interviewing her. She has thought through her experiences, strengths, weaknesses, and values, and she reviewed her database. Jocelyn has researched questions and prepared a list of sample answers. She has practiced interviewing and feels prepared.

The only problem is deciding what to wear. Jocelyn has worked as a fashion model and loves to wear the latest styles. She doesn't own a suit and feels that corporate dressing is boring. She wants to make her own fashion statement and likes leather mini-skirts, very long hair, and lots of jewelry.

Problem Solving The following ten questions are designed to help solve problems and make sound decisions. You can use these questions to find solutions to your own problems. Put yourself in Jocelyn's place and consider these questions from her point of view.

- What is the problem?
- Do I have enough information?
- Can I make the decision by myself?
- Have I brainstormed alternatives?
- Have I looked at likely consequences?
- Have I identified all the resources and tools needed?
- Have I developed and implemented an action plan?
- Have I identified the best solution?
- Have I assessed the results?
- Have I modified the plan, if necessary?

What solution would you suggest to Jocelyn? Write your answer on the lines below.

_____

_____

_____

_____

_____

_____

STRATEGIES Online

Find out more about your interview image by visiting this book's Web site at strategies. glencoe.com

Interview Homework

As with all aspects of the job search, you must do your homework and be prepared. When you prepare for the job interview, start by researching yourself, the company, and the specific job description. Write down this information using the following categories:

- Educational history:

  _____
  _____
  _____

- Work and volunteer experiences:

  _____
  _____
  _____

- Skills, personal qualities, competencies, talents, and abilities:

  _____
  _____
  _____

- Career goals:

  _____
  _____
  _____

- Information about the company and specific job:

  _____
  _____
  _____

- Skills and qualities that would add value to the company and job:

  _____
  _____
  _____

CHAPTER 6

The Interview

Winning Points

- Present a professional and appropriate appearance.
- Use good verbal and nonverbal communication skills.
- Project a positive attitude and enthusiasm.
- Be confident, poised, and friendly.
- Be well prepared and knowledgeable.
- Be respectful, well mannered, and a good listener.
- Communicate how your skills and strengths would benefit the company.
- Ask good questions.

■ Introduction

Throughout this book, preparation has been stressed as a key factor for success in the job-search process. Chapter 5 covered the importance of preparing for the interview. If you have researched the company, matched your skills with the company's needs, planned a professional image, developed questions, and rehearsed, you have done much to ensure a successful interview.

In this chapter we will discuss what to expect and what to do during the interview, including the following:

- How to relax and channel stress into a positive force
- How to make a positive and lasting first impression
- How to build rapport
- How to stress your strengths and reinforce your skills
- How to ask questions
- How to readjust and close the interview

You will learn to manage the interview process to achieve the results you want.

Chapter 6 Objectives

After you have completed this chapter, you will be able to:

- Explain how to relax and overcome fear and anxiety
- Explain the importance of the first impression
- Describe how to build rapport and respect
- Explain how to conduct a successful lunch or dinner interview
- Describe how to listen and ask thoughtful questions
- Explain the importance of personal qualities
- Summarize how to clearly show how your skills will benefit the company
- Identify what an employer really wants in an employee
- Describe how to readjust and close an interview

Interview Evaluation

Knowing what to expect when you have your interview can reduce the fear of the unknown. Most companies use an evaluation sheet to rate applicants during the interview. Before examining Steps 4–9 of the interview process, this section will explore and discuss the *evaluation system*, which typically covers the following areas:

- Competence
- Clearly defined career goals
- Communication
- Enthusiasm and positive attitude
- Leadership
- Personal qualities
- Problem solving
- Overall appearance

Competence

Competence includes work experience, knowledge of the field, achievements, and grades. The following paragraph is an example of a good response to a question concerning competency.

> I earned a 3.2 GPA while working part-time, being very involved in the Accounting Club and volunteering for the chamber of commerce. My internship, work experience, and volunteer experience were just as valuable as my formal education. I learned a great deal about accounting and teamwork and made many valuable contacts in my field.

Clearly Defined Career Goals

Employers want to be sure that you have a clear sense of where you are going and that you know what you want to do. The following paragraph is an example of a good response that demonstrates career maturity.

> Since I have been around small business all my life, I have always been interested in all aspects of business. In high school, I took an accounting class and knew this was what I wanted to do. I started helping my dad with his books. I chose Brady Business School because it has a good accounting department. There is no doubt that accounting is the field I want to pursue.

Communication

Since communication is such an important job skill, employers are interested in how well you speak. Some interview evaluation forms have categories for speaking in an articulate, clear, concise, and logical manner.

> My dad owned his own business, so I was involved in business for as long as I can remember. I did stock work in the summers and helped with marketing and sales. I never viewed any job as boring or menial. I wanted to learn every aspect of our business.

Enthusiasm and Positive Attitude

A positive attitude is one of the most important factors in job success. Employers are looking for someone who shows enthusiasm and interest and who has an upbeat outlook.

> I was very interested in reading about your overseas branch office. I took French and Spanish in high school and have always loved different cultures. Your training program also emphasizes the opportunities for international trade. I am very interested in learning new skills so that I can grow with the company.

Leadership

Since hiring is a big investment, many companies want to hire employees who have leadership potential.

> I was vice president of the Accounting Club and was instrumental in starting the first mentor program for freshmen. This resulted in a 14-percent increase in the retention rate of freshmen. I would love to be involved in any way with programs designed to retain employees.

Personal Qualities

Employers are very interested in personal qualities, such as honesty, integrity, commitment, dependability, maturity, responsibility, and fairness.

> I was the oldest of four children, and both my parents had jobs that required travel. I learned to be responsible, hardworking, and dependable. I also tried to set a good example for my younger brothers and sisters. I wanted them to look up to me, and I wanted to teach them good values. One time when I was 14, we had all just gotten home from grocery shopping. I discovered that the clerk had undercharged me. We all walked back to give the clerk the $5.00 that we owed.

Problem Solving

Analytical ability and logical inquiry are important to employers. Indicate how you use critical thinking to make decisions and solve problems.

> I have good business judgment and common sense. Recently I was responsible for locking up the store at night, and the power went out on one of the machines. I went through a logical process to solve the problem. I found the manual and had the power restored.

Overall Appearance

Your overall appearance makes a big first impression. If you are neat, clean, and professionally dressed, and if you walk and talk in a confident manner, you will project a professional image. Use direct eye contact; a confident, clear voice; and effective communication.

The Next Steps

In Chapter 5, the three steps of preparing for the interview process were explained:

1. Research.
2. Remember image.
3. Rehearse.

Now that you have fully prepared, what can you do during and after the interview to ensure success? This chapter will answer that question by examining Steps 4–9 of the interview process:

4. Relax.
5. Build rapport.
6. Review basic questions and answers.
7. Reinforce your skills and strengths.
8. Respond with questions.
9. Readjust, correct, and close.

Chapter 7 will discuss Step 10, the last step of the interview process.

Step 4. Relax

Most people feel a bit nervous and apprehensive before they go to a job interview. For some people, however, the interview stage causes such extreme fear that they experience severe anxiety and apprehension. They are so stressed out that they either become paralyzed and tongue-tied, or they nervously talk themselves right out of a job. Companies want confident and polished employees who can perform even in stressful situations and can communicate effectively. If you stammer, shake, and appear nervous, chances are you won't be hired.

However, it is normal to experience some jitters. After all, instead of dealing with paper and phones, an interview requires you to face a real person and sell yourself. In a sense, you are on stage. You are the center of attention, and all eyes are on you to see if you fit into the organization. This can cause mild to severe stage fright. Interviewing is a lot like public speaking, causing similar types of stress. Stress, however, can give you a rush of energy. In fact, many performers and athletes say that it is the controlled stress that makes for an outstanding performance.

Preparation is the key! When you are well prepared, you feel more confident and in control. Being well prepared for the interview will help you channel and reduce stress and will greatly increase your chances of success.

You also have to overcome your fear of speaking and of being rejected. Effective communication skills are vital not only in the interview but throughout your career. The higher up you go in an organization, the more you will need to make presentations, interview others, and chair meetings. Imagery, positive self-talk, and relaxation techniques can make a big difference in learning to channel stress, fear, and stage fright. You want to give your best performance as you communicate your strengths and value.

Top athletes know that they can improve performance when they manage anxiety and stress. Techniques used in sports psychology help them improve their focus and concentration through relaxation, imagery, and positive self-talk. You can use the same techniques discussed in the following sections to **relax and overcome fear, anxiety, and shyness** to im-prove your performance during your job interview and entire job search.

Relaxation

First, learn how to relax and quiet your mind. Find a quiet place. Sit with your legs uncrossed and your arms at your side. Take several deep, slow breaths and exhale slowly. Close your eyes and relax your entire body. Drop your shoulders, roll your head, and breathe all the tension from your body. Clear your mind of all chatter and concentrate on deep breathing. Feel your muscles relax and your body grow heavy. Drop your jaws and shoulders. As your breathing becomes slower and deeper, you will become more relaxed and centered. Do this relaxation technique several times before your interview.

Remember, one of your best resources is strategies.glencoe.com

Imagery

Clearly visualize yourself being interviewed. Imagine every detail of the interview. See yourself looking and feeling confident and polished. Picture yourself speaking calmly and answering all questions with a graceful and convincing style. You are self-assured and are making an impact on the employer. Visualize yourself relaxed and fully in the present. You are focused on the questions as you communicate directly with the other person. Imagine a positive outcome.

Positive Self-Talk

People who suffer from anxiety and stage fright may talk themselves into a state of panic. Panic can cause shallow breathing, sweaty palms, butterflies, and even more negative self-talk. You may begin to question your sense of worth. You can stop this cycle of negativity and create a cycle of success. You do have control over your thoughts and can reprogram your mind for success. By jotting down a few of the negative sayings that flit through your mind, you'll become more aware of ways in which you are creating your own fear and anxiety. The examples in **Figure 6.1** on page 164 show how you can reshape your thoughts by using positive self-talk or affirmations. Set goals, practice positive habits, and increase your skills. Your self-esteem will improve, and you will feel more confident and competent.

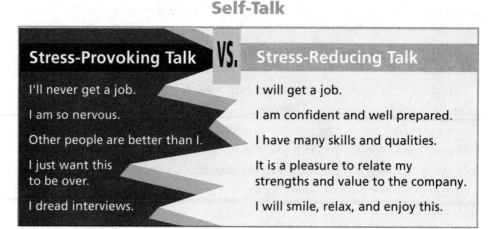

Step 5. Build Rapport

Since the decision to hire someone often comes down to the simple factor of being likable (the résumé screens out candidates who are not qualified), it is important to build rapport with the interviewer. Rapport is the ability to find common ground with another person. People who are good at building rapport have a way of making others feel comfortable and good about themselves. They are good at reading nonverbal cues and adjusting their communication to achieve real understanding. They know how to build rapport in a sincere and genuine manner. Whether rapport is established can often depend on the first few minutes of contact.

First Impressions

First impressions are extremely important and difficult to change. Studies indicate that interviewers make up their minds quickly about a job candidate. It is during the first minute or two that the interviewer makes an initial decision about how well you would fit into the company. The first few minutes also set the tone for the entire interview. From the time you walk in the door, judgments are made about your personality, character, competency, and style. This initial impression is based on dress, eye contact, body language, posture, and verbal communication. Nonverbal communication can influence the first impression even more than words.

Body Language

Many job searchers spend hours finding just the right verbal response and forget about the importance of nonverbal communication. Body language carries over 90 percent of the meaning you are trying to convey. Gestures, body stance, facial expressions, clothes, hairstyle, jewelry, walk, and posture all work together to create an image. Assess your body language:

- Do you have direct eye contact without staring?
- Are your facial expressions warm, sincere, and expressive?
- Are your gestures relaxed and natural, or do they seem forced?
- Do you walk confidently and sit straight?

You can say all the right words, but an incongruant or out-of-synch body language or tone of voice will send people double messages. For example, a candidate may be interviewing for a job and talk about the importance of teamwork and sensitivity and yet be sitting in an aloof manner, using little eye contact, and speaking in a flat tone of voice. The disparity will be noted and questioned.

Assess your consistency. You may want to videotape yourself and have a good friend watch it with you, or ask several people to give you their honest opinions. Ask yourself the following questions:

- Do you come across to others as honest and forthright?
- Do people tend to trust you?
- Take note of your tone of voice, body language, and words. Are they consistent?
- Do you come across as a good listener?
- Are you misunderstood often?

The purpose of the building-rapport stage is to put you at ease. The interviewer wants to get a picture of the real person behind the résumé. The question being asked during this stage is: *Are you poised, confident, and professional looking?* Your challenge is to present a professional and polished first impression.

A Confident Image

Use positive body language, and walk tall with your shoulders back and your head high. Maintain direct and frequent eye contact. Smile and show warmth and attentiveness. Say, "Hello, I'm John McAllen (first name and last name). It's a pleasure to meet you." Use a firm, yet gentle, handshake. Relax while sitting straight. Don't fidget or engage in nervous habits, such as playing with your hair, keys, coins, or pen.

Practice these five essential habits for projecting a confident image and creating a positive first impression:

- Smile.
- Maintain direct eye contact.
- Repeat the person's name.
- Give a firm handshake.
- Walk and sit tall, straight, and relaxed.

Casual Conversation

Be prepared to talk about yourself. A typical question is: *Tell me about yourself.* (See Chapter 5.) Don't start with the story of your life. Instead, choose a recent job experience and relate your achievements. For example:

> I just graduated from Benson Business College with a certificate in industrial technology. I worked last summer as an intern at Bio Products Corporation, and by the end of summer, I was a member of a team that redesigned the computer-training manual.

Confidence and Poise

Be enthusiastic and assertive and take an active role in the interview. For many people, interviewing is frightening, and they react to the fear by acting passive. You don't want to come across as arrogant, but acting overly submissive will lose you points. You are an equal human being. You want to be viewed as a professional and part of the team. Therefore, it is important to be confident and well prepared. Review the tips for overcoming shyness during an interview listed in Staying Power on page 183.

If you focus on having a positive attitude, you will be able to overcome your fear of interviewing. Focus your attention on the questions. Be ready for open-ended questions. Most interviewers don't ask yes or no questions since they want you to talk and explain your background. Open-ended questions allow you to stress your skills and give specific examples of how you have demonstrated them. Be alert. Develop a vocabulary that is positive and action oriented. Relate your skills and assets to the job. Strong verbal skills help you create a confident image.

Verbal Skills

WORDS

Many prospective employers form an impression of you by your choice of words. Assess the words you use and ask yourself these questions:
- Do you have a good vocabulary?
- Do you know the language or buzzwords of the job?
- Do you use sexist or racial slurs?
- Do you use slang or overused words?
- Do you use irritating or filler words, such as *like, you know, uh?*
- Do you use loaded words, such as *honey* or *dear?*
- Do you use formal names and titles when you first meet others?
- Do you have facts and figures to back up your material?
- Can you make small talk?

- Do you use direct and assertive words, or do you use qualifiers such as *kind of* or *sort of?*
- Are you brief and to the point, or do you ramble?
- Do you use common, concise words, or do you try to impress others with fancy or overly technical jargon?

VOICE

What does your voice sound like? What are the positive aspects of your voice? Ask a good friend to be honest with you and let you know if you have annoying phrases or mannerisms that detract from your effectiveness as a communicator. Listen to yourself for a few days and jot down phrases that you tend to repeat.

After you have assessed your voice, set up an action plan to rid yourself of annoying habits. Join Toastmasters (a public speaking organization), take a speech class, go to a speech therapist, or ask a friend to help you improve.

Testing Your Voice

EXERCISE 6.1

Tape-record yourself and then listen carefully. Analyze your voice.

Positive Aspects of Your Voice	Yes	No
Calm	____	____
Pleasant	____	____
Energetic	____	____
Confident	____	____
Reassuring	____	____
Crisp pronunciation	____	____
Warmth in tone	____	____
Other_____		

Negative Aspects of Your Voice	Yes	No
Shrill	____	____
Strident	____	____
Grating	____	____
Strained	____	____
Raspy	____	____
Harsh	____	____
Breathy	____	____
Nasal	____	____
Abrasive	____	____
Slurred	____	____
Other_____		

Positive Attitude

Your attitude at the beginning of an interview is the one factor that will most affect its outcome. Chapter 2 discussed the importance of motivation and positive attitude for building contacts, staying enthusiastic, and making a good first impression.

It is also critical to create a relaxed and positive mental state before and during the interview so that you will **project a confident, positive, and professional image.** If you have a negative outlook or go into an interview with a sense of doom, it will affect not only your thinking but also your body language, eye contact, tone of voice, and behavior. Learn to relax by preparing, getting organized, rehearsing, and taking deep breaths.

Warmth and Humor

People who have a knack for building rapport are friendly and relaxed. They are able to laugh at themselves and life. Humor can put people at ease by bringing a light atmosphere to even a tense situation. Humor, warmth, and a sincere smile create a comfortable climate.

Respect and Etiquette

It is important to **be respectful and use good business etiquette.** Let's look at a few points of etiquette that are not only proper and nice but also essential for an effective interview. (See also **Figure 6.2.**)

Arrive on time. If you're late for the interview, you've already "said" too much. Being late indicates you are inconsiderate, disorganized, or not serious about the job. If an emergency occurs, try to call and reschedule. Make certain you arrive at the office about 15 to 30 minutes before your scheduled interview. Use that extra time to walk around, survey the area, read notes on bulletin boards, get a cup of coffee, check yourself in a mirror, and relax. Use the power of deep breathing to relax, project positive thoughts, and calmly review your notes about the company. Don't check in with the receptionist if you are more than 20 minutes early. Check in about 5 to 10 minutes before the interview. Chat with the receptionist; turn in an application if you have been asked to submit one. Be pleasant and positive.

Remember to get a good night's sleep and be sure to get up early enough to have a healthy breakfast and avoid traffic problems and needless rushing.

It is best to go on interviews alone. Unless your spouse or a guest is invited to a special event, bringing anyone with you for support is unprofessional. Also, it might indicate a lack of confidence that you don't want to project.

Be respectful. While you understand your own nervousness, it is important to be sensitive to the interviewer and recognize that he or she may be a bit nervous, too. Civility means respect and sensitivity to the other person.

Interview Etiquette	
Do:	**Don't:**
• Always be on time.	• Don't chew gum or smoke.
• Walk tall and use relaxed body language.	• Don't drink alcohol or go to an interview with alcohol on your breath.
• Relax while sitting straight.	• Don't sit until the employer indicates the appropriate spot.
• Do everything you can to create a supportive climate. If you are offered coffee, have a cup.	• Don't fidget or engage in nervous habits, such as playing with your hair, keys, or coins.
• Follow your host in a subtle manner—if formal, be more formal; if relaxed, be more casual.	• Don't look at your watch.
• Smile.	• Don't use first names unless you are invited to do so.
• Take several deep breaths and focus on the positive.	• Don't look fearful, anxious, overeager, arrogant, bored, or too passive.
• Be confident. You are a professional.	
• Make direct eye contact.	
• Give a firm handshake.	

LUNCH AND DINNER INTERVIEWS

In some instances, employers may conduct job interviews during lunch or dinner. Keep in mind that eating while you are being interviewed is especially difficult. Not only is the interviewer concerned with good answers, he or she is also concerned with your table manners, poise, confidence, and ability to make small talk. Your personality, demeanor, and attitude are the focus.

Here are a few tips that can help:

1. **Stay on guard.** With light conversation, you might be tempted to slip into the role of being out for lunch with a friend, especially if you hit it off, discover you have several things in common, and share a few good laughs. Remember, however, that you are always being interviewed. Maintain a professional demeanor: Avoid taking a firm stance on politics or religion. You are here to get a job, not make a new best friend or persuade someone to follow your beliefs. Answer all questions professionally and use discretion. Follow the lead of the interviewer. Don't answer questions that haven't been asked. Don't go into great detail about your personal life. Refrain from saying anything negative about your past jobs or people with whom you have worked.

2. **Concentrate on the interview, not the meal.** Order something light and easy to eat. Don't worry if you don't get full; you can grab a regular meal later when you are not distracted. Don't order ribs, corn-on-the-cob, or any food that is messy and that you have to pick up with your fingers. Remember, your first priority is to land the job, not to have a culinary experience.

3. **Use your best table manners.** Know which silverware to use. Put your napkin on your lap. Don't start eating until others have been served. Don't talk while eating; chew with your mouth closed. Yes, these are all things our mothers nagged us about, and they are critical in a job interview. Companies are concerned that employees make a good impression and know how to use good manners. This is especially important if you are dealing with the public or working with foreign markets, or if the company has an image that demands proper etiquette from all of its employers.

4. **When ordering, take your lead from the interviewer.** Ask for what is recommended or the specialty of the restaurant. If in doubt, order something at a medium price. Don't go for the most expensive or the least expensive item on the menu. Don't order something like toast if your interviewer is having a full meal.

5. **Don't reach for the check.** Even if the interviewer leaves it there for what may seem like a long time, you should not pick up the check. Remember, you are a guest.

6. **Don't smoke or drink.** When dining outside or in a smoking section of a restaurant, don't smoke even if you are invited to do so. Smoking will not enhance the interview. (However, if you are a non-smoker, don't make a fuss if the interviewer smokes.) Nicotine and alcohol may cause you to appear jittery, nervous, or offguard. In general, it's best to refrain from drinking alcohol. However, occasionally, some interviewers may offer wine or other alcoholic beverages with dinner as part of a social function or special event. If it is appropriate to accept, drink very moderately. Remember that in this relaxed setting, you may forget that this is an interview. Be careful not to let your guard down.

Listening Skills

A large part of building rapport involves listening, not talking. Effective listening can make the difference between success and failure, not only in the job process, but in your career as well. Listen to the questions carefully. Pause before you jump in with your response. Don't interrupt the interviewer or change the subject. Communicate that you are interested by maintaining good eye contact, nodding, smiling, and giving other signals that show you understand. Active listening means listening to the intent of the speaker, not just to his or her words or tone. **Build rapport by being a good listener.**

Mirroring

One method of building rapport is to use the subtle technique of *mirroring*. Match your rate of speech, posture, eye contact, phrases, and style to that of the interviewer. You are not mimicking the interviewer's actions in a phony manner but building a common bond through respect and nonverbal communication.

Stand in front of the chair or sofa to the left of the interviewer until he or she asks you to be seated. Cross your legs and face the interviewer, leaning slightly forward. You are creating a position that says, "See, we really are alike." People generally relate to others who are similar. Build rapport by focusing on similarities. If possible, it is better to sit next to the interviewer rather than to sit with a desk in between. The desk creates a barrier that focuses on the roles you are each playing. Compliment the interviewer on some positive aspect of the company that you discovered in your research or on something in the office.

In Chapter 3, we discussed how people learn, think, and relate using different styles. You can often tell a person's style by his or her nonverbal behavior, choice of words, and overall appearance. Listen carefully to how the interviewer frames questions.

If the interviewer appears to be primarily a **thinker,** make certain you are accurate, more formal, and thoughtful in your responses, stressing facts and detail. The overall message you want to send is: *I do it right.* The interviewer may pose a question such as: "Do you think...?"

If the interviewer is primarily a **creator,** be idea oriented, flexible, friendly, and warm. The overall message you want to send is: *I am innovative, flexible, and creative.* The interviewer may use a phrase such as: "Do you see...?"

If the interviewer is primarily a **relator,** be supportive and approachable, stressing harmony and cooperativeness. The overall message you want to send is: *I am compassionate, supportive, and a team player.* The interviewer may pose a question such as: "How do you feel...?"

If the interviewer is primarily a **director,** be results oriented, logical, and stick to the subject. The overall message you want to send is: *I get results and am action oriented.* The interviewer may pose a question such as: "What have you accomplished?"

Step 6. Review Basic Questions and Answers

The interviewer will ask basic questions, and you will be expected to restate qualifications and expand on certain areas. **Respond with good answers.** The purpose of this stage is to see how well you can communicate your skills, personality, and qualifications. If you have prepared for questions and practiced answering them, you will do well during this stage. Refer to Chapter 5 to refresh your memory about the most commonly asked questions and good responses. Your main goal is to relax and focus on the questions with the intention of answering them in a direct and honest manner.

The question behind the interviewer's question is: *Can you communicate in a direct and thoughtful manner?* Your challenge is to have confident and thoughtful answers to basic questions and to clarify your skills and experiences. You must demonstrate that you have the necessary communication skills to speak in a clear, direct, and concise manner.

Step 7. Reinforce Your Skills and Strengths

At one stage in the interview, the questions will become more intense and probing. Remember, the résumé has already screened out people who are not qualified for the position. The basic question-and-answer session has clarified your skills. The interviewer now wants to know if you are the best person for the job. The purpose of this stage of the interview is to determine what specific skills and personal qualities you can bring to the company that would match their needs.

The question behind the interviewer's question is: *Why should we hire you?* **Demonstrate how you will benefit the company** and that you are the best applicant for the job. Determine the ways you can relate your accomplishments to specific situations. Be sure to include school, internship, and volunteer experiences as well. Mention accomplishments that relate to you skills. Some examples might include:

- Group problem-solving experiences.
- Helping to save a department from major cuts.
- Cost-cutting measures that you initiated.
- Tough deadlines that you met.
- Extra effort of working as a team.
- Training someone in new methods or new responsibilities.
- Increasing profits.
- Instituting a new system in manufacturing, marketing, accounting, and so on.
- Increasing sales by a certain percentage.
- Developing a new product or program.
- Developing relationships with new clients, affiliations, customers, or generating new business.
- Ability to work with diverse groups of people.

Focus on Personal Qualities

Most companies look beyond job skills. That "something extra" is character coupled with personality traits that are considered important for job success. Remember, the résumé and cover letter are used to screen out unqualified candidates. The interview is designed to discover your personality and personal qualities. The interviewer is attempting to assess your attitude, character, potential for growth, poise, communication skills, maturity, energy, temperament, and ability to solve problems. The employer wants to know if you are a good match for the job.

You must communicate that you have something unique to offer, that you can satisfy the company's needs, and that you really are the best person for the job. In order to sell anything, it is important to know what the buyer wants. Most companies ask the same questions:

- Will this person fit in?
- Can this person solve problems?
- Can this person make sound decisions?
- Does this person have a positive attitude and enthusiasm?
- Can this person increase profits and/or decrease spending?

Here are a few general traits, or personal qualities, that most employers value in employees. How would you describe yourself and your work experiences to an interviewer to highlight and focus on these and other important traits?

- **Dependability** You have the ability to keep agreements and follow through on commitments. You are on time.
- **Determination** You have the desire and commitment to see a situation through to completion even when problems or difficulties arise. You are persistent and get results.
- **Motivation** You are enthusiastic and have the desire to achieve and be resourceful.
- **Honesty** You have a strong moral sense. You are trustworthy.
- **Integrity** You take responsibility for your actions and hold your ground.
- **Empathy** You have the ability to understand, actively listen, and build rapport with others.
- **Cooperation** You get along, are friendly, and work well with others.
- **Energy** You have the health and stamina to give time and effort to follow through on projects.
- **Confidence** You are poised, friendly, and self-assured but not self-important or arrogant.
- **Persuasiveness** You have the ability to speak and write in a clear, concise, effective, and influential manner.
- **Organization** You are efficient and effective and use the resources available to plan and achieve results.
- **Hardworking attitude** You are willing to go the extra mile, have demonstrated an industrious nature, and work in a consistent and sustained manner.
- **Initiative** You have the ability to take initiative, to see what needs to be done, and to take action.
- **Flexibility** You are adaptable and can change directions when necessary. You will pitch in and help out on different assignments.

▨ ## Connecting Traits and Experiences

Review the list of personality traits in the previous section. On the lines provided, write your responses. The following is an example that demonstrates the personal trait of *initiative:*

I helped my auto shop instructor grade papers and worked with him in the shop during labs. One time he didn't show up for class. I knew his wife was overdue on her delivery date for their first child. This was a night class and no administrators were on campus. I felt comfortable meeting the class. I gave the class several sample problems. I also gave them a demonstration on motor repair since that is my area of specialty. My instructor was very appreciative that I took the initiative to go ahead with the class. The students said they enjoyed the demonstration and were kept on target with the class schedule. Because of this experience, I am more confident. I am careful not to overstep my bounds of authority, but I also know there are times when it is important to take the initiative to get the job done.

1. The personal trait I most want to highlight is:

   _____

   _____

   _____

2. I have demonstrated this trait in the following ways:

   _____

   _____

   _____

   _____

   _____

   _____

3. Because of this quality, my work was affected in the following manner:

   _____

   _____

   _____

   _____

   _____

   _____

Surveying Your Qualities

Make a list of the personal qualities, skills, and abilities that you most want to get across in the interview. Next to each quality, write the experience that demonstrates your quality or skill. Review the self-assessment exercises in Chapter 1 and the work you did in Chapter 3 in translating your experiences into job skills. Make certain that your experience is true and that it demonstrates a positive quality. Remember, these personal qualities and skills do not have to be work related. You can show how a life experience, a sport, a club event, travel, or a volunteer job helped you develop character, determination, skills, and so on. For example:

Quality	Demonstration
Hardworking attitude	I grew up on a farm, and I worked very hard before and after school, on weekends, and during summers.
Dependability	I have a part-time job and have never been late or missed a day of work.
Ability to deal with stress	When my dad lost his job, we had to really pull together. At the same time, my grandmother was very ill. Everyone was under a lot of stress. I dealt with it by chipping in. I got a part-time job and helped take care of my grandmother. I learned a lot about budgeting my time, getting my priorities and values straight, and being a supportive part of a team.

_____   _____
_____   _____
_____   _____
_____   _____
_____   _____
_____   _____
_____   _____
_____   _____
_____   _____
_____   _____
_____   _____
_____   _____
_____   _____
_____   _____
_____   _____

Step 8. Respond With Questions

The interviewer wants to see if the applicant can ask intelligent questions. Now is the time to **ask your prepared questions.** The purpose of this stage is to give you a chance to assess how well you have done, to clarify certain points, clear up any miscommunications, and make certain you understand the job. The question is: *Can you leave a lasting positive impression by asking good questions?* Your challenge is to ask thoughtful, intelligent, and probing questions.

Questions to Ask

Interviews are not one-sided. You are also probing for information and determining if a job is right for you and your career. Asking good questions also indicates to the interviewer that you have done your homework and that you are concerned about your career.

Be prepared to ask a few questions about the company, to whom you would be reporting, the commitment to training and education, how important this position is to the company's mission, and so forth. During the interview, other questions may occur to you. Add them to a list of written questions. Don't try to memorize the questions you want to ask. **Figure 6.3** lists some suggested questions to help you assess whether this job is a window of opportunity or a closed door.

Of course, you will want to see a written job description; understand your key assignments, to whom you will be reporting, who reports to you, travel requirements, and the company's performance review procedure. Also, find out the office location.

Questions Not to Ask

Do not mention salary, vacations, benefits, or sick leave until the interviewer brings them up or until you are offered the position. You should, however, have in mind a realistic salary that is acceptable to you. Find out what the going rate is for similar jobs at various companies. Differentiate between what you desire and what you will accept. If you are asked what you expect, you can respond with a range.

Questions a Job Interviewer Should Not Ask You

You may be asked questions that are inappropriate and, in some cases, illegal, as prohibited by the Americans With Disabilities Act of 1990. How you answer such questions—your body language and demeanor— is just as important as the words you use. Answering such questions in a tactful way will be a challenge.

It is best not to become defensive or angry. Most interviewers are attempting to gather information about you in such subtle areas as personality, attitudes, and general ability to learn and change. Look beyond

Questions to Ask

1. How does my position fit with the mission of the organization? What are the key responsibilities of this job?

2. What are the major challenges or concerns that face this organization in the near future?

3. Is the company planning major changes in the future? If so, how would they affect my department? My position?

4. With whom would I be working most closely? Does this company use working teams?

5. Ideally, what would you like me to contribute to this organization? What skills and personality characteristics are most important for success at this company?

6. How would you describe the corporate culture at this organization? The management style?

7. Who are your major competitors?

8. What is the major difference between this company and your competitors?

9. What do you wish you had known about this company when you interviewed for your position? What is it about the company that attracted you or has caused you to stay?

10. How do you view company morale? What is the company's philosophy about motivating employees?

11. Besides making a profit and offering good service, what values are most important at this company?

12. I have read your mission statement. How do you manifest this philosophy on a daily basis for your employees and customers?

13. I plan on working hard and contributing to the company. What advancement do you see for me in five years if I have proven myself?

14. What are the major goals of this company in the near future?

15. How many people have held this job in the last ten years? Where did they go?

Figure 6.3
The Right Questions Asking the right questions will not only give you needed answers, but it will also tell the interviewer that you're a serious, well-informed candidate. *Think of a particular job you might want: Which of the sample questions in this figure would most apply in an interview?*

the question and attempt to determine what the interviewer is trying to get you to reveal. Remember, the employer is trying to find a "fit"— someone who will be an integral part of the team. Given that most employers have honorable intentions, get beyond the question to what they really want to know.

Laws change, but the following are some sensitive areas that are taboo or at the very least inappropriate.

1. **Age:** Federal law protects against age discrimination. *How old are you? How old are your children?* or other questions that attempt to determine age are inappropriate and taboo. Special laws, however, do exist for

the employment of minors and for people older than 70. If you are young, the employer may want to determine if you are mature; if you are self-disciplined and have time management skills; and if you have the necessary experience and wisdom to make sound decisions. If you are an older applicant, the employer may want to determine if you are set in your ways; if you have enough energy to do the job; if you have health problems associated with growing older; if you can relate to younger staff and customers; and so on.

2. **Marital status:** The general rule is that a woman should not be asked any question that wouldn't also be asked of a man and that all questions should be job related. Questions about children, child care, spouse's employment, and birth control are illegal. If an interviewer is concerned about a married candidate's ability to travel extensively, it is appropriate to ask: *Will extensive traveling be a problem for you?* It is not appropriate to ask: *Does your husband mind if you travel?* The employer may also be trying to find out if you are someone who is dependable; if you can give a lot of time and energy to the job; and if you would be willing to relocate.

3. **Sexual preference:** It is taboo to question someone's sexual preference and ask: *Would your lifestyle be an embarrassment to this company?* The employer may be concerned about how discreet you are about your private life and if you will offend other staff or customers.

4. **Religion:** You should never be asked about your religion (unless you are applying to a religious organization). However, if an interviewer is concerned, for example, about whether you will be able to work at certain times, it is appropriate to ask: *Can you work occasionally on Saturday, Sunday, or certain holidays?*

5. **Race or national origin:** You should not be asked to identify your race or nationality. Nor should you be asked for a picture of yourself.

6. **Disabilities:** You should not be asked questions about a physical or mental disability unless it will directly affect job performance. You can be asked questions such as: *This position requires long hours sitting at the computer. Do you have any physical limitations that would directly affect your job performance?*

7. **Financial matters:** Questions about your financial affairs, such as *Do you own your own home?* are taboo. However, in many states, employers are allowed to run standard credit checks on potential candidates. Employers may be trying to assess an applicant's stability.

8. **Criminal record:** You should not be asked: *Have you ever been arrested?* However, it is not illegal to ask if you have ever been convicted of a crime. Employers value honesty and want to feel assured that they can trust employees.

How to Respond

Hiring and training new people is expensive. Therefore, employers are concerned about getting the best possible candidate and finding out as much as possible about that person. You may get asked some questions that make you feel uncomfortable. If you want the job, the best advice is to remain calm and respond in such a way that lets the interviewer know you can read beyond the inappropriate question. Don't get defensive. Let's say you are asked how many children you have. You know that the interviewer wants to find out if you will be dependable. You might reply as follows:

> I have three children. I understand that this job would require me to work weekends and nights. That will not be a problem. I have excellent day care and several backup caretakers. I am committed to getting the job done and producing excellent results. That often means putting in additional hours. I am dependable and only missed two days of work last year as a result of illness at my last job.

Career Directions

BusinessWeek

The Tender Issue of Age?

It is generally illegal in a job interview for employers to ask questions—even indirect ones such as when you got your high school diploma—that can be used to determine your age, says employment attorney Louis DiLorenzo, who heads the labor department at Bond, Schoeneck & King in Syracuse, N.Y. But whether it's smart to stand up and cry foul in the middle of an interview if you really want the job is another issue.

The Age Discrimination in Employment Act (ADEA) bars employers from using age as a basis for hiring, firing, and other employment considerations, such as promotions and compensation. The protection generally applies to workers age 40 and above, but individual states can pass laws that protect even younger employees.

There are some fuzzy areas, however. An employer can ask you when you graduated from college if the question is related to the job.

Otherwise, sniffing around to find an employee's age is pretty much verboten.

Of course, if you're persuaded that you have been discriminated against because of your age, then you may want to seek counsel or file an EEOC complaint. One thing to remember, though, is that discrimination in hiring cases is among the hardest to prove.

"It's definitely in a candidate's best interest to be as honest as possible," says Bobbi Moss of Management Recruiters International. Moss thinks the best way to deal with an employer's concerns is to anticipate them and counter them in an interview.

—By Eric Wahlgren

Excerpted from December 17, 2001, issue of BusinessWeek Online by special permission, copyright © 2000-2001, by The McGraw-Hill Companies, Inc.

Career Case Study As a reentry student majoring in marketing, Ron Villarosa was excited about a new career. Previously, he had managed a supermarket for 15 years. After graduating, he went to a job interview at a company that sold video games. However, he was greeted coolly by the 28-year-old supervisor. Ron expected to be viewed as being older but believed his skills could overcome doubts about his ability to relate to a younger market. ***What do you think Ron said to persuade the prospective employer to hire him?***

Remember, this is not a battleground to prove who is right. You do not have to allow anyone to intimidate or embarrass you, but you can also learn to respond with tact and respect.

Since everyone has some characteristic or situation that may be perceived as a handicap, it is often better to bring it out in the open in a positive light and discuss how you would deal with it. For example, assume you are 20 years old and just graduated from a certificate program in real estate. You can anticipate that the interviewer may have concerns and ask a question about your lack of experience and youth. Instead of hiding from this issue, face it and respond directly:

> I have a lot of energy and stamina. I am eager to learn, open to change, and have not formed negative habits. I am enthusiastic, hardworking, and am willing to work very hard to learn this business. I work well with people of all ages and do not mind taking orders or following directions.

Suppose you are a single woman who has sole custody of four small children. Rather than hide from the issue, bring up the quality of dependability and assure the interviewer that you are adequately prepared:

> I have day care as well as family and friends who help in case of an emergency. In my last position, I only took off a few days because of family illness, and even then I was able to complete work at home. I am dependable and committed to my profession.

Make certain you are prepared to discuss questions that assess your potential weaknesses. Review **Exercise 6.4** and give careful consideration to good responses.

EXERCISE 6.4   **Responding to Difficult Questions**

Respond to the following questions. Make up other questions and responses that you think you may be asked on the lines provided.

1. Can you explain why your grades were not very good in school?

   _____

   _____

   _____

   _____

2. Your job experience is limited to the fast-food industry. Have you had any other experiences that demonstrate your skills?

   _____

   _____

   _____

   _____

   _____

3. Do you think your lack of a college degree will hinder your career goals?

_____

_____

_____

_____

_____

4. _____

_____

_____

_____

_____

_____

5. _____

_____

_____

_____

_____

_____

6. _____

_____

_____

_____

_____

_____

EXERCISE 6.4

continued

Step 9. Readjust, Correct, and Close

As you are interviewing, pay attention to eye contact and body language. You may notice when someone is giving you the signal to move on, or you may pick up clues that he or she is confused or disagrees with what you are saying. Of course, you don't want to waffle in your presentation, but you should be sensitive to body cues and feedback, and then adjust your answers accordingly. For example, if you are getting a puzzled look, ask the interviewer if examples or clarification would be helpful. The important thing to remember at this stage is to be sensitive, aware, fully

CHECK

in the present, and flexible. Successful people have the ability to adjust and adapt to different situations.

Generally, when the interview is winding down, it's time for you to **review, assess, and close your interview.** The interviewer will ask if you have any questions. In addition to asking questions, this is the time to summarize your strengths and stress how they relate to the job. For example:

> Thank you for the opportunity to discuss how my strengths in organization and writing and my computer skills relate to this position. I know I could make a real contribution to your company. I am very excited about this position and how well it matches my strengths.

Here are a few other tips to make the closing a success:

1. **Etiquette and good manners.** Many interviews require a great deal of time, cost, and coordination. Express your appreciation to your host. Make certain that you recognize the hospitality and professionalism of the staff. For example, you might say, "Thank you for the opportunity to interview for this position. I very much appreciate your time and the professional way you handled the interview."

2. **Follow up with interest.** You may find yourself exhausted from the trip, questions, and tour, but keep up your energy and attention. Show your interest and enthusiasm for the job right through to the end of the interview. Take note of any new developments, equipment, or programs that are mentioned or noticed during a tour or discussion and refer to them at the end of the interview.

3. **Follow up with questions.** You will usually be asked if you have any final questions, so have a few ready. Ask specific questions about the company and the job when appropriate. Demonstrate that you have done your homework.

4. **Follow up with details.** Make certain you know what is expected next. Ask when you might expect to hear about the decision and who will call you. Be sure the company has your phone number and knows where and when you can best be reached. The interviewer will usually indicate an approximate date for notification. If not, ask when you might hear and if you could call in a week or so.

Generally, you will not be offered the job on the spot. If you are, however, indicate that you would like a few days to think about it. Ask when the company needs an answer. Reassessing the interview, follow-up, and negotiating salary will be covered in Chapter 7.

STAYING POWER

Listen and Relax

*C*ongratulations! A potential employer has responded to your cover letter and résumé, and you have just scheduled an interview. Unfortunately, what you've been trying so hard to arrange now seems like your biggest nightmare. You begin to wonder if it's the job you really want. You may even begin to doubt your qualifications— and have a sneaking suspicion that the person who called you must have made a mistake.

These are all normal symptoms of anxiety about a job interview. However, it's important not to let the fear of failure or "stage fright" cause you to dwell on your fears and imagine worst-case scenarios. Create the impression you want to make by visualizing a successful, confident job interview as you take inventory of the qualities and qualifications that make you the right person for the job.

It's important to be clear about what you want to say, but you can also project a relaxed, respectful attitude by paying attention to the interviewer. You can use shyness to become an effective listener. When you focus on making the interviewer feel comfortable and concentrate on the interview, your self-consciousness may disappear.

Try This...

Being comfortable during your job interview can suggest to a prospective employer that you will be comfortable in the working environment. Focus on these strategies:

- Make sure your body language shows that you are attentive and respectful of the interviewer.
- Make eye contact as you listen to questions and give answers.
- Don't overact or fawn, but listen with genuine curiosity and attentiveness.
- Observe the way people around you speak. Be a better listener every day, and you will be a better listener during interviews.
- Decide what habits and techniques work well for you and practice them.

CHAPTER 6 *Review*

Skill Check Recap

- Relax and overcome fear, anxiety, and shyness.
- Project a confident, positive, and professional image.
- Be respectful and use good business etiquette.
- Build rapport by being a good listener.
- Respond with good answers.
- Demonstrate how you will benefit the company.
- Ask your prepared questions.
- Review, assess, and close your interview.

Self-Check List

Keep track of your progress. Read the following and mark *yes* or *no*.

	Yes	No
• I have practiced relaxation to overcome fear.	_____	_____
• I have learned how to create a positive first impression.	_____	_____
• I have practiced nonverbal communication.	_____	_____
• I have practiced verbal communication.	_____	_____
• I know how to answer basic questions with clear, concise answers using good grammar.	_____	_____
• I know how to reinforce my skills and achievements.	_____	_____
• I can give examples of my skills and experience.	_____	_____
• I can connect my achievements with the needs of the company.	_____	_____

Review Questions

1. What are eight factors used to evaluate you as a prospective employee?

   _____

   _____

2. What are three ways to overcome major anxiety?

   _____

   _____

3. Which four strategies will you use for establishing rapport?

   _____

   _____

4. What is the interviewer's purpose behind asking basic questions?

   _____

   _____

5. When the interviewer's questions become more intense and probing, what is his or her question behind the question?

   _____

   _____

6. What are six things to remember during a lunch or dinner interview?

   _____

   _____

7. Which of the personal qualities listed on page 173 would you find easiest to demonstrate in an interview?

   _____

   _____

8. What do your questions tell an interviewer about you?

   _____

   _____

Critical Thinking

9. Think about two skills you already have. For each skill, write down how you will be able to demonstrate it on the job.

   _____

   _____

Cooperative Learning

10. Form groups of four students. Each student will role-play being interviewed. Using the personal qualities listed in question 7, demonstrate these characteristics. Critique one another.

Anticipating the Interview

Gary is 20 and has just graduated from a community college with an associate of arts degree in heating, air conditioning, and technology. He is eager to start working full-time and wants to work at the same company where he has worked part-time while attending school. He has put together a résumé and a good cover letter and has prepared good questions and answers for an interview.

Gary is well prepared. However, he is very shy and has always avoided any kind of public speaking. He is terrified of the interview and breaks out in a sweat just thinking about it. He is afraid that his anxiety may overshadow his qualifications and other personal qualities during his interview—and that he won't get the full-time job.

Problem Solving The following ten questions are designed to help solve problems and make sound decisions. You can use these questions to find solutions to your own problems. Put yourself in Gary's place and consider these questions from his point of view.

- What is the problem?
- Do I have enough information?
- Can I make the decision by myself?
- Have I brainstormed alternatives?
- Have I looked at likely consequences?
- Have I identified all the resources and tools needed?
- Have I developed and implemented an action plan?
- Have I identified the best solution?
- Have I assessed the results?
- Have I modified the plan, if necessary?

What solution would you suggest to Gary? Write your answer on the lines below.

_____

_____

_____

_____

_____

_____

_____

_____

_____

STRATEGIES Online

Find out more about building condence for your interview by visiting this book's Web site at strategies.glencoe.com

Interview Rehearsal

Practice interviewing out loud and as often as possible with friends, with career-center staff, and on tape. Review how you perform and ask others for feedback.

- Do you have good eye contact?

  _____

  _____

- How is your body language?

  _____

  _____

- Do you reveal self-confidence?

  _____

  _____

- How is your ability to answer questions?

  _____

  _____

- Make a list of questions to ask the interviewer.

  _____

  _____

  _____

  _____

  _____

- On the lines provided, write down the points you wish to improve and speech patterns to overcome.

  _____

  _____

  _____

  _____

CHAPTER 7

Following Up

Winning Points

- Continue a self-assessment program.
- Keep organized and detailed written records.
- Follow up on all contacts.
- Write thank-you notes.
- Expand your job search effort to include small and large companies.

> "It's the constant and determined effort that breaks down resistance, sweeps away all obstacles."
>
> —Claude M. Bristol
> Motivational writer

Introduction

After the interview, you may be tempted to breathe a sigh of relief and believe the only thing you have left to do is wait. However tempting it is to take a break, it is crucial that you stay active, involved, and focused. Waiting is not the final step to getting the job. In the previous chapters, you have completed nine of the steps of interviewing. Now is the time to take the tenth and final step: Reassess and follow up.

This chapter will look at the importance of following up with the seemingly small details that can make the difference in a successful job search:

- Interview assessment
- Follow-up thank-you notes
- Continued networking and record keeping
- Negotiation
- Reevaluation

Chapter 7 Objectives

After you have completed this chapter, you will be able to:

- Describe how to reassess the interview process
- Explain the importance of follow-up letters, calls, and contacts
- Write thank-you notes
- Identify how to clarify expectations and agreements
- Explain and apply effective negotiation strategies

Step 10. Reassess and Follow Up

Why is follow-up so important? Following up on details is an essential part of the job search. In fact, following up on the interview is almost as important as the interview itself. Without follow-up, your cover letter and résumé may end up lost, set aside, buried on someone's desk, or forgotten. You may have had a great interview, but as weeks pass, the interviewer may forget which candidate said what or how impressive your skills really are. A thank-you note will help the interviewer remember your strengths and achievements, and he or she may take a second look at your résumé.

In addition to writing thank-you notes, follow-up means assessing your interview performance and progress, writing letters in response to rejections, following up with phone calls, and sending out more résumés—in short, follow-up means staying active in the job search until you get and accept an offer. As the old saying goes, "It's not over until it's over." Even when you have a solid offer, follow-up continues to be important. Negotiating the best salary, making a sound decision about whether to accept the offer, and keeping good records are all follow-up tasks that are important for your career.

Reassessment

As soon as possible after the interview, find a quiet spot and jot down your immediate thoughts concerning the interview. Make certain you have the correct names and spelling of everyone who interviewed you or key people to whom you were introduced. If you need to send in additional material or information or were given a date when a decision will be made, jot this down and follow through.

When you have more time, sit back and, in a nonjudgmental and detached way, **review and reassess the interview.** The point of this reviewing is not to worry or fret, but to improve. You can use a checklist, like the one in **Exercise 7.1,** to review each aspect of the interview. Also, ask yourself the following questions:
- Which questions made you feel most comfortable?
- Which questions made you feel least comfortable?
- What questions were surprises?
- What did you feel comfortable about?
- Did you feel you had rapport?
- What did you do that worked?
- Were you able to say what you had planned to say?
- What would you do differently if you could?
- What was your overall feeling about the interview?

Evaluating Your Interview

Review your job interview by filling out this form.

Date_____ Company_____

Job Position_____ Interviewer's Name_____

Questions	Yes	Somewhat	No
1. I researched the company.	___	___	___
2. I researched the industry.	___	___	___
3. I focused on the employer's needs.	___	___	___
4. I made a positive first impression.	___	___	___
5. My greeting was professional and friendly.	___	___	___
6. I communicated my achievements.	___	___	___
7. I listened carefully and responded sincerely.	___	___	___
8. I adjusted my verbal and nonverbal communication when needed.	___	___	___
9. I emphasized personal qualities.	___	___	___
10. I successfully channeled excess energy and was relaxed and calm.	___	___	___
11. I related personal traits and strengths to the position.	___	___	___
12. I showed courtesy, respect, and good manners.	___	___	___
13. I expressed focused career goals.	___	___	___
14. I showed energy and enthusiasm.	___	___	___
15. I adapted to the interviewer's style.	___	___	___
16. I answered difficult questions with poise.	___	___	___
17. I asked good questions and gathered valuable information.	___	___	___
18. My closing was strong and focused.	___	___	___

Following Up With a Thank-You Note

After you have finished your initial assessment of the interview, take time to write and **follow up with a thank-you note.** A thank-you note not only communicates good business etiquette, it communicates your attention to detail and ability to build rapport. Express your favorable impression of the company, your appreciation for the interview, and your continued interest in the position. You can cite specific examples.

Because few people take the time to write them, a thank-you note is a great way to set yourself apart from others who have interviewed for the same position. It is also a written reminder of who you are and will solidify your image in the mind of the interviewer.

Consider sending a thank-you note not only to the interviewer but to anyone who was especially helpful, such as the receptionist, department head, professionals in your field, someone in your network, or potential coworkers who took time to meet with you. These people may be able to give you a recommendation, provide leads on another job, or keep you in mind for the future.

Your thank-you note can be either handwritten or typed. See **Figure 7.1** for an example of a typed thank-you note and use the following guidelines for all thank-you notes:

- Send a thank-you note within 24 hours.
- Make certain spelling and grammar are correct.
- Check the proper spelling of people's names and titles.
- Keep notes short and concise but sincere.
- Mention your interest in working with the company.
- Thank anyone who has been helpful.
- Make your notes personal and individual.

STRATEGIES Online

Remember, one of your best resources is strategies.glencoe.com

Formal Thank-You Note

Figure 7.1
Business Etiquette Use the standard format for a business letter—the same format you followed for cover letters—for a formal, typed thank-you note. *What information is included in this letter that demonstrates the job applicant's specific interest in the company?*

April 28, 2004   **Date (1-2 inches from top of paper)**

4-6 spaces

Ms. Lynn Redfield
Director, Human Resources
Capital Industry   **Inside address**
2202 Bend Street
Pinecrest, AL 23993

2 spaces

Dear Ms. Redfield: **Salutation**

2 spaces

Thank you for an enjoyable interview last Friday. You conducted the interview professionally, and everyone I met was helpful and pleasant. I enjoyed learning more about Capital Industry and have a sincere desire to work for this progressive and supportive company. I was most   **Body** impressed with your training program.

2 spaces

If additional information is needed, please let me know. I look forward to hearing from you.

2 spaces

Sincerely,   **Complimentary Close**

3-4 spaces

Daniel E. Page   **Signature**

Daniel E. Page
2910 Riverton Drive   **Return address**
Troy, MI 8002

By using computers or a word processor, it is easy to create a letterhead with your return address; or you can put your address under your name and signature as in the sample in **Figure 7.1.** Many word-processing programs have automatic templates for standard business-letter format that will automatically arrange the sections of a typical business letter:

- Date
- Inside address
- Salutation
- Body of letter
- Complimentary close
- Signature

Practice writing on your computer, or simply use pen and paper.

Following Up Systematically

After your interview and as you continue your job search, you can decrease frustration and increase effectiveness if you continue to use the systematic record-keeping system discussed in Chapter 2. Don't rely on your memory or feel that once you have gone through this process and reached this point that you can forget the required steps to keep good records. **Follow up with good record keeping.** Most people change jobs several times in their careers. If you set up an effective record-keeping system, you will be able to review the process easily, minimizing frustrations, and enhancing your confidence and job-search skills.

Keeping meticulous records will also help you be successful in your job and get promoted. For example, keep records of your goals, achievements, successful projects, letters of appreciation, and so forth. These will be important during performance reviews and for your own goal setting.

Job-Search Journal

It is difficult to remember what you have accomplished and the progress you're making in your job search. Write down details, names, dates, important information, and your emotional highs and lows as they occur. A journal can be extremely valuable throughout your job search and in your career.

Networking

Networking isn't just a job-search activity—it's a vital part of career success. Review your network often and follow up with information concerning your job search and your career. Set goals for meeting new people and nurturing long-term professional contacts. Be supportive of coworkers, professional contacts, and friends. Send thank-you notes, articles of interest, notes of concern, or congratulations for achievements to your network when appropriate. Listen actively and be available when people need support.

Let your references and the key people who helped you in your job search know if you have interviewed for a job and how your job search is going. They may be able to give you information about other jobs. **Continue to network.**

Telephone Follow-Up Lists

It is critical to keep a complete list of companies that have received your résumé and companies where you've interviewed. Be sure to **follow up with phone calls.** If you haven't gotten an interview, indicate in your cover letter that you will call to schedule a time to meet. Make your calls promptly as a reminder that you sent your résumé, are interested in the position, and would very much like an interview. During the interview, indicate that you will be calling to follow up on the interview itself. Polite persistence is a major factor in getting a job.

Other Follow-Up Letters

If you call and cannot reach the person who has the power to hire, follow up with another letter indicating your interest and a time when you will call again. It may not be enough to send your cover letter and résumé when making an initial inquiry for a job. You may need to follow up in a week or so to keep your name recognized by sending another résumé with a follow-up letter such as the one in **Figure 7.2.**

Sample Follow-Up Letter to Request an Interview

July 7, 2004

Ms. Lynn Redfield
Director, Human Resources
Capital Industry
2202 Bend Street
Pinecrest, AL 23993

Dear Ms. Redfield:

On June 30, I applied to Capital Industry for a position as sales representative in the Midwest region. As I haven't heard from you, I wanted to let you know that I am still very interested in working for your company.

Over the last few months, I have done considerable research into Capital Industry. I am impressed with the progressive marketing and quality of products. Customer service is stressed and your distributor in Austin expressed support for your training and service.

As my résumé indicates, I have demonstrated the following:

- A positive attitude and outgoing personality
- Effective communication skills and success in working as a team
- Self-motivation and a willingness to learn by continually taking courses and workshops since earning an associate's degree in business
- Capacity for hard work, dependability, and responsibility

I am confident I can make a real contribution to Capital Industry. I would appreciate the opportunity to meet with you and discuss these ideas. I will call next week to see if we can arrange a mutually convenient time. Thank you for your consideration.

Sincerely,

Daniel E. Page

Daniel E. Page
2910 Riverton Drive
Troy, MI 8002

Figure 7.2
Assertive Communication It's a fine line between being professionally assertive, becoming a nuisance, or appearing desperate. Employers receive many résumés and can get bogged down. Taking an extra step in following up can sometimes be rewarded. *Why might writing a second follow-up letter be ill advised? Be advantageous?*

You Got the Job!

SKILL CHECK →

Congratulations! When you graduate from applicant to new employee, you will usually receive a call from the interviewer offering you the job. At this time you may be offered a specific salary, or the interviewer may ask you to come in to discuss salary and benefit details. At this time you can also **find out the expectations and essential details of the job.** The phone call, or negotiation meeting, is usually followed by a formal letter that outlines the salary agreement, the starting date of the job, and where to report on the first day.

Before you accept a job, spend some time thinking about not only salary but all the factors to be considered with a job offer (see **Figure 7.3**). Ask yourself several questions about any company before you make a final commitment:

- Is the company economically stable?
- Is it the right size and in the right location for me?
- Are the pay and benefits adequate?
- Is the company technologically current?
- Is there emphasis on research and development of new products?
- Is there a good training program?
- Can I work toward my long-term career goals at this company?
- Is family and leisure time important to the company?
- How much travel is expected?
- Is there a strong commitment to corporate ethics?

Figure 7.3

No Surprises The time to clarify expectations is before you sign the acceptance letter or contract. Make certain you and your new supervisor agree on the details, and you will avoid future misunderstandings and dissatisfaction with your job and your boss. *Which three factors, besides salary, would be the most important to you when considering a job offer?*

Beyond Salary: Factors to Consider

✓ Salary	✓ Responsibilities and expectations
✓ Benefits	✓ Supervisor
✓ Vacation and holidays	✓ Performance review policy
✓ Insurance	✓ Raises and promotions
✓ Retirement plan	✓ Daily schedule and overtime
✓ Starting date	✓ Travel
✓ Office space	✓ Travel reimbursement procedures

Negotiations

The time has come to negotiate your salary. The question to ask yourself is: *"How much am I worth?"* Your answer will likely affect the outcome of your salary negotiation. You must convince both yourself and the employer of the value that you will bring to the job so that you can **negotiate the best possible salary.**

Researching the market value of your field, your employer, your position, and your skills is crucial. Come up with a range of high and low salaries that employees in similar positions are earning. Several resources will be useful in identifying current salaries:

- Professional trade organizations
- Business magazines
- Company literature
- Contacts in the field

Career Directions · BusinessWeek

Negotiating the Minefield of Multiple Offers

Job offers are a little like romance, our experts say. You wait by the phone for months and no one calls—then suddenly everyone wants you. So, get used to grappling with the ethics of multiple offers, says Mike Sweeny, a managing director at T. Williams Consulting.

The most important rule, our experts stress, is for you to do what's best for your career. Howard Hegwer, managing partner for Management Recruiters of Seattle [says] "People really have to manage their own career, wrap their arms around it, and take full responsibility for making things happen—or not."

It does matter how you handle the process, because careless offenses—such as cavalierly using multiple offers to play salary games

with potential employers— can come back to haunt you.

Should you approach your manager with the outside offer and [try] to negotiate? "That's situational," says Dan Hayes, an e-services consultant at the recruiting firm Hall Kinion in Minneapolis. The answer depends on whether this approach might work in your particular office culture and whether you're dealing with the kind of

manager who would hold it against you.

Job candidates also need to keep in mind that counter-offering can have some brutal consequences. "Bidding wars are no fun," Hayes says. "They make you look greedy, and to be honest, companies really get bitter about it."

And now that all that's settled, maybe you can get some work done.

By H. J. Cummins

Excerpted from January 12, 2001, issue of BusinessWeek Online by special permission, copyright © 2000-2001, by The McGraw-Hill Companies, Inc.

Career Case Study Trudy Norman had been working as a clothing buyer for three years with little hope of advancement, despite her valuable contributions. Then she was offered a less interesting but higher-paying job. She was doubtful about leaving but needed more money. She decided to tell her boss to see if she could get a raise. Unfortunately, because the company viewed employees as interchangeable parts, her boss did not counter the offer but said she could leave within three days. ***Did Trudy do the right thing by telling her boss? Why?***

Check with your local library for additional resources. Keep a file of salary ranges and job descriptions in career areas of interest to you. This file should be kept and updated throughout your career.

Always keep in mind that salaries will vary by geographical locations. So check out the cost of living for the location where you wish to work and then make comparisons. Government offices also have standardized salary schedules, which are published by the U.S. Department of Labor. You can also find this information online using salary calculators. Go to **strategies.glencoe.com** to find such Web sites.

During negotiations you may be asked to tell the employer what salary you have in mind. Avoid presenting your requirements first. Respond by saying that you need to know more about the job assignment, advancement possibilities, and training. Ask the employer to provide you with a range for entry-level jobs at the company and compare the range with your research. Discuss the following factors regarding your salary:

- Your worth
- Value you will add to the company
- Experience
- Skills
- Personal qualities
- Education

Be careful not to paint yourself into a corner. If you state a salary that is too low, the employer may question your worth. You may also be resentful later if you settle for less money than other people are making with your experience and background. If you state a salary that is too high, however, it may disqualify you. If you already have a job, you will generally want to increase your salary.

You might say, "I would expect to make what other customer service reps make with my training and experience and am certain that your offer would come into that range. I am most concerned about a good commission plan and that my salary will reflect my ability to produce results." If you are offered the lowest salary, and you think your training and experience are worth more, counter with a higher salary that keeps you within the standard salary range for that job. Show that you have self-worth and negotiation skills in this situation.

Writing an Acceptance Letter

As soon as you have made a rational and sound decision, it's time to write an acceptance letter. Writing this type of letter will be a rewarding part of your job search. An acceptance letter provides a formal written record for both you and the employer, and it will be considered a contractual agreement.

Sample Acceptance Letter

Daniel E. Page
2910 Riverton Drive
Troy, MI 48002

April 28, 2004

Ms. Lynn Redfield
Director, Human Resources
Capital Industry
2202 Bend Street
Pinecrest, AL 23993

Dear Ms. Redfield:

Thank you for your call Tuesday informing me that I have been chosen for the position of sales representative. I am eager to become part of the team at Capital Industry and am confident that I will contribute to the company.

I have appreciated your consideration during the interview process. The entire job process was made enjoyable because of your professional style.

I will arrive for work in three weeks (May 15). I can be reached at my parents' home until then. Their address and phone number are:

Jan and Bill Page
331 Sweetbriar Lane
Pinecrest, AL 23993
(202) 839-0032

Thanks again for your support. I look forward to working with you.

Sincerely,

Daniel E. Page

Daniel E. Page

Figure 7.4
Looking Forward Writing an acceptance letter should be an enjoyable task, especially because all of your job-search efforts have paid off. *What is one important feature of an acceptance letter that you should be sure to include?*

Review the sample acceptance letter in **Figure 7.4** for an example of a typical letter of acceptance. Be direct about accepting the job offer and include these elements:

- Your statement of acceptance of the position
- A restatement of the terms of employment (e.g., job title, location, and salary)
- The date you will begin your job
- Expression of your appreciation and positive anticipation about the position
- Your address, phone number, or other contact information

When You Don't Get a Job Offer

Even if you don't do well in an interview, or you hear that the job was offered to someone else, write thank-you notes to those companies that you still find interesting. You never know when another opening will occur. The interviewer will think of you and your well-written thank-you note, recognizing your grace and professionalism. This type of thank-you note should express appreciation for the interview, continued interest in the company, and best wishes for the company's success. The following letter shown in **Figure 7.5** is an example of a response to a rejection letter.

Sample Response to a Rejection Letter

Figure 7.5

Keeping the Lines Open In spite of being turned down, you still can take advantage of the new contact you have made. *Why should you bother writing a letter to a company that has rejected you for a job?*

> Daniel E. Page
> 2910 Riverton Drive
> Troy, MI 48002
>
> April 28, 2004
>
> Ms. Lynn Redfield
> Director, Human Resources
> Capital Industry
> 2202 Bend Street
> Pinecrest, AL 23993
>
> Dear Ms. Redfield:
>
> Thank you for sending me the letter informing me that you have chosen another candidate for the position of sales representative for the Midwest division of Capital Industry.
>
> I was treated with professional courtesy by everyone I met, and the entire review process was enjoyable. You have been most helpful and considerate.
>
> I wish you the best with the new candidate. If another position does open up in the near future, please keep me in mind. I am still very interested in Capital Industry and believe I could make a real contribution.
>
> Thank you again for your time and consideration.
>
> Sincerely,
>
> *Daniel E. Page*
>
> Daniel E. Page

Time to Reevaluate

What is going right and wrong with your job search? Are you making progress? Start logging replies and your analysis of interviews, and begin the process of determining whether your plan of action is effective. Your goal is to get invited for an interview and get a job offer. If you are working hard at the job search but are becoming discouraged, this is the time to reevaluate your efforts. Use the Job-Search Checkpoint form in **Exercise 7.2** on page 202 to assess your job-search process. Find out what is keeping you from being successful. **Reevaluate and readjust regularly.**

Review the exercises you've done throughout this book for help in assessing interests and skills, as well as writing and presentation skills. Assess possible reasons why you are not getting job offers. Were you late for an interview? Are there strategies you need to practice? You may not be realistic in applying for certain jobs; or you may be falling victim to one of the reasons listed below in **Figure 7.6**. Use the Self-Check Lists in the Chapter Review sections at the end of each chapter and apply the Skill Check strategies for a successful job search, and you will be rewarded for your time and effort.

Applying Strategies

10 Common Reasons for Job Rejection

1. Unprofessional appearance
2. Indifference and lack of enthusiasm
3. Excessive nervousness
4. Know-it-all attitude
5. Little eye contact and lack of poise and self-confidence
6. Lack of preparation and did not do homework on company
7. Poor communication skills
8. Did not relate skills and strengths to job
9. Poor manners
10. Misrepresented qualifications

10 Strategies That Work

1. Improve your appearance. *(Chapter 5)*
2. Work on having a positive, enthusiastic attitude. *(Chapters 5, 6, 7, and 8)*
3. Relax. *(Chapter 6)*
4. Focus on building rapport. *(Chapter 6)*
5. Be confident and poised with direct eye contact. *(Chapters 5 and 6)*
6. Be well prepared. *(Chapters 1, 2, and 5)*
7. Practice effective verbal and nonverbal communication skills. *(Chapters 5 and 6)*
8. Effectively relate skills and strengths to job. *(Chapters 1, 3, 4, 5, and 6)*
9. Practice good manners and be an effective listener. *(Chapters 5 and 6)*
10. Be honest and display integrity. *(Chapters 3 and 5)*

Figure 7.6
The Good News All the reasons for rejection can be countered by the effective strategies and guidelines presented in this book. Use the list of 10 Strategies That Work as a guide for reviewing what you need to do to increase your chances of success. *Which skills and traits do you need to improve and how would you do that?*

▓ Job-Search Checkpoint

Are you getting interviews? Have you been prepared for the interviews? Use the following guidelines to assess your job-search process. Write your responses to these statements on the lines provided. You can also copy and incorporate this checklist into a daily log.

Date_____

1. I have done my homework and completed research for the following companies:

_____

_____

_____

_____

_____

_____

2. I have sent out résumés and personalized cover letters and prepared for interviews for the following companies:

_____

_____

_____

_____

_____

_____

3. I have prepared for interviews and interviewed for the following positions:

_____

_____

_____

_____

_____

_____

4. My feelings about today's interviews are:

_____

_____

_____

_____

_____

STAYING POWER

*A*fter constantly looking for jobs, thoroughly researching companies, sending out countless applications, and being disappointed by several interviews, you finally get a job offer. Ideally, you will feel excited about advancing your career. However, you may feel like taking the job because you desperately need the money. You may also feel apprehension over taking the job, asking yourself if you are ready for it or if you really want it.

Before you allow your emotions to dictate your response to the job offer, it's important to take a moment to think about your options and your long-term goals. Ask yourself: Are you ready to commit to the position? Do you think the salary or rate that is offered to you is fair? Will this job take your life in the direction you want it to go?

By honestly evaluating your situation and looking at the "big picture," you will help ensure that you make the right decision for your future. Just as importantly, you will make certain that the company hires the right person for the job. Being hired is a two-way street, and it's important to think about how you will contribute to the business to make it a mutually beneficial relationship.

Try This...

- Think about your values. Knowing what you want out of life and having specific goals will help you determine if a particular job is right for you.
- Conducting research ahead of time will help you make decisions when it's time to accept a job.
- As part of your research, ask people who have jobs in your career area what an average day is like, what skills are required, and how much money they make.
- Continue responding to other job opportunities, so you will have alternative possibilities if a current prospect falls through.

CHAPTER 7 Review

Skill Check Recap

- Review and reassess the interview.
- Follow up with a thank-you note.
- Follow up with good record keeping.
- Continue to network.
- Follow up with phone calls.
- Find out the expectations and essential details of the job.
- Negotiate the best possible salary.
- Reevaluate and readjust regularly.

Self-Check List

Keep track of your progress. Read the following and mark *yes* or *no*.

	Yes	No
• I have followed up on the interview assessment.	_____	_____
• I have followed up on job-search goals.	_____	_____
• I have written thank-you notes.	_____	_____
• I have followed up after sending out more résumés.	_____	_____
• I have followed up on cover letters sent out.	_____	_____
• I have followed up on contacts.	_____	_____
• I have updated my résumé.	_____	_____
• I have followed up on interviews.	_____	_____
• I have followed up on salary and benefits arrangements.	_____	_____
• I have reevaluated my job search.	_____	_____
• I have adjusted my strategies where necessary.	_____	_____

Review Questions

1. Why is follow-up important?

   _____

   _____

2. What are the two most important follow-up activities?

   _____

   _____

3. What three things should thank-you notes express?

   _____

   _____

4. What three things should you continue to do after an interview?

   _____

   _____

5. Why is researching the market value of a prospective job critical?

   _____

   _____

6. What might occur if you suggested a salary that was too low or too high?

   _____

   _____

7. What factors might you negotiate besides salary?

   _____

   _____

8. If you don't receive any job offers, what should you do?

   _____

   _____

Critical Thinking

9. Look at the list of 10 Common Reasons for Job Rejections on page 201. Which factor applies to you? How can you correct it?

   _____

   _____

Cooperative Learning

10. In pairs, review and assess each other's portfolios. Suggest ways to improve.

Settling for the Best Offer?

Maria has a degree from a prestigious architectural school, good grades, key leadership activities, and impressive references. She followed a focused job-search strategy by carefully completing her self-assessment and creating an active network, an effective résumé, and cover letters. Maria only applied to large, impressive companies. She assumed that with her qualifications it would be easy to get a top job at a major company. After being turned down twice, she applied to a small company and was promptly offered a good job. The salary is not as high as she expected, but the opportunities for advancement are excellent.

Maria is torn between accepting a job at a small company and holding out for a job at a major, prestigious firm.

Problem Solving The following ten questions are designed to help solve problems and make sound decisions. You can use these questions to find solutions to your own problems. Put yourself in Maria's place and consider these questions from her point of view.

- What is the problem?
- Do I have enough information?
- Can I make the decision by myself?
- Have I brainstormed alternatives?
- Have I looked at likely consequences?
- Have I identified all the resources and tools needed?
- Have I developed and implemented an action plan?
- Have I identified the best solution?
- Have I assessed the results?
- Have I modified the plan, if necessary?

What solution would you suggest to Maria? Write your answer on the lines below.

_____

_____

_____

_____

_____

_____

_____

_____

_____

_____

STRATEGIES Online

Find out more about accepting job offers by visiting this book's Web site at strategies. glencoe.com

Your *Career* Portfolio

Follow-Up

After every job interview, use the following questions to help evaluate your interview. Add this page to your career portfolio.

- What is your assessment of the job interview?

  _____

  _____

- What are the pros and cons of the job?

  _____

  _____

- Can you determine whether you will accept a job offer?

  _____

  _____

- What can you determine is a feasible salary for the position?

  _____

  _____

- What job requirements are most important to you?

  _____

  _____

- What are your main priorities?

  _____

  _____

- What are your strengths and abilities?

  _____

  _____

- What are some new questions you want to follow up on?

  _____

  _____

CHAPTER 8

Job Success Strategies

- Take time to learn the corporate culture.
- Be a lifelong learner.
- Develop positive habits and personal qualities.
- Take charge of your career.
- Take charge of your performance reviews and get feedback.
- Create high visibility.
- Develop a strong network.
- Realize that your job depends on the value you create.

Introduction

A new job usually presents an exciting opportunity for a better salary and professional growth. Your first few months on the job can also set the tone for your career at a company. As in the job interview, first impressions are very important!

There are basic strategies that can help you succeed in your new job. Of these strategies, a positive attitude and effective listening skills are the most important. Be enthusiastic, but follow the company's policies and procedures to the letter. Ask questions and listen attentively to your supervisor and coworkers. Make certain you have a clear understanding of your responsibilities, expectations, and limits. Your first year on the job can lay a foundation for your entire career, so take advantage of this orientation period.

Chapter 8 Objectives

After completing this chapter, you will be able to:

- Explain the importance of the first year on the job
- Describe and apply success strategies and positive habits
- Summarize how to manage your career
- Define the best strategies for getting promoted
- Describe how to prepare for the changing world of work

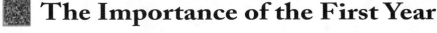

The Importance of the First Year

You've signed the contract; assembled neat and appropriate clothes for the job; and celebrated getting the job you want. Now is the time to follow a path to advancement and success.

The first year is a critical transitional time and can make or break your career. You are no longer a student but are not yet one of the seasoned professionals. During this orientation period, your supervisors and coworkers will be evaluating you to see how well you adapt to the job routine. The question they will ask is: "Did we make a mistake or a good choice?" Your actions will be watched. Focus on strategies and habits that can help you succeed during your first year on the job.

> "I maintained my edge by staying a student; you always have something to learn."
>
> —Jackie Joyner-Kersee
> Olympic Gold Medal
> winner

The Corporate Culture

Every organization has a climate of norms or values that define acceptable behavior. These unwritten rules are almost never discussed but are very real. For example, at some organizations, it is understood that you can call the supervisors by their first names, date other employees, send jokes through e-mail, or wear blue jeans on Friday. At other organizations, these practices would not be tolerated. It is critical that you **learn the corporate culture** and understand how you are expected to behave. Keep your eyes open, listen, and ask questions. When in doubt, keep your behavior and appearance professional and conservative.

Observe and Listen

During the first few months, observe and listen more and talk less. This is especially important when it comes to jokes and gossip. A standard rule that will save you embarrassment and career setback is: Don't take part in gossip. It is never apparent who has the real power in any organization or who is related to or good friends with whom. During the first few months, it's better to observe and listen nonjudgmentally. You can listen to—but don't join in on—office gossip.

Watch colleagues and observe how things are done. You want to fit into the culture, and this takes time and patience. Some people make the mistake of coming into a new job eager to share their feelings and opinions. They want to show their boss and coworkers how creative and smart they are, so they suggest major changes, criticize established procedures, and love telling people the "right" way to do things. Their attitude says, "How did you manage before I joined this company?"

Don't be a show-off or know-it-all. Even if you have some great new ideas for how to make the company run better, take time to know the company before you try to impress people with your clever and creative mind. Give yourself a few months to study and observe. Take time to **listen, be aware, and ask questions.** The more you know about the

work environment, the product, the competition, the corporate culture, office politics, your boss, your clients, and your customers, the easier it will be to offer really sound solutions. Making a big splash, becoming too familiar, and trying too hard to impress rarely work and can ruin a career.

Here are a few questions to help you assess the corporate culture of your new workplace:

- What are the basic procedures in this office?
- What problems keep the company from being more efficient?
- Who really has the power and knowledge?
- Who uses critical thinking to make decisions?
- Who confronts problems directly and solves them?
- Who avoids problems until a crisis occurs?
- Who pulls together the team, and who is highly visible?
- What office games are going on? Are certain people excluded from meetings?
- Who likes to spread rumors and gossip? Who runs to the boss to tattle?
- Whose ideas are listened to and acted upon?
- Does someone steal ideas or take the credit for the work of others?
- Whose doors are open, and where do you go for support?
- Are resources and assistance given to help employees meet their goals?
- Is teamwork encouraged, or are game playing, suspicion, and rumors allowed?
- What behavior gets rewarded: cooperation and direct communication or hidden messages, power games, and one-upmanship?
- Were you hired over someone who wanted a promotion?
- What were some new ideas that worked in the past?
- How do people get recognized at this organization?
- Do you know office procedures? Whom do you notify if you have a meeting, doctor's appointment, or if you are ill?
- What is the office policy regarding dating and socializing among employees?

Know Dating Policies

Dating is one of those sensitive areas that varies from company to company. Follow the basic rule of taking time to get to know the corporate culture, and don't get overly friendly with anyone for a few months. If you learn that dating is acceptable between coworkers in different departments, be discreet and professional. Leave your personal life at home. In general, a supervisor should never date or room with a subordinate. Even though the supervisor may be very fair, others could perceive favoritism. Finally, you don't have to leave your personality at the office door, but be aware that overly flirtatious behavior will undermine your credibility and leave you open to office gossip and rumors.

Positive Work Attitudes and Image

Your attitude at the beginning of a job is the most critical factor for success. Be upbeat, optimistic, and attentive. **Develop a positive attitude and work habits.** As we've discussed throughout this book, positive habits are thoughts and actions that you have practiced consistently and that you do without thinking. Everyone goes through career setbacks and disappointments. Therefore, it is important to develop a habit of being positive. Professionals bounce back and look for the good side of every situation. If you are enthusiastic, positive, and motivated, you will outshine the average employee.

Create a Professional Image

Be professional. Create a professional and positive image. Put away your student-casual wardrobe and make certain you are dressed in a neat, clean, and businesslike manner. Review the guidelines in Chapter 5 on putting together a professional business wardrobe. Occasionally take a hard look at yourself in the mirror and periodically assess if you look like a polished professional.

Be a Lifelong Learner

Learning new skills and getting additional training will be key for success. Peter Drucker, author of *Management: Tasks, Responsibilities, Practices,* writes that there are three conditions for excellent work:

1. Productive work
2. Feedback
3. Continual learning

Don't wait for the company to send you to school. Determine your needs and ask about the company's training program. If they don't have one, sign up for classes at a local college. Put a high priority on learning new skills and on personal growth and professional development. Learn new software technology and improve interpersonal and writing skills. **Be a lifelong learner.**

CONTINUE TO LEARN NEW TECHNICAL AND JOB SKILLS

Take classes and advanced training. Read books, professional journals, and management articles. Learning new computer and telecommunications skills can make you very valuable to the company. Cross-learn other jobs. Take an interest in learning sales, marketing, production, and various other tasks and procedures around the company. Study the competition. What are their strengths and weaknesses?

IMPROVE YOUR VERBAL COMMUNICATION AND LISTENING SKILLS

The higher up you go in any organization, the more important communication skills are to your effectiveness. Mean what you say, and say what you mean. All companies value the employee who can speak in a concise, clear, and direct manner. Learn to get your points across effectively and give effective speeches and outstanding presentations. Join Toastmasters or take a college class and practice often. As with any other skill, you must commit yourself to learning the basics and then practice with diligence.

A large part of communication involves listening. Be an active listener who listens for understanding and for the intent of the speaker. Paraphrase what the speaker has said to verify that you both understand. Never interrupt others. Be patient and allow them to finish before you make your points. By doing these things, you will **improve communication and listening skills.**

LEARN GOOD WRITTEN COMMUNICATION SKILLS

It is vital that you demonstrate the ability to write in a clear, concise, and direct manner. Practice writing and take classes. Collect good memos and reports to use as models.

LEARN PROBLEM-SOLVING AND DECISION-MAKING SKILLS

Learn about the problems and concerns of the company and brainstorm solutions. Learn from your experiences and from others. Listen to how people you admire have handled problems and made decisions.

Being known as a person who can solve problems and make sound decisions will give you an edge in advancing your career. Every job involves problem solving and decision making. You will want to find out the perimeters of your accountability. Study problems in your group so that, when the time comes, you will have the information to offer solutions. Employees who see change and problems as challenges to overcome and opportunities for growth tend to be more productive and happy.

By following the same step-by-step procedure we've been using to make decisions in the job-search process, you will be known as a person who is a creative problem solver and who uses critical thinking to make decisions. Use the following steps:

1. State the problem.
2. Gather information.
3. Brainstorm creative solutions.
4. State the consequences of each solution.
5. Clarify your purpose. (What results do you want?)
6. Select the best alternative.
7. Review the pros and cons of the best alternative.
8. Act on the best alternative.
9. Evaluate situations based on critical thinking.
10. Adjust as necessary.

When you have a problem, come up with several solutions. Choose the one you think is best and try to determine the likely consequences. Your boss will know that you have good problem-solving and critical-thinking skills but are not too arrogant to ask for advice or approval when necessary.

You can have competent job skills, technical knowledge, and commitment, but success will elude you if you don't have a positive attitude and the ability to work effectively with others. Employers want to know if you have confidence, enthusiasm, perseverance, health and energy, intelligence, maturity, diligence, a positive attitude, initiative, creativity, and the ability to relate and work with different people.

Ask for feedback. When starting new projects, get advice. Review how you have handled projects and problems in the past. What have you learned about yourself? Ask for feedback from others and be open to growth. Take charge of your career. Set goals for learning new skills, assess your progress, and map out a plan of action.

Personal Qualities and People Skills

Employers always value people who have people skills. They place a great premium on the ability to work effectively with people and to adapt to the workplace environment (see **Figure 8.1**). Employers value the following personal qualities:

- Honesty
- Compassion
- Commitment
- Courtesy
- Loyalty
- Integrity
- Fairness
- Concern for others
- Respect
- Openness to change
- Sensitivity
- Devotion to the truth
- Trustworthiness
- Courage

Cubicle Awareness

Figure 8.1
Adapting to Cubeland Cubicles are a fact of modern work life, with many companies providing a combination of cubicle and office space for their employees. *What other issues might arise out of the cubicle workspace?*

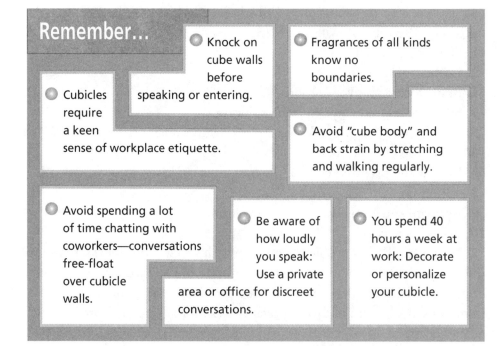

Remember...

- Cubicles require a keen sense of workplace etiquette.
- Knock on cube walls before speaking or entering.
- Fragrances of all kinds know no boundaries.
- Avoid "cube body" and back strain by stretching and walking regularly.
- Avoid spending a lot of time chatting with coworkers—conversations free-float over cubicle walls.
- Be aware of how loudly you speak: Use a private area or office for discreet conversations.
- You spend 40 hours a week at work: Decorate or personalize your cubicle.

Develop Ethics and Integrity

Business ethics require that you not only follow obvious moral and legislated laws, such as not stealing from the company or lying, but that you also conduct yourself with integrity in daily actions. Nothing is as important as your reputation. While ethics encompass a code or system of moral principles, integrity refers to your adherence to individual principles of good character. For example, accepting gifts from your clients may be legal and even acceptable under the ethical code of your office, but your own sense of integrity may not allow it. You may be faced with a situation where your supervisor says it is acceptable to omit certain information, but you may consider the omission to be lying, an action that would not fit in with your sense of moral character or integrity.

Having integrity and business ethics means you are honest, aboveboard, and straight with people. You don't lie or stretch the truth just to make a sale or impress others. You keep your word and honor your agreements. You admit when you are wrong and never blame others or cover up when you make a mistake. Ethical people take responsibility for their actions and behaviors. They never intentionally hurt other people and are aware of the consequences of their decisions. They are critical thinkers who make decisions based on fact but also consider the human factor. **Be ethical and take responsibility for your actions.**

Like ethics, civility is the cornerstone of a supportive and productive climate. Treat everyone with respect and kindness. Profanity, sexual or racial remarks, gossip, one-upmanship, and tactless behavior should not be part of the workplace.

Assess your personal qualities and make a commitment to follow the highest ideals in all areas of your life. Be truthful, reliable, responsible, and diligent in the effective use of company resources. Before you make a remark or a decision, ask yourself these questions:

1. **Is this action legal?** Does it comply with the company's policies, procedures, and values? If my parents, spouse, or child were here, would I say or do this?
2. **How would I feel later?** How would my actions or behavior make me feel about myself?
3. **How would others see me?** If my actions were written in a news article and put on the front page of the paper, what impression would the public, my family, my coworkers, and my friends have of me?
4. **Is this action fair?**
5. **Would this action be hurtful?** Would this remark or action cause someone to be hurt or embarrassed?

Take Responsibility for Your Actions

Everyone makes mistakes. No one expects you to be perfect, but you should be responsible and honest. When mistakes do occur, don't justify, blame, or cover up; just take responsibility and apologize.

Take responsibility for making the company more successful. Never say, "This isn't my job," or "Sorry, I only work here. I don't make the policy." Notice small things that can be done and, when possible, take steps to create lan outstanding company.

Take responsibility for your community. Get involved and contribute your talents and time. Join a worthwhile community project or board and gain visibility through community service so that people in the community, company, and industry know who you are.

Be Known as a Doer

Get organized and do first things first. Some people talk a good game but don't produce results. Be results oriented. Get projects done and done on time. Follow through on commitments and practice good organizational and time-management skills that will help you be more successful. **Figure 8.2** lists many other positive work habits that can improve your working life. Managing your time better can help you achieve these advantages:

- Be more effective at work.
- Enjoy your job.
- Improve your health.
- Lower your stress.
- Have more time for family, friends, and hobbies.
- Increase your self-esteem and sense of competency.

Assess Your Time and Resources

Take stock of your day. Ask yourself: What are your time wasters? Are you putting a lot of time into low-priority items or areas that do not produce results? Could your office, equipment, or scheduling be rearranged to help you be more productive? Are you trying to work hard and think creatively during low-energy times? Are you opening the mail and doing mundane tasks during high-energy time? Assess how organized and effective you are.

Invest in the resources and equipment that can help you be more effective at home and in the office. A new computer, software, printer, organizer, answering machine, fax, or car phone may help you increase productivity.

Get Organized

Take time to get organized. Sometimes, it is necessary to work on Saturday morning or over lunch for a few days to get yourself organized. Make certain that files are in the right place and that you have the needed data for your projects. Look at the arrangement of your office. Could it be set up more efficiently?

Stress Savers

Make the Transition

Starting a new job involves more than learning new tasks and responsibilities. You are also adjusting to a new company culture with unfamiliar people and customs. Apply these strategies to make a successful transition:

- Get enough rest and get up early.
- Allow yourself initial transition time of several months.
- Spend some extra time organizing your work when necessary.
- Listen to and observe your new office culture.
- Avoid office gossip.
- Be willing to pitch in when needed.

Positive Work Habits

- ★ Arrive on time or a few minutes before a meeting or appointment.
- ★ Do first things first and respond quickly to requests for information.
- ★ Take careful notes and keep track of deadlines.
- ★ Meet all deadlines.
- ★ Write down all appointments.
- ★ Review procedures in a small group.
- ★ Project the most likely consequence of a decision.
- ★ Assess and adjust when necessary.
- ★ Be a follow-through person.
- ★ Write notes to yourself.
- ★ Return phone calls.
- ★ Write action steps for projects.
- ★ Follow up on all details.
- ★ Do the unpleasant but necessary things that you tend to avoid.
- ★ Remind team members, tactfully, to finish projects.
- ★ Don't make promises you can't keep.

Figure 8.2
Strategies That Add Up
Responsibility and dependability are just two attributes of a promotable person. *What three work habits listed would most help you become better at doing your job?*

Use the Power of Teamwork

Too many people think they must be solitary corporate stars and want to work alone. Most companies, however, require team effort. Participate in group projects and activities. **Create effective work relationships.** It is critical that you develop a team-player mentality and learn to work effectively with a variety of people. Working as a team member can enhance your productivity, foster creative ideas, and help you solve problems and make decisions. Learn to have a positive attitude even when you are working with difficult people. Appreciate differences in people and bring out their best qualities. Don't expect people to be perfect. Accept people and look for the best in them to get good results.

Becoming Visible and Action Oriented

You will not be valued if you are not visible. People need to know what you are doing and contributing. If no one knows you are doing great things, you might not get promoted. Employees who may be diligent but never come out of their offices usually don't get promoted. **Increase your visibility** by volunteering for new projects, giving presentations, or writing an article for a trade publication. Don't kid yourself that if you are patient and work hard, promotions and salary increases will be automatic. Unfortunately, workplace decisions are often not fair or equitable. When possible, let top management know what you have accomplished. Get involved in the company.

Be confident and don't undermine your sense of worth by saying, "Oh, it was really nothing." You need not be arrogant, but quietly enhance your visibility by speaking up for yourself. It is important to know and appreciate your own worth and accomplishments and speak about them in a direct manner.

Have lunch with different people from various areas of the company. Volunteer to be on committees for office projects or to organize social events. This will demonstrate that you work well as a team member and will increase your visibility within the company. If the opportunity should arise, offer to chair meetings. Remember, it is important to increase your visibility among your coworkers as well as gain visibility with your supervisors.

Ask your boss for more exposure. You might ask if you can give speeches, make presentations, arrange meetings, and take on new projects. As we discussed in Chapter 2 on networking, find a boss, mentor, or role model who is committed to your development and who will help you enhance your visibility.

Give It All You've Got the First Year

You not only have to work smart, you have to work hard and put in some extra hours at a new job. Be mindful, however, that frequent overtime may be discouraged at some companies. So always be sensitive to the individual corporate culture and company policy. Commit yourself to the company and show loyalty, excitement, and old-fashioned hard work. There is a certain focus that occurs when you throw your whole heart into your job. Give it all you've got from day one. Be on time to all meetings, be alert, and be actively involved. Make certain your desk is cleared off at the end of the day and spend a few minutes reviewing the next day's priorities.

Pay Your Dues

As a new employee, you may be asked to perform many tasks: running errands, making coffee, taking notes, making copies, setting up a room for presentations. You may get the most undesirable office equipment and assignments. Don't let your ego get in the way. Every job has its unpleasant task, and as you demonstrate your willingness to do whatever needs to be done to achieve your objectives, you will move up in the company. It is expected that new employees pay their dues. You might offer to stuff envelopes, take packages to the mailroom, or be a greeter at receptions. Volunteer to help with new assignments or projects. This is a better way to learn about a new company than just asking questions or reading manuals. You will also become visible, get to know a lot of people, and be known as someone who is not afraid to roll up his or her sleeves and help.

Continue to Network

Networking is vital for making contacts and creating a professional support base. You can use contacts in your network to help solve problems, gain advice and guidance, and gain and give support. To review, some of the people in your network may include:

- Supporters
- Professionals
- Promoters
- Role models
- Mentors

Keep an updated résumé in your file at all times in case one of your contacts asks to see it. It is important that you have a well-organized, professional, concise, and attractive résumé to enhance your marketability. Even if you are not looking for a new job at this time, you need to know that you are marketable.

In Chapter 2, we discussed how important networking is for professional survival and for advancement. Networking can also boost your visibility. As you **continue to network,** you will find that you gain leadership skills and visibility by getting actively involved in professional organizations. In a sense, you are managing your own image and career development. Networking can help you stay visible, knowledgeable, current, and on top of job opportunities in the workplace.

Getting Promoted

Create an Effective Relationship With Your Supervisor

Most employees know the importance of working effectively with others and managing their careers. Few relationships, however, will be as critical as the one you develop with your boss. You will want to develop effective communication, create trust, and support the people with whom you work. Your supervisor is the one person who is responsible for rewarding your performance, helping you to be more visible, and promoting you to a new position. Therefore, creating a good working relationship with your boss is a key skill in managing your career. (See **Figure 8.3** on page 220.)

Creating a solid work relationship means working together to solve the company's problems and developing mutual respect and trust. From day one, ask your boss which assignments and job duties are most important and which decisions should be discussed together. You want to be seen as a self-starter, but you don't want to overstep your bounds of authority.

Building a Good Relationship
Create a positive working relationship with your boss:
➤ Set mutual goals and clarify expectations.
➤ Keep your boss informed.
➤ Understand your and your boss's duties, concerns, projects, and goals.
➤ Assess both your and your boss's strengths and weaknesses. How can you support your supervisor?
➤ Understand and respect your boss's personal style.
➤ Maintain clear, direct, and honest communication. Ask for feedback.
➤ Acknowledge and praise good work accomplished by your supervisor and coworkers.
➤ Understand the performance-review system and evaluate yourself.
➤ Keep an accurate record of meetings and dates projects are due and submitted.
➤ Keep a file of memos sent, performance evaluations, list of achievements, and letters of appreciation.

Understand Performance Reviews

Performance-review systems vary from company to company, but few are considered excellent or motivating. Many companies use a standard form and conduct a performance review once a year. Therefore, it is up to you to **manage your performance reviews** and career growth. You don't need to wait to be formally evaluated. Prepare for your appraisal so you can make it as accurate, pleasant, and helpful as possible. Be realistic, but expect the best. To prepare, use the following guidelines and ask yourself self-assessing questions:

1. **Review your formal job description.** Update it when you take on more assignments and projects. Do you exceed requirements for your job? What job assignments could you take on that would enhance your position? What relationships could you develop that would help you do your job better? What new skills could you learn that would improve your performance?

2. **Get a copy of the company's performance review.** Ask personnel for a copy of the standard performance-review document the company uses. (See **Figure 8.4** on page 222 for a sample form.) Review the criteria and make certain you understand areas in which you will be rated. Most appraisals look at the following areas:

- **Objective results** Which goals and duties do you perform that can be measured by results? Keep accurate records of production, sales quotas, cost budgets, number of customers helped, and so on.
- **Behavior** Do you put forth the effort to achieve? Do you appear confident and professional? Do you handle stress well?
- **Attitude** Do you have a positive attitude? Are you enthusiastic?
- **Teamwork** Do you work well with others? Are you willing to do more than your share of the work to get a project completed? Do you need to get all the credit, or do you focus on team effort?
- **Deadlines** Do you meet deadlines?
- **Office policies and procedures** Do you come to work on time and work hard all day? Do you observe office procedures concerning overtime, travel expenses, time off, and vacations?

3. **Assess your performance.** Make certain your work is up to your own and your supervisor's standards of excellence. Develop professional credibility. You want to achieve a reputation for competence that is acknowledged by your coworkers and your supervisor. Compare your evaluation of your performance with the standard performance-review form in **Figure 8.4.** on page 222. Do you have measurable results? What have you accomplished that is outstanding? In what areas do you think you need to improve?

4. **Establish good communication with your supervisor.** Set up a time to review your performance with your supervisor on a regular basis. After projects, make certain you have feedback on how you can improve. Place letters of appreciation from customers in your file. Ask your supervisor how to improve.

5. **Make an action plan.** Develop an action plan for how you are going to improve. Do you need to develop new skills? What training programs or classes are available? Do you want to go on for a degree or just learn new skills? How can you prepare for greater responsibility?

Net Advantage

Continuing Education A good way to demonstrate competence and a positive attitude is to take the initiative and develop new job skills. If you've taken a class, point that out to your boss during a performance evaluation. If you haven't, include retraining as part of your action plan for improvement. Many adults return to school to brush up and develop new skills. There are many sources for continuing education, including online courses, community colleges, and trade and technical schools.

For information on continuing education and career advancement, go to strategies.glencoe.com for links to related Web sites.

How can developing your job skills benefit you even if you're not getting a promotion?

Figure 8.4

Assess and Progress By reviewing
this performance review form before
having an actual on-the-job review, you
can identify areas where you need
improvement and develop an action
plan. *Are there any other criteria
that should be added to the sample
form that might be useful for your
particular job?*

Sample Performance Review Form

PERFORMANCE REVIEW

NAME _____ POSITION _____ DIV/DEPT. _____ APPOINTMENT DATE _____

FROM _____ TO _____ Return to personnel office before _____
    (Rating Period)   *(Date)*

SECTION A Rate only those factors that apply to this position. Immediate supervisor must check each appropriate factor in the proper columns. Additional factors may be added as appropriate to the position.

	Unsatisfactory	Satisfactory	Not Rated
1. Observance of work hours			
2. Attendance			
3. Public contacts			
4. Employee contacts			
5. Communication with others			
6. Knowledge of work			
7. Work judgments			
8. Planning and organizing			
9. Job-skill level			
10. Quality of work			
11. Acceptable work volume			
12. Meeting deadlines			
13. Accepting responsibility			
14. Accepting direction			
15. Operation and care of equipment			
16. Initiative and creativity			
17. Learning ability			
18. Work station appearance			
19. Safety practices			
20. Accepting change			
21. Effectiveness under stress			
22. Work coordination			
23.			
24.			
25.			

Any unsatisfactory rating must be explained in **Section C.**

For employees who supervise others:

26. Planning and organizing			
27. Scheduling and coordinating			
28. Training and instructing			
29. Productivity			
30. Evaluating subordinates			
31. Judgments and decisions			
32. Leadership skills			
33. Operational skills			
34. Supervisory control			
35. Compliance with affirmative action rules			

ROUTING:

White–Personnel

Canary–Department

Pink–Employee

SECTION B Record job STRENGTHS and performance incidents.

SECTION C Record work performance DEFICIENCIES or job behavior requiring improvement or correction.

SECTION D Record specific GOALS or IMPROVEMENT PROGRAMS to be undertaken during next evaluation period.

SECTION E Do you recommend retention at this time?
    YES ☐   NO ☐

SECTION F This employee is eligible for Merit Salary Adjustment on _____. In my judgment, the employee's job performance:

___ meets the level of quality and quantity expected. I recommend that the employee be granted a merit salary adjustment.

___ does not meet the level of quality and quantity expected. I recommend that the employee not be granted a merit salary adjustment and have so informed the employee.

SECTION G The last position description on file in this office is dated _____
    (Date)

Is this description accurate? _____

We have no position description for this position. ☐

I certify that this report represents my best judgment.
RATER

_____ _____ _____
(Rater's Signature)   *(Time)*   *(Date)*

DEPARTMENT HEAD/DEAN:

_____ _____ _____
(Rater's Signature)   *(Time)*   *(Date)*

EMPLOYEE: I certify that this report has been discussed with me. I understand my signature does not necessarily indicate agreement.

Comment: _____

_____

_____

_____ _____
(Employee's Signature)   *(Date)*

Manage Your Performance Reviews

Throughout this book, the benefit factor has been stressed. You will want to continue to find ways to add value to the organization or company that employs you. Doing so will only work to your advantage. In fact, you should ask yourself regularly, "How do I demonstrate value to the company?" One way to monitor your contribution is to use the performance-review form to evaluate your progress.

Part of managing your career is to take control of and manage your performance reviews. Too often people avoid or dread performance reviews. Your performance review, however, provides the feedback you need to assess your strengths and concerns and set goals.

Career Directions | BusinessWeek

Your Performance Review: Make It Perform

In flush economic times, many companies treat performance reviews as little more than the paperwork required before granting annual raises. When the economy turns down, however, companies use these evaluations to weed out their weakest staff.

You'll look especially strong if you can show how your work bolsters the bottom line.

Rather than dwell on what you didn't do during the past year, focus on mapping out your future plans. At most companies, employees and supervisors work together to set the employee's goals. The key is to be as specific as possible and to ask for any help or training you need.

Even the best workers should prepare to hear some criticism. Don't act defensively. Instead, discuss what you learned from a failure and how you'll do things differ-

ently, says Robert Gorden, co-author of *The Complete Idiot's Guide to Performance Appraisals.*

Typically, companies rank employees on a scale of 1 to 5 or give them an A, B, or C. When supervisors have sole discretion over the evaluation, they tend to give above-average marks. That's why a growing number of companies have switched to "forced ranking" systems, which require supervisors to put a percentage of their staff into each rating category.

Forced ranking or not, you needn't accept a poor evaluation. Immediately contact your human resources department to see if your company has a formal objection process, suggests Tom Coens, a Lansing (Mich.) labor lawyer and co-author of *Abolishing Performance Appraisals.*

Done right, performance reviews motivate and keep everyone focused. In today's chilly business climate, your job could depend upon it.

By Susan Scherreik

Excerpted from October 22, 2001, issue of BusinessWeek Online by special permission, copyright © 2000–2001, by The McGraw-Hill Companies, Inc.

Career Case Study The rumor was circulating that the annual raise would be dropped due to the poor economy. So, David Pressman was nervous about his upcoming performance evaluation. With the new forced ranking system, he suspected he'd be given an average rating so the company could justify no raises. He had worked hard in the last year as a graphic designer and didn't want his efforts to be wasted. *What strategies could David use when he discusses his evaluation with his manager?*

Assess Your Job Description

Begin by reviewing your job description. What functions do you perform that add value to the company? How would you rank this value? Make certain you have a detailed job description. You should know what is expected of you and what specific skills, functions, and personal qualities are required or desired for your position. Determine what skills and qualities can be measured and how you can determine results.

Ask for Feedback

Tell your supervisor that you want to be told of concerns and problems when they occur. Stress that you cannot grow professionally or change your behavior if you are not aware of issues until the yearly performance review.

Set Your Goals and Objectives

Usually, you will set your goals and objectives with your boss. Even if your boss doesn't give you guidance, you can develop your goals and objectives based on your job description and shared discussions with your supervisor and work team members. Send a copy to your supervisor and ask if these are agreeable expectations.

Create Your Own Evaluation System

Conduct your own performance review by setting goals and initiating a time frame using a matrix system, such as the one in **Exercise 8.1.** Focus on these categories:

- **Job Function:** Determine the functions that you perform that are of value to the company.
- **Value:** Assign a value of this function to the company, "A" being most valuable, and so on.
- **Steps:** Determine the necessary steps you would take to translate this function into a series of action steps.
- **Measured Results:** Ask customers, coworkers, professional peers, and supervisors to review your actions. Feedback can only help you succeed.

What barriers have you encountered, and what changes occurred after setting your goals? If you met your goals on time, what factors and resources helped you? If you didn't meet your goals, what factors and barriers got in your way? Adjust your goals based on the data you have collected. Then adjust and modify your goals and objectives for next year.

Having measurable objectives and results concerning your performance and a systematic plan of action in hand will help you assess your own progress and set future objectives. You will be taking control of your career and not just reacting to feedback from your supervisor.

Review your job description and the main functions of your job. Review the goals you have set for the first six months and indicate how you will measure outcomes. Determine how you can evaluate each stage of the process to help you produce the results you want. Check the company's performance-review form and add criteria you think are important.

Functions 1 and 2 give examples of the steps needed to improve performance in each function area, as well as how improvement can be measured.

For a job you've had in the past, choose three functions and list steps for improvement and criteria to measure results as you fill in the matrix below.

Function	Value	Steps	Measured Results
1. Meeting customer needs	A	• Return phone calls. • Provide status reports. • Assess input from customers. • Clarify customer needs.	• Positive feedback • Increased business • Improved rapport • Positive reports
2. Keeping commitments	A	• Create a follow-up file. • Establish a to-do list. • Set written goals. • Monitor progress of each phase.	• Increased productivity • Reputation for keeping agreements • Increased customer calls • Positive responses and letters of recognition

Leaving a Job

Be Careful About Job Hopping

Throughout your career, you will want to continue to assess your interests, skills, job satisfaction, and performance. If after evaluating your job, you believe you've made a big mistake, or if you think your company is involved in unethical activities, look for a new job. However, resist the urge to job hop at the first sign of dissatisfaction. You can damage your career by having too many jobs in a short period. There will always be something you don't like about every job. In addition, if you're experiencing your first full-time job, be aware that it is a big transition. Becoming accustomed to long hours that are usually not flexible is a major adjustment. Consider your options carefully before you quit.

EXERCISE 8.2   Evaluating Your Job

Assess how well your job meets your needs. Put a check next to what you have and what you want in a job. A greater number of checks in the *What You Have* column means your job is a good match for you.

Job Factor	What You Have	What You Want
1. Career advancement	_____	_____
2. Personal growth	_____	_____
3. Independence	_____	_____
4. Opportunity to learn	_____	_____
5. Good pay	_____	_____
6. Good benefits	_____	_____
7. Travel	_____	_____
8. Flexible hours	_____	_____
9. Job security	_____	_____
10. Opportunity to use creative problem solving	_____	_____
11. Challenging	_____	_____
12. Opportunity to use my skills	_____	_____
13. Good working relationships	_____	_____
14. High visibility	_____	_____
15. Opportunity to work as a team	_____	_____
16. Education and training	_____	_____
17. Good relationship with supervisor	_____	_____
18. Good mentor relationship	_____	_____
19. Sense of contributing to the world	_____	_____

Don't Burn Your Bridges

At some point in almost everyone's career, it is necessary to leave a job. Today's workers can expect to change jobs at least four times or more. There are, of course, many reasons for choosing to leave a job. Your spouse may have relocated through his or her job to another part of the country. You may have heard about another job that seems like a real career booster, is more challenging, or looks like a better fit with your talents and your career goals. Your interests may have changed enough to make your current job seem less desirable. In some cases, the time frame for promotion at your current company may not suit your expectations. To evaluate your job satisfaction, complete **Exercise 8.2.** You can also ask yourself the following questions to assess your position:

* Do my coworkers ignore me or leave me out?
* Do I feel that I'm wasting my time?
* Do I wonder what life would be without this job?
* Is being sick a relief to me because I don't have to go to work?
* Do I feel that I don't have a future with this company?
* Do I have trouble sleeping due to my job?

When the time comes to leave your job, do it with grace and professionalism. Don't burn your bridges by leaving on a negative note, even if you haven't enjoyed working with some of your colleagues. Continue to act like a professional even as you clean out your desk.

Negative comments within the workplace often get back to people, and you may end up looking bad even if your comments are factual. If you need to air complaints, don't do it at work; speak with a trusted friend or counselor in confidence. In addition, your colleagues may change companies, and you may find yourself working with them again someday. Always treat others with civility and respect even if they are being unreasonable.

Do your best to leave your job in good shape. Give enough notice and finish major projects. Leave details of your assignments and let other people in the office know what you have been working on. Let them know that you can be reached by phone if there are questions. In short, be responsible.

One way to ensure a smooth exit is to give your notice by writing a clear and thoughtful letter of resignation, such as the sample in **Figure 8.5** on page 228, that acknowledges your supervisor and thanks him or her for the chance to work at the organization and learn new skills. Again, be gracious—this isn't the time to vent frustrations. Send a note to your coworkers, thanking them for working with you. After a few weeks on your new job, call and see how things are going and if they have any questions about your former projects.

Figure 8.5

Parting Words Though you may never cross paths with your former co-workers and boss after taking a new job, there is a greater chance that you will—if you remain in the same career. *What other advantages might warrant writing a thoughtful letter of resignation?*

January 17, 2003

Mr. Walter Knapp
Director of Sales and Marketing
Bechtel Information Services, Inc.
P.O. Box 1372
Savannah, GA 31402

Dear Mr. Knapp:

Please accept this letter as my official notice of resignation. I have accepted a position with Abbott International as Field Supervisor for Sales. I will begin my new assignment February 1.

It has been a pleasure to work with you the past three years. I have appreciated your continual support, guidance, and unfailing good humor. I have learned a great deal about customer service from your example and commitment. I plan to continue making customer satisfaction a top priority in my new position.

I wish you continued success.

Sincerely,

Barry

Barry T. Kason
723 Pine Street
Savannah, GA 31402

Workplace Trends

Employees may change jobs due to numerous causes, including larger economic forces. Shifts in the economy and corporate buyouts may result in layoffs, mergers, downsizing, forced retirement, and job changes. The workplace of tomorrow will be an entirely different place. Flexibility and the ability to learn new skills will be key. Even though career professionals know it is important to adapt to change, many people resist change and fear going beyond the comfort zone. It is important to change your perception of security and develop ways to gain the skills, personal qualities, and education that will make you more marketable and give you a sense of competency. As you grow professionally, it will be even more important to be aware of job trends. Here are a few trends that are affecting the workplace.

Decentralized Problem Solving

The computer age, beginning in the early 1990s, placed valuable information—once the domain of top management—in the hands of all workers. The entry-level clerk can access information at the flip of a laptop. Self-direction is replacing the old mode of only doing what you are told to do. Previously, a store manager may have been told what products would be sent from headquarters. Now data are customized and received via laptops through reports generated at headquarters. Local managers can access information on sales, profits, new products, and trends. This new technology, plus the elimination of many middle managers, means that people closest to the customers may be making decisions. In some cases, employees may gain more autonomy, greater responsibility, and more control over what they do.

Diversity

The workplace of the future will be more diverse and will reflect the changing national racial profile. In 1990, whites comprised 84 percent of the American population. U.S. Census Bureau projections indicate that by the year 2025, that percentage will drop to 62 percent. Hispanics, African Americans, Asians, Native Americans, and other ethnic groups will make up well over a third of the entire population. Border states, such as California, presently reflect an even greater racial mix. Minorities and women are entering the labor force in greater numbers. In fact, over half of all workers entering the workplace during the next decade will be comprised of immigrants from all over the world or the children of immigrants. It will be increasingly important to pay more attention to cultural and gender diversity in the workplace. The successful employee must be able to work with people of different ethnic and racial backgrounds, genders, ages, physical abilities, and lifestyle preferences.

DIVERSITY STRATEGIES

1. **Value the differences.** It will be important to not only tolerate differences but to also learn to value and appreciate diversity.
2. **Take an interest.** Learn about other cultures, religions, and races. Attend workshops and be aware that people learn, solve problems, and relate to others in many different ways.
3. **Create an open mind-set.** Be tolerant and get into the habit of understanding other people. See things from different points of view.
4. **Review policies and procedures on diversity.** Be sure that your organization has policies that ensure respect and protect people from discrimination. If not, you may question whether you want to work for a company that doesn't value diversity; or you may want to take a

leadership role in developing programs, policies, and procedures to help support cultural diversity.

5. **Create diverse work teams.** Look at work teams in your office in new ways. A diverse team is necessary to approach problems in creative ways. Make a commitment to create a climate of respect and understanding.

SEXUAL HARASSMENT

Sexual harassment is behavior that has a sexual connotation; is unwelcomed, unwanted, and demeaning; and creates a hostile or abusive work environment. The U.S. Supreme Court in 1993 ruled that a "hostile work environment" doesn't have to be psychologically injurious but only reasonably perceived as abusive. Sexual or cultural harassment is illegal, unnecessary, and destructive in the workforce. It is also costly. Besides incurring expensive legal costs, the work climate suffers from loss of productivity, low morale, and distrust. Managers are responsible for ensuring that appropriate guidelines are established and posted and that they are in compliance with the law. The corporate climate must respect differences in gender, race, culture, and religion. As an employee, you should know company policies and procedures. Does your company follow these general guidelines?

1. **Does the company have a written policy?** Does the company have a posted written policy concerning sexual harassment, describing how to file a complaint and the disciplinary actions that may result because of inappropriate behavior?

2. **Is there a designated person?** Has the company assigned a person who is knowledgeable, fair, and approachable to handle complaints concerning sexual harassment?

3. **Is the company in compliance with policies and laws?** Are employee behaviors and work practices in compliance with the company policy and federal and state laws?

AIDS

Employees need to have the facts and accurate information on AIDS in the workplace. Fear and discrimination can be eliminated if facts replace rumors and misinformation. Employees need to know and practice effective procedures on how to protect themselves from the virus, especially in high-risk situations.

Alcohol and Drug Abuse

The effects of alcohol and drug abuse as well as smoking can be devastating and staggering to employees. In fact, substance abuse is one of the most common—and expensive—employee problems.

1. **Know the cost involved.** The National Institute of Drug Abuse has estimated that drug and alcohol abuse cost the U.S. economy over $150 billion every year in lower productivity, medical care, lost wages, higher insurance premiums, and property damages.

2. **Keep up on the laws.** In most states, smoking is prohibited anywhere in the workplace due to the harmful effects of secondhand smoke. Some companies are even reluctant to hire smokers because of the increased health risks of cancer, chronic bronchitis, and emphysema. As an employee, know the laws regarding safe work environments, hiring guidelines, drug testing, and treatment programs.

3. **Get help.** If you have a problem, get help. Employees should know the signs of substance abuse. Some warning signs of substance abuse include these behavioral changes:
   * Difficulty in recalling and following instructions
   * Frequent tardiness or absence from work
   * Frequent disappearances from the job location
   * Taking too many cigarette or restroom breaks
   * Taking extended lunch and work breaks
   * Difficulty getting along with coworkers
   * Increased mistakes on the job
   * Accidents off the job that affect job performance
   * Dramatic changes in personality or work performance during the day, especially after taking a break

   Employee assistance programs (EAPs) offer resources for treatment. Developed in the 1940s by large companies, EAPs were originally alcoholism treatment programs in association with Alcoholics Anonymous. Expanded to include all substance abuse and life issues, EAPs are a less controversial and more effective alternative to drug testing alone.

Training and Education

Another significant job trend is the increasing importance of education and training. The amount of available information and the ways in which we can retrieve it are growing in leaps and bounds. Adaptable employees need to know how to stay on top. If you want to go into management or supervision, it is even more important to continue to learn new skills and to keep up on new trends.

1. **Get more education and training.** Keep yourself up-to-date by taking classes at a local college, attending training programs and conferences, and keeping active in professional associations.

2. **Learn new skills.** Skills in computers, grant writing, negotiation, foreign language, fiscal management, marketing, innovative delivery systems, customer relations, and human relations will make you more marketable.

3. **Learn and consistently practice good habits.** Qualities such as enthusiasm and a positive attitude, tolerance, perseverance, and hard work are vital for job success.

4. **Cross-train.** Learn other jobs at your company. Ask how other departments do certain jobs. Volunteer to take on new projects.

Focus on Success

Just as you plan and take charge of your job search, you need to carefully manage your first year on the job. **Increase your energy and balance** as you start your day so that you will form positive work habits:

- **Get organized.** The night before, arrange your clothes and put your briefcase and keys by the door. Get up early. Don't get stressed out by being late or looking for lost items.

- **Get plenty of rest.** Get to bed early at about the same time every night. Give up your late nights and establish a regular routine of sleep so that you are at work early, feeling energized, focused, clear-headed, and enthusiastic.

- **Eat healthy foods.** You can't have energy if your diet is poor. Eat a balanced diet of foods rich in vitamins and fiber, such as whole grains, vegetables, fruits, low-fat milk, and protein. Keep healthy snacks in your desk to help you avoid that tempting donut with your coffee break.

- **Get regular exercise.** Nothing increases your energy like exercise. In order to build lasting energy and health, you need regular, aerobic exercise. Get up early enough to do 10 or 15 minutes of exercise. Take a brisk walk at lunch or instead of a coffee break, or work out in a gym a few times a week. Do yoga or stretching exercises at night to relax.

- **Do something you enjoy every day.** Take time to read for pleasure, visit with friends, write, play sports, and enjoy simple pleasures.

- **Avoid energy drainers.** Alcohol, cigarettes, and drugs will sap your energy. Too much caffeine will also cause your energy to dip.

- **Use positive images and self-talk.** Visualize yourself as competent, caring, positive, and professional. Mentally walk through your day before you get out of bed. See yourself handling any problem in a calm, positive, and creative matter. Keep a list of affirmations in your desk and say them often. Remember, self-esteem is something that you can give yourself; it is a habit that you can create through positive self-talk, visualization, learning new skills, and positive habits.

Throughout your career, you will want to develop a reputation for being a competent and responsible professional who creatively solves problems and uses critical thinking to make decisions. You form this professional image by consistently applying positive habits and by demonstrating skills, good personal characteristics, and high standards of ethics.

If you apply these strategies successfully, and you've faced the challenges of the job-search process, you're well on your way to experiencing growth and prosperity as a result of all your efforts.

STAYING POWER

Handling Culture Shock

*E*ven if you have been hired for your dream job, adjusting to it may be difficult. You will be coping with both external and internal stressors. A stressor is a situation or event that causes the body to react. Working lengthy hours, having to deal with a new office culture, navigating office politics, cooperating with abrasive personalities, and handling work-related stress can be a shock. In addition, you may have to face a steep learning curve, a long commute to and from work, or little vacation time. The stress of a new job can take a toll on your mind, body, and spirit, and affect your performance on the job as well as the quality of your life.

In the face of the many adjustments that come with having a new job, it's important for first-year employees to maintain a positive attitude and a long-term outlook. Challenges should be seen as opportunities for growth; dilemmas should be kept in perspective; and all efforts should be made to appreciate the positive aspects of a job.

Ask yourself: What are you learning? How are you growing? Where will your career grow? Realize that personal growth is not always easy, and that the most meaningful lessons can often be difficult.

Try This...

Taking care of yourself is a critical step in avoiding burnout on the job.
- Increase your physical energy by exercising regularly, getting enough rest, and eating healthy food.
- Maintain your mental health by being organized at the workplace, using positive affirmations on a daily basis, and having a group of friends to support you in and out of the workplace.
- Continue to do the things you enjoy—sports, hobbies, or crafts.
- Maintain your sense of humor. Finding humor in workplace struggles can make the most difficult situations bearable.

CHAPTER 8 Review

Skill Check Recap

- Learn the corporate culture.
- Listen, be aware, and ask questions.
- Develop a positive attitude and work habits.
- Be professional.
- Be a lifelong learner.
- Improve communication and listening skills.
- Be ethical and take responsibility for your actions.
- Create effective work relationships.
- Increase your visibility.
- Continue to network.
- Manage your performance reviews.
- Increase your energy and balance.

Self-Check List

Keep track of your progress. Read the following and mark *yes* or *no*.

	Yes	No
• I have developed a positive attitude.	_____	_____
• I understand the corporate culture.	_____	_____
• I am knowledgeable about the company.	_____	_____
• I have a professional image.	_____	_____.
• I am learning new skills.	_____	_____
• I am developing solid work relationships.	_____	_____
• I am a creative problem solver.	_____	_____
• I use critical thinking in decision making.	_____	_____
• I manage my performance reviews.	_____	_____
• I have increased my visibility.	_____	_____
• I manage and adapt to change.	_____	_____
• I understand work trends.	_____	_____
• I follow up on career advancement and success.	_____	_____

Review Questions

1. What is meant by the term *corporate culture?*

   _____

   _____

2. What is the major advantage of observing and listening?

   _____

   _____

3. What are four areas where you can truly be a lifelong learner?

   _____

   _____

4. Which two personal qualities and skills do you need to develop?

   _____

   _____

5. What are the five questions you should ask yourself to determine the ethics and integrity of an action?

   _____

   _____

6. Which three Positive Work Habits will be hardest for you to practice?

   _____

   _____

7. What five steps should you take to prepare for the performance review?

   _____

   _____

8. What are five strategies to help ensure healthy workplace diversity?

   _____

   _____

Critical Thinking

9. Self-assessment is one of the key tools for finding and keeping a good job. Review ways self-assessment can help you get a job and keep it.

Cooperative Learning

10. In groups of four, discuss five types of problems that might occur on the job. Rate each problem:
    1) Severe enough to warrant resigning from the job
    2) Severe but should be watched
    3) Possible to solve by _____

Moving Ahead

Dana graduated several years ago with a certificate in architectural drafting and design. She does her job well and is competent, but she hasn't been promoted. Dana believed that once she got her certificate and performed the duties of her job description, she would automatically get promoted. She's beginning to think that it is time to reassess her skills, personal qualities, and achievements and take control of her career.

Dana knows she either has to make herself more visible and valuable at her present job or more marketable for a new job. However, she's not sure where to begin or what steps to take.

Problem Solving The following ten questions are designed to help solve problems and make sound decisions. You can use these questions to find solutions to your own problems. Put yourself in Dana's place and consider these questions from her point of view.

- What is the problem?
- Do I have enough information?
- Can I make the decision by myself?
- Have I brainstormed alternatives?
- Have I looked at likely consequences?
- Have I identified all the resources and tools needed?
- Have I developed and implemented an action plan?
- Have I identified the best solution?
- Have I assessed the results?
- Have I modified the plan, if necessary?

What solution would you suggest to Dana? Write your answer on the lines below.

_____

_____

_____

_____

_____

_____

_____

_____

_____

_____

_____

STRATEGIES Online

Find out more about updating skills and getting promotions by visiting this book's Web site at strategies. glencoe.com

First Year on the Job

Keep a log of events during the first year on your job. Reassess regularly.
Use the following questions to assess your job success and adjustment.

- Do I understand my employer's expectations? What are they?

  _____

  _____

- What are the limits of my authority and responsibility?

  _____

  _____

- Do I ask questions if I am unsure?

  _____

  _____

- Do I bring my supervisor up-to-date on progress and deadlines? How?

  _____

  _____

- How have I demonstrated that I am a self-starter?

  _____

  _____

- How have I contributed to the company?

  _____

  _____

- Am I always on time? Do I put in more hours than expected?

  _____

  _____

- Do I work well with other people?

  _____

  _____

APPENDIX 1

More Résumé Samples

The next few pages contain more examples of résumés that are clear, concise, and complete. These models show résumés written in chronological style, functional style, and a combination style. One of these styles will work for you, whether you have a great deal of work experience, little work experience, or have recently reentered the job market.

Chronological Résumé

Laura L. Lewis
613 Park Avenue
Wales, NY 20992
(914) 621-9882

Education

1998   Maryland Institute of Art   Baltimore, MD
              Bachelor of Arts
                  in Commercial/Graphic Arts

Work Experience

2000–present **Freelance Artist**   Wales, NY
              Designed numerous brochures, illustrated
              posters, photographed series on food preparation
              for weekly magazine. Edited home show articles.

1998–2000   *Ellis Graphics, Inc.*   Baltimore, MD
              Graphic Artist and Assistant Editor
              Produced printed illustrations, brochures,
              business cards. Supervised layout productions,
              covered home shows. Planned displays for
              metropolitan garden show. Responsible for all
              layouts, photo displays, and original drawings.
              Worked directly with the editor-in-chief.

1997–1998   *National Home and Garden Magazine* Baltimore, MD
              Intern Staff Photographer
              Designed setups and photographed homes and
              gardens. Illustrated articles on interior design.
              Photographed indoor and outdoor scenes and
              nature close-ups. Edited articles on interior design.
              Taught basic photography to staff.

Awards

1999   *Home and Garden Magazine*
              Creative Photography Award

Chronological Résumé

CRAIG L. CHAMBERLAIN
19 Central Avenue
Cleveland, OH 44112

CAREER OBJECTIVE: To acquire a paralegal position that will utilize my administrative, legal, and computer skills.

WORK EXPERIENCE

2001–present	Municipal Court of Ohio	Cleveland, OH

Legal Secretary
- Responsible for contract negotiations, preparation of legal documentation and correspondence, mergers, and acquisitions.
- Prepare budget and compile tax-filing information. Maintain court calendar.

2000–2001	Allen Stokes and Partners	Cleveland, OH

Paralegal Intern
- Handled pretrial arrangements, drafted summons and complaints, took depositions, drafted court decisions, and researched cases.
- Developed data communication network that increased billing efficiency by 15 percent.

SKILLS
- Fluent in Spanish
- Proficient in IBM and Apple MAC II
- Motivated, hardworking self-starter
- Excellent organizational skills
- Demonstrated ability to work with diverse clients and coworkers

EDUCATION

2001	Ohio Career School	Cleveland, OH

Paralegal Studies Degree
Notary Public Training for State of Ohio

Chronological Résumé

Dennis L. Yates
237 Park Lane
Raleigh, NC
(205) 561-1231

EDUCATION

2002	DUKE UNIVERSITY	Raleigh, NC

Bachelor of Science in Occupational Therapy
- Grade Point Average 3.8/4.0
- Academic Dean's List
- Earned 100 percent of college costs

WORK EXPERIENCE

2001–2002	DUKE UNIVERSITY HOSPITAL	Raleigh, NC

Intern Occupational Therapist
- Specialized in pediatrics play therapy.
  Worked with developmentally delayed, autistic,
  learning disabled, and cerebral palsy patients.
  Developed schedules, assisted with treatment,
  motivated and coached patients.

1999–2000	MENTAL HEALTH CENTER	Raleigh, NC

Medical Secretary
- Performed research, filed reports, typed,
  entered data processing.
- Installed and trained staff in database computer
  system. Resulted in reduction of estimated 12 hours
  per week of reporting.

MEMBERSHIPS AND COMMUNITY SERVICE
- American Occupational Therapy Association
- Sunset Senior Citizens Home: assisted director
  in developing and implementing programs

(little experience)

Chronological Résumé

EMILY CHAN
902 12th Street
Grand Lakes, MN 55002

CAREER SUMMARY: Accounting supervisor with eight years experience in accounting, computer systems, and administration.

EMPLOYMENT HISTORY

1999–present	Rockford Company	Grand Lakes, MN

Accounting Supervisor
Responsible for all accounting functions.
Accomplishments:
- Designed and implemented computer-based accounting system. Saved 20 percent of accountants' workload.
- Developed new training program for audit programs and wrote procedure booklet.
- Secured $150,000 grant for worker training.

1997–1999	Trenton Accounting Agency	Trenton, MN

Accountant
Analyzed all accounting records and budgets.
Accomplishments:
- Designed computer payroll system.
- Redesigned reporting procedures to comply with new state and federal regulations.

EDUCATION

1997	Trenton State College	Trenton, MN

Bachelor of Science in Accounting

1998	Certified Public Accountant, Minnesota (passed first time)

1998	Trenton Community College	Trenton, MN

Continuing Education Computer Science Program

AFFILIATIONS AND MEMBERSHIPS

1999–present	Trenton Business and Professional Women
1997–present	American Association of Accountants
2001	American Cancer Society Board of Directors
2000	President, Trenton State College Accounting Club

(more experience)

Functional Résumé

Jan A. Berg
354 Pinehill Street
Aspen, CO 83992
(607) 839-2883

EDUCATION

2002   MOUNTAINVIEW COLLEGE   Aspen, CO
Bachelor of Science in Industrial Technology
- Management emphasis with focus on manufacturing processes, quality control, CAD/CAM, industrial design.
- Business minor: Course work emphasis on statistics, finance, economics, accounting, and management.

SKILLS

- Skilled in interpersonal communication.
- Proficient in Macintosh and DOS formats and a variety of software, including spreadsheets, word processing, and database.
- Hardworking, self-motivated, and positive.
- Demonstrated ability to work effectively in teams.

EMPLOYMENT HISTORY

2001–present   INSTITUTE FOR INDUSTRIAL TECHNOLOGY   Aspen, CO
Personal Assistant to Vice President
- Prepare cost estimates, contracts, and regular progress reports.
- Set weekly agenda.
- Review and modify work performance forms.
- Created employee database system improving efficiency and reliability in scheduling. Increased profits by 15 percent in one year.

2000–2001   INSTITUTE FOR INDUSTRIAL TECHNOLOGY
Intern Manufacturing Staff
- Interacted with clients, researched needs, and developed industrial designs.
- Assisted in advertisement and promotional program.

AFFILIATIONS

2000–present   Industrial Technology Institute

Functional Résumé

Thomas R. Kason
903 Greewood Lane
Bennet, Maine 01223

MECHANICAL SKILLS

Brake systems	Electrical systems
Front ends	Tire rotation
Engine tune-up	Electrical fuel injection
Heating	Air conditioning
Engine performance	Shock absorbers

CUSTOMER RELATIONS AND SALES

- Excellent rapport with customers.
- Designed successful customer satisfaction form to improve customer service and feedback.
- Motivated and hardworking (Sales increased by 25 percent in one year).
- Improved repeat customers (over 15 percent increase).

WORK EXPERIENCE

2000 – present   Melvin's Auto Shop   Bennet, MN
Mechanic
- Diagnose and repair various vehicles.
- Responsible for bodywork, tune-ups, ignition repair, transmission repair, and maintenance.
- Develop a good working relationship with customers.
- Prepare billings and follow up on customer concerns.

EDUCATION

2001   Bennet Community College   Bennet, MN
Associate of Science in Automotive Technology
GPA 3.6/4.0

CERTIFICATE

2002   Sterling Training Programs
Certificate of Training on Foreign Cars

(little experience)

Combination Résumé

Maria M. Perez
2839 Elm Drive
Evans, Illinois 80392
(702) 883-1231

TECHNICAL SKILLS

Knowledge of:
- Key systems
- Network topologies
- Software Lotus, MS/DOS

Experience with:
- Traffic analysis
- Digital multimeters
- Query system setup

CUSTOMER SERVICE SKILLS

- Effective team skills (Managed two college team projects).
- Ability to work with variety of people.
- Effective written and oral communication (Published senior project).
- Creative problem solving (Solved traffic analysis problem).
- Hardworking and persistent: Worked 40 hours a week while attending school at night.

WORK EXPERIENCE

2000–2001
Data Entry Clerk
Baylor Corporation   Evans, IL

Intern Telecommunications Specialist
Baylor Corporation   Evans, IL

EDUCATION

June 2000
Redwoods Institute of Technology   Evans, IL
- Associate of Science
- Major: Telecommunications
  Minor: Computer Science
- GPA 3.6

SENIOR PROJECT

Systems Documentation and Network
for a Telecommunications Company

(re-entry student with little work experience)

APPENDIX 2

Job Description Glossary

Academic Department Head
Administers affairs of an academic department. May administer department's budget and recruit academic personnel. Conducts meetings to discuss current teaching strategies and obtains recommendations for changes within the department.

Account Executive
Responsible for the development of and service of a customer account. Brings business to the firm. Consults with the client and collaborates with associates to find best strategies for servicing clients.

Account Executive *(Advertising)*
Meets with clients. Participates in meetings with other departments on the ideas for a campaign. Plans overall strategy for clients. Keeps up-to-date on media rate changes and new media outlets. Serves as a link between the agency and the clients.

Account Executive *(Food Service)*
Initiates and signs new customers, which includes scouting new business, helping survey clients' needs, writing formal request letters, and making formal presentations, usually accompanied by management representative(s). Representative of the food service contractor who deals directly with the liaison designated by the client.

Account Executive
(Public Relations)
Meets with clients to determine needs for public relations program. May review company strategies and goals, current customer base, and reputation with the public. Recommends public relations program. Keeps up-to-date on new and existing programs and policies. Serves as a link between the public relations firm and the clients.

Account Executive *(Telemarketing)*
Organizes and manages a program internally once it has been brought in by a telemarketing representative. Coordinates script writing, script testing, list preparation, forms design (to record sales and customer data), and client reports. Monitors the project and provides regular reports for the client.

Account Executive Trainee
(Advertising)
Fields material from other departments. Takes calls from clients. Keeps in touch with traffic department on schedules for ads and spots.

Account Manager

Develops an efficient coverage pattern for the territory. Decides on the call frequency for major accounts. Develops a sales plan for the territory. Promotes, sells, and services product line. Reviews customer-call reports. Coordinates activities at individual key customer locations.

Accountant

Helps businesses and individuals set up financial recordkeeping. Examines, analyzes, and interprets accounting records for the purpose of giving advice or preparing statements. Estimates future revenues and expenditures to prepare budget.

Accountant *(Food Service)*

Prepares and analyzes financial reports that furnish up-to-date financial information. Accountants employed by large restaurant firms may travel extensively to audit or work for clients or branches of the firm.

Accountant *(Hospitality)*

Sets up the financial recordkeeping for the hotel or other lodging facility. Estimates future revenues and expenditures to prepare the operation's budget for each year.

Activities Coordinator *(Cruiselines)*

Plans and implements activities for passengers on cruiselines.

Actuarial Trainee

Works for insurance companies analyzing statistics to determine probabilities of accident, death, injury, earthquake, flood, fire, etc., so that the rates charged for insurance policies will bring in profits for the company while still being competitive with those of other insurance carriers.

Actuary

Uses mathematical skills to predict probabilities of events that will be used for insurance plans and pension programs.

Adjuster

Investigates and settles claims of losses suffered by policyholders of all kinds of insurance.

Adjuster Trainee

Assists with investigations and settling claims of losses suffered by policyholders of all kinds of insurance.

Administrative Analyst/Planner

Responsibilities include developing any new systems and setting up any long-range planning systems; responsible for the planning group, which actually plans each day's shipment to distribution centers. Works on product allocation and inventory control. Responsible for anything that might affect the distribution centers. Works on product allocation and inventory control. Responsible for anything that might affect the distribution area.

Administrative Assistant

An administrative support job performed with little or no supervision, and one that is a step higher than an executive secretary. Handles dissemination of contract information or works with a chief officer of a company in preparing corporate reports. Often involves supervision of others.

Administrative Dental Assistant

Checks office and laboratory supplies; maintains waiting, reception, and examination rooms in a neat and orderly condition; answers telephones; greets patients and other callers; records and files patient data and medical records; fills out medical reports and insurance forms; handles correspondence, schedules appointments, and arranges for hospital admission and laboratory services. May transcribe dictation and handle the bookkeeping and billing.

Administrative Dietitian

Responsible for training and supervision of food service supervisor and assistants in food preparation and formulating policies, enforcing sanitary and safety regulations. Buys food, equipment, and other supplies, so must understand purchasing and budgeting.

Administrative Manager

Provides maximum support to all divisions through the regional or district distribution centers and ensures that timely, cost-effective service is provided to those units and their customers. Supervises personnel, equipment, materials, facilities, product handling, inventory control, building services, customer relations, order processing, office services, and district operations.

Administrative Medical Office Assistant

(See **Administrative Dental Assistant**)

Administrative Secretary

Handles everything except dictation and typing. Duties range from filing and setting up filing systems, routing mail, and answering telephones to more complex work such as answering letters, doing research, and preparing statistical reports.

Administrative Support Manager (*Word Processing*)

Responsible for the operation of the entire word processing center.

Administrator (*Education*)

Directs the administration of an educational institution, or a division of it, within the authority of the governing board. Develops or expands programs or services. Administers fiscal operations such as a budget planning, accounting, and establishing costs for the institution. Directs hiring and training of personnel. Develops policies and procedures for activities within area of responsibility.

Administrator (*Education*)

Involved with curriculum and program development and directing teaching personnel of the school system. Confers with teaching and administrative staff to plan and develop curriculum designed to meet needs of the students. Visit classrooms to observe effectiveness of instructional methods and materials. Evaluates teaching techniques and recommends changes for improving them. Conducts workshops and conferences for teachers to study new classroom procedures, new instructional materials, and other aids to teaching.

Advertising Manager

Plans and executes advertising policies of an organization. Confers with department heads to discuss possible new accounts and to outline new policies or sales promotion campaigns. Confers with officials of newspapers, radio, and television stations and then arranges billboard advertising contracts. Allocates advertising space to department. May authorize information for publication.

Aerospace Engineer

Designs, develops, tests, and helps manufacture aircraft, missiles, and spacecraft.

Agent (*Insurance*)

Sells traditional life insurance to clients. May also sell mutual funds and other equity-based products. Many agents also qualify as financial planners after obtaining certification. Explains financial products in detail to prospective clients. Processes necessary paperwork when closing a sale.

Air Patrol Officer

Patrols areas, by air, where the military is located.

Airline Schedule Analyst

Reviews schedules for all incoming and outgoing flights. Makes recommendations for changes in schedules to ensure maximum service while still maintaining strict procedures.

Airport Manager

Responsible for operating a safe facility and for fundraising. Keeps the public informed on safety decisions affecting the area surrounding the airport.

Airport Operations Agent

Customer service agent responsible for assigning boarding times, lifting tickets; coordinates baggage service; announces flight arrivals to main desk.

Airport Security Officer

Notes suspicious persons and reports to superior officer. Reports hazards. Inspects baggage of passengers. Assists passengers with lost luggage claims. Directs passengers to appropriate boarding areas. Warns or arrests persons violating ordinances. Issues tickets to traffic violators. Maintains overall security of the airport.

Analyst (Marketing)

(See **Market Research Analyst**)

Anthropologist

Studies the development of humans and human society.

Arborist

Plants, cares for, and maintains trees; diagnoses and treats diseased trees.

Architect

Involved with all aspects of the planning, design, and construction of buildings. Prepares proposals that include illustrations and scaled drawings. Draws the structural system as well as the other elements that go into the project. Provides advice about choosing contractors.

Area Manager (Retail)

Manages a selling center within a store. This would include a small group of departments carrying related merchandise.

Area Sales Manager (Hospitality)

Responsible for sales promotion for a group of hotel properties in a specified geographic area.

Assistant Hotel Manager

Assists with supervising the operations of the different departments of a hotel: food service, housekeeping, front office, and maintenance. Ensures the smooth functioning and profitability of the hotel by maintaining the property and quality guest service.

Assistant Manager (Food Service)

Performs supervisory duties under the manager's direction. Must be capable of filling in when the manager is absent, thus needs good management skills and knowledge of the operation.

Assistant Marketing Director (Travel)

Assists with the development of competitive strategies for clients. Reviews services and products being offered and evaluates client's market position. Assists companies with monitoring themselves to make sure they are delivering what is promised.

Assistant Media Planner

Learns to interpret rate cards of various media. Analyzes audience ratings. Writes letters and, memos. Compares media alternatives. Prepares and delivers presentations to clients. Talks with sales representatives from various media. Evaluates media buying.

Assistant Professor

A designation of faculty rank used to refer to faculty members with some, but not extensive, teaching experience in their area of expertise. (See **Professor**)

Associate Media Director

Makes decisions on media buying. Reviews alternative selections and results of ratings to determine decision.

Associate Professor

A higher designation of faculty rank than assistant professor; used to refer to faculty members with more extensive teaching experience in their area of expertise. Often, this ranking is

also marked by research work, publications, or industry experience.
(See **Professor**)

Associate Research Director
(Advertising)
Evaluates information published by government, trade, or other groups as relates to individual ad campaigns. Evaluates suggestions and findings of the research account executive to determine best approach to each ad campaign. Keeps campaign operating within specified guidelines.

Association Account Executive
(Hospitality)
Responsible for the development of and service of professional or trade association business coming into the hotel or other related facility.

Attractions Specialist
Has specific knowledge of local attractions and how to promote them. Provides input on target population for promotional effort.

Auditor *(Hospitality)*
Examines and analyzes accounting records of hotel or food service operation and prepares reports concerning its financial status and operating procedures. Analyzes data to check for duplication of effort, extravagance, fraud, or lack of compliance with management's established policies.

Baker
Prepares all the baked items that are not desserts, such as breads, rolls, muffins, and croissants for use in dining rooms of hotels and restaurants and related facilities. Depending on the size of the staff and the operation, may also make pies, cakes, and some pastry items.

Bank Guard
Responsible for security in banks.

Bank Manager
Manages, directs, and coordinates activities of workers engaged in accounting and recording of financial transactions, setting up trust or escrow accounts, probating estates, and administering trust or mortgage accounts. Develops relationships with customers, business, continuity, and civic organizations to promote goodwill and generate new business.

Bank Officer Trainee
Gains experience in the main functions of the banking business. These include the trust department, where money is invested for families, institutions, or other businesses; the credit department, where decisions are made on loaning money to customers; and operations where all of the normal business functions (data processing, personnel, public relations, and accounting) are monitored.

Banquet Captain
May greet the host, hostess, and guests. Ensures that everything is as ordered. Ensures that all party rooms are in order at all times and checks before and after a function to make sure that the patrons are satisfied. Presents the bill for signature or payment when the function is over. Pays employees at the end of the function.

Banquet Manager
Arranges banquet and food service functions. Arranges banquet details after they have been agreed upon by the catering manager and the customer. Prepares and updates banquet menus. Reports inventory needs to purchasing agent and storeroom, and may supervise the scheduling of staff to work the functions.

Bartender
Mixes and serves alcoholic and non-alcoholic drinks for patrons of a bar following standard recipes. Mixes ingredients such as liquor, soda, water, sugar, and bitters to prepare cocktails and other drinks. Serves wine and draft or bottled beer. Collects money for drinks served. Orders or requisitions liquors and supplies. Places bottled goods and

glasses to make an attractive display. May slice and pit fruit for the garnishing of drinks. May prepare appetizers, such as pickles, cheese, and cold meat.

Benefits Coordinator

Administers various employee benefit programs such as group insurance—life, medical, and dental; accident and disability insurance; pensions; investment savings; and health maintenance organizations. Initiates medical and option forms and/or affidavits; arranges for their completion and submission within time limits. Implements new benefit programs; arranges and conducts employee information presentations and enrollments. Ensures program compliance with governmental regulations.

Beverage Manager

Responsible for compiling statistics of liquor costs, sales, profits, and losses. Inventories the bar as needed, sometimes daily, and prepares the daily consumption report that is forwarded to the auditing office. Issues merchandise to all bar areas, but usually does not buy liquor. Instead, forwards purchase orders to a central purchasing agent, who may order for several hotels in a chain.

Border Patrol Officer

Responsible for guarding all U.S. points of entry to detect and prevent illegal entry into the United States. Inspects commercial carriers, terminals, and traffic checkpoints to stop those who attempt to enter the country without proper clearance. Also responsible for deportation actions.

Branch Manager

Plans, coordinates, controls the work flow, updates systems, strives for administrative efficiency, and is responsible for all functions of a branch office.

Branch Sales Manager

Makes a direct sales effort to the customers in the area to sell a product line. Provides management with sales and booking forecasts on a monthly, quarterly, and annual basis. Keeps abreast of prices and performance of competitors' products in his or her territory. Handles service and related problems as they arise. Trains and supervises sales staff.

Broadcast Technician

Performs the work of an electronics technician, specifically on various types of broadcast equipment. (See **Electronics Technician**)

Butcher

Responsible for cutting, boning, and otherwise caring for and preparing meats for cooking.

Buyer (Production)

Responsible for placing orders, expediting back orders, and processing paperwork for stock and nonstock supplies. This includes processing requisitions, researching products, clarifying specifications, typing purchase orders, following up on back orders, selecting vendors, maintaining up-to-date product information files, and utilizing computer terminals and hand-held order entry devices to place order.

Buyer (Retail)

Selects the goods to be sold by retail stores or wholesale outlets. Buyers also help to plan the selling programs for the goods they have purchased. They normally specialize in one type of goods such as men's clothing, housewares, or accessories.

Buyer Trainee (Retail)

Assists supervising buyer. Places orders and speaks with manufacturers by telephone. Supervises the inspection and unpacking of new merchandise and overseeing its distribution.

Cafeteria Manager

In charge of a unit with as few as one employee to as many as 70 or more. Oversees all employees, sometimes giving limited on-the-job training.

Has hiring and firing responsibilities. Purchases what is needed for unit, usually from a central purchasing office, and keeps records of the same.

Camp Manager

Directs and coordinates activities of workers concerned with preparation and maintenance of buildings and facilities in residential camp; coordinates through staff or personally directs staff in preparing and maintaining such camp facilities as dining halls, etc., used by resident employees. Schedules purchase and delivery of food supplies. Enforces safety and sanitation regulations.

Captain

An officer ranking above a first lieutenant and below a major.

Carpenter

Cuts, fit, and assembles wood and other materials in the construction of buildings, highways, docks, boats, and other structures.

Case Manager (Law)

Organizes a case's pleadings, oversees the mechanics of producing documents and maintaining documents library. Experience as a litigation paralegal usually required.

Catering Manager

Works with the Executive Chef on menus, food quality, or service problems. Responsible for arranging any catered functions held at the establishment, from weddings to conventions, from banquets to dances. Draws up necessary contracts. Helps customers select menu, decorations, and room arrangement and transmits these requirements to various departments for execution.

Chef

Supervises, coordinates, and participates in activities of cooks and other kitchen personnel engaged in preparing foods for a hotel, restaurant, cafeteria, or other establishment. Estimates food consumption, and requisitions or purchases foodstuffs. Receives and checks recipes. Supervises personnel engaged in preparing, cooking, and serving meats, sauces, vegetables, soups, and other foods. May employ, train, and discharge workers. In small establishments, may maintain time and payroll records.

Chief Accountant

Responsible for the supervision and control of the general accounting functions. This includes general ledger, payables, payroll, property, budget reporting, and statistical accumulation. Responsible for financial statement and report preparation and budget reviews. Supervises and trains employees in accounting, payroll, and accounts payable.

Chief Accountant (Hospitality)

Responsible for the supervision and control of the general accounting functions of the hotel. This includes night audit functions, general ledger, payables, payroll, property, budget reporting, and statistical accumulation. Responsible for financial statement and report preparation and budget reviews. Supervises and trains hotel employees in accounting, payroll, and accounts payable.

Chief Actuary

Oversees the calculation of probabilities of death, sickness disability, injury, property loss, fire, and other hazards. Evaluates and analyzes relevant statistics. Determines the rate of expected losses due to the issuance of various types of policies. Determines the various provisions contained in insurance policies.

Chief Financial Officer

Develops corporate financial objectives. Establishes policies and procedures for the effective recording, analyzing, and reporting of all financial matters. Directs the controller, treasury, and corporate financial services activities to ensure that each of these functions meets established goals and provides effective service to the corporation as a whole.

Chief Tourism Officer

Oversees the staff engaged in tourism development for a particular area. Works within established budgets. Approves promotional campaigns.

Claims Examiner

Analyzes insurance claims to determine extent of insurance carrier's liability and settles claims with claimants in accordance with policy provisions. Investigates questionable inquiries.

Claims Representative

Reviews insurance claim forms for completeness; secures and adds missing data; and transmits claims for payment or for further investigation.

Clinical Dental Assistant

Reviews patients' records and presents them to the dentist; obtains information needed to update medical histories; takes patient X rays; assists the dentist in examining patients; instructs about medications.

Clinical Medical Assistant

Receives patients' height, weight, temperature, and blood pressure; obtains medical histories; performs basic laboratory tests; prepares patients for examination or treatment; assists the physician in examining patients. Instructs patients about medication and self-treatment, draws blood, prepares patients for X rays, takes EKGs, and applies dressings.

Club Manager

Estimates and orders food products and coordinates activity of workers engaged in selling alcoholic and non-alcoholic beverages for consumption on the premises. May manage staff involved in operating club with recreational facilities for private groups or the general public. Responsible for grounds and buildings, payroll, and promotion.

Coder

Converts routine items of information obtained from records and reports into codes for processing by data typing using predetermined coding systems.

Coder-Editor

Synthesizes the results of questionnaires or mail or telephone surveys. The results are then reviewed by the research analyst.

Coding Clerk Supervisor

Supervises and coordinates activities of workers engaged in converting routine items of information from source documents into codes to prepare records for data processing. Modifies, revises, or designs forms and initiates procedures to develop more efficient methods of data input.

College Recruiter

Interviews college graduates on campus. Works in conjunction with the policies and standards approved by the Employment Manager.

Colonel

A military officer ranking above a lieutenant colonel and below a brigadier general.

Commis

A professional assistant in the kitchen or dining room.

Commissioner of Tourism

Promotes overall tourism efforts. Generates new sources for funding. Interfaces with businesses in the community to gain support for tourism development.

Communications Equipment Technician

Performs the work of an electronics technician specifically on various types of communications equipment. (See **Electronics Technician**)

Communications Technician

May direct activities of production, circulation, or promotional personnel.

May prepare news or public relations releases, special brochures, and similar materials. Assigns staff member, or personally interviews individuals and attends gatherings to obtain items for publication, verify facts, and clarify information.

Composer

Creates original music such as symphonies, operas, sonatas, or popular songs. Transcribes ideas into musical notation using harmony, rhythm, melody, and tonal structure. Composes using musical instruments, pen and paper, or computers.

Computer Operator

Operates computer equipment to ensure that tasks are processed in accordance with a schedule of operations. Maintains and completes daily logs. Maintains an accurate report of equipment and/or software malfunctions.

Concierge

Handles guests' problems in a hotel, makes reservation requests with restaurants and transportation facilities, arranges tours, procures theater tickets, and handles a host of other activities.

Conference and Meeting Coordinator

Coordinates the planning and execution of conferences and meetings on and off site. Notifies attendees of details. Makes necessary facilities arrangements. Makes travel arrangements if required. Oversees the function and conducts post-meeting evaluation.

Conference Planner

Compiles list of individuals or groups requesting space for activities and schedules needed facilities. Notifies program participants of locations assigned. Maintains schedules and records of available space, space used, and cancellations. Requisitions needed equipment. Arranges for services during the conference. Follows up with client after the conference for evaluation of services provided.

Conference Reporter

Attends conferences at the request of the conference coordinator. Records minutes of the meetings and activities that occur during the conference. Types up summaries and distributes to requesting parties.

Conference Service Coordinator

Books meetings, services them, and follows up with post-meeting evaluations.

Consultant

Consults with client to determine need or problem, conducts studies and surveys to obtain data, and analyzes data to advise on or recommend a solution. Advises client on alternate methods of solving problem or recommends a specific solution. May negotiate contract for consulting service.

Consultant Advisor (Paralegal)

Assists the legal publisher in planning new kinds of books to be written either about the paralegal profession or the procedures utilized by paralegals in law offices.

Consumer Product Safety Commission Investigator

Responsible for enforcing compliance with all regulations that protect the consumer against unsafe products.

Controller

Directs financial affairs of an organization. Prepares financial analyses of operations for guidance of management. Establishes major economic objectives and policies for the company. Prepares reports that outline company's financial position in areas of income, expenses, and earnings based on past, present, and future operations. Directs preparation of budgets and financial forecasts.

Convention Center Manager

Manages the building, does marketing and public relations for events at the center. Responsible for entire budget for the center and supervises personnel.

Convention Planner

Arranges space and facilities for convention. Keeps exhibitors and attendees informed of procedures and policies for participation. Assigns troubleshooters to be available to provide needed services during the convention and minimizes situations that may result in a safety, legal, or logistical problem.

Convention Sales Manager

Responsible for generating business conventions at hotels, civic centers, or other appropriate facilities. Oversees sales staff. Approves advertising and rate packages. Handles projections on business and expected income. Works within established budgets.

Cook

Prepares, seasons, and cooks soups, meats, vegetables, desserts, and other foodstuffs for consumption in hotels and restaurants. Reads menu to estimate food requirements and orders food from supplier or procures it from storage. Adjusts thermostat controls to regulate temperature of ovens, broilers, grills, and roasters. Measures and mixes ingredients according to recipe, using a variety of kitchen utensils and equipment, such as blenders, mixers, grinders, slicers, and tenderizers to prepare soups, salads, gravies, desserts, sauces, and casseroles. Bakes, roasts, broils, and steams meat, fish, vegetables, and other foods. Observes and tests foods being cooked by tasting, smelling, and piercing with fork. Carves meats, portions food on serving, plates, adds gravies or sauces, and garnishes servings to fill orders.

Coordinator of Membership Sales

Maintains prospect lists for membership in travel clubs or travel associa-tions. Coordinates marketing programs to solicit new membership. Explains membership policies and benefits and receives payment of membership dues. Makes decisions on appropriateness of membership.

Coordinator/Scheduler

Word Processing)

Sees that there is an even flow of work to the word processor.

Coordinator of Scheduling

(Retail)

Prepares production schedules. Determines type and quantity of material needed to process orders. Issues work orders. Calculates costs for manufacturing.

Coordinator/Travel Information Center

Supervises and coordinates activities of workers engaged in greeting and welcoming motorists at state highway information center. Provides information, such as directions, road conditions, and vehicular travel regulations. Provides maps, brochures, and pamphlets to assist motorists in locating points of interest or in reaching destination. May direct tourists to rest areas, camps, resorts, historical points, or other tourist attractions.

Copy Chief

Supervises one or more copywriters in an advertising agency, department, or service, whose function it is to assign the work of preparing the textual matter for advertisements; supervises the actual writing and transmits the completed work in accordance with the existing traffic arrangement in the firm. Coordinates copywriting activities with the layout, art, and production departments of the organization.

Copywriter

Writes original advertising material about products or services for newspapers, magazines, radio and television, posters, or other media.

Corporal

The lowest-ranking non-commissioned officer, just below a sergeant.

Corporate Account Executive
(Hospitality)

Responsible for the development of and service of corporate (business and industry) business coming into the hotel.

Corporate Paralegal

Drafts minutes, forms and dissolves corporations, works with the Securities and Exchange Commission (SEC), reviews Blue Sky laws, oversees mergers and acquisitions, assists with leveraged buyouts.

Corporate Recruiter

Recruits corporate-level staff for the organization. Works in conjunction with the policies and standards approved by the Employment Manager.

Corporate Travel Manager

Sets up travel budget, establishing policies for employees to follow; acts as a liaison with an outside travel agency that actually handles the arrangements; also involves personnel relocation as well as meetings and convention planning. May administer corporate aircraft, transportation to training programs, the car pool, and possibly group recreational trips or vacations for employees; may also negotiate discounts with travel suppliers.

Correctional Officer

Responsible for maintaining security in prison facilities and overseeing the safety of the inmate population.

Counselor

Helps people handle personal, social, educational, and career problems.

Court Reporter

Makes accurate records of what is said during proceedings of all types. Memorizes and then reproduces the appropriate symbols involved in shorthand and machine reporting. All types of recordings—manual, machine, and tape—are transcribed accurately and typed in the required format.

Cosmetologist

Shampoos, cuts, colors, chemically treats, and styles hair; gives manicures, pedicures, and facials; applies makeup.

Creative Director

Develops basic presentation approaches and directs layout design and copywriting for promotional material. Reviews materials and information presented by client and discusses various production factors to determine most desirable presentation concept. Confers with heads of art, copywriting, and production departments to discuss client requirements and scheduling, outlines basic presentation concepts, and coordinates creative activities.

Credit Manager

Responsible for the collection of accounts deemed to be delinquent and for determining when the accounts should be referred to an outside agency for further collection efforts. Generates reports on a daily and monthly basis. Posts cash on a daily basis.

Crime Lab Technician

Collects and examines evidence from crime scenes and submits results to be used as evidence in criminal cases.

Criminal Investigator

Conducts investigations of collusion, bribery, conflicts of interest, thefts from government jurisdictions, and offenses specified in the acts protecting government personnel and procedures.

Cruise Director

Supervises all activity on board the cruiseline. Responsible for overall safety and service of passengers. Oversees staff on board.

Customer Service Agent (Travel)

Arranges for car rental on-site at rental company by phone with travel agent or in person with individual customer. Processes contracts and arranges billing upon return of the rental vehicle.

Customer Service Manager (Retail)

Responsibilities include making certain that shipments take place as scheduled. Acts as a liaison between customers and the sales force. Spends most of the time on administrative duties, including reviewing performance standards. Also trains personnel.

Customer Service Representative

Responds to customer inquiries and performs a variety of duties related to customer service. Works with customers to offer alternatives to unresolvable problems. Receives, researches, and answers customer inquiries and requests regarding accounts, products, rates, and services. Develops and maintains company's image and corporate philosophy in the community.

Customer Service Representative (Airlines)

Duties include onward flight reservations, securing hotel and car reservations, and ticketing passengers in flight.

Customer Service Representative (Retail)

Resolves customer complaints and requests for refunds, exchanges, and adjustments. Provides customers with catalogs and information concerning prices, shipping time, and costs. Approves customers' checks and provides check-cashing service according to exchange policy. Issues temporary charges. Keeps records of items in layaway, receives and posts customer payments, and prepares and forwards delinquent notices.

Customs Agent

Examines incoming travelers' luggage, registers weights of incoming vessels, and enforces approximately 400 laws and regulations for the federal government. Ensures that revenue is paid for incoming goods and prevents prohibited goods from entering or leaving the country.

Dancer

Dances alone, with a partner, or in a group to entertain an audience.

Data Entry Operator

Operates keyboard machine to transcribe data onto magnetic tape for computer input. Examines forms and source documents to determine work procedures.

Data Entry Supervisor

Accountable for quality, productivity, cost-effectiveness, and timeliness of work to ensure efficient and effective conversion and verification of data into readable forms. Directs distribution of work; prioritizes allocation of resources to meet schedules. Sets performance standards and reviews policies for data entry personnel.

Dean

Develops academic policies and programs for college or university. Directs and coordinates activities of academic department heads within the college. Participates in activities committees and in the development of academic budgets. Serves as a liaison with accrediting agencies that evaluate academic programs.

Demographer

Plans and conducts demographic research and surveys to study the population of a given area and affecting trends.

Dental Assistant

Helps dentist during the examination and treatment of patients. Sets up and maintains instruments, arranges appointments, and keeps records of patients.

Dental Hygienist

Licensed to clean teeth under the supervision of a dentist. Instructs patients in dental care, diet, and nutrition for proper mouth care.

Dentist

Helps patients take care of their teeth and gums, either to correct dental problems or to advise patients on ways to prevent future cavities and gum problems.

Department Manager (Office)

Directs and coordinates departmental activities and functions utilizing knowledge of department functions and company policies, standards, and practices. Gives work directions, resolves problems, prepares work schedules, and sets deadlines to ensure completion of operational functions. Evaluates procedures and makes recommendations for improvements. Assigns or delegates responsibility for specific work.

Department Manager (Retail)

Supervises and coordinates activities of personnel in one department of a retail store. Assigns duties to workers and schedules lunch, breaks, work hours, and vacations. Trains staff in store policies, department procedures, and job duties. Evaluates staff. Handles customer complaints. Ensures that merchandise is correctly priced and displayed. Prepares sales and inventory reports. Plans department layout. Approves checks for payment and issues credit and cash refunds.

Deputy Commissioner of Tourism Development

Establishes goals, policies, and procedures of tourism development for a given area.

Deputy Sheriff

Performs patrol services and investigates offenses. Serves as bailiff in the courtroom. Serves orders or civil papers of the county courts, including subpoenas, show cause orders, property seizures, and garnishments. Collects legal fees assigned by the courts.

Design Assistant (Textile)

Researches colors by contacting color forecasting services. Visits color forecasters to see presentations. Finds new garments on the market and in stores. Contacts fabric salespeople by phone for fabric samples. Keeps records, does patterns, and keeps design room organized.

Design Technician

Tests and assists in the design of all kinds of electronics equipment developed by Electronics Design Engineers. Performs the work of an electronics technician. (See **Electronics Technician**)

Designer (Drafting)

Makes design drawings to assist in developing experimental ideas evolved by research engineers, using specifications and sketches, and employing knowledge of engineering theory and its applications to solve mechanical and fabrication problems.

Destination Promoter

Sells meeting and convention planners, tour operators, and wholesalers on the idea of choosing a destination for their program. Services individual travelers with information and products that will make their business or pleasure trips more satisfying.

Detective

Continues investigative work started by patrol officers, identifies and apprehends offenders, recovers stolen properties and completes official reports, and prepares testimony and evidence for court presentation.

Dining Room Captain

Works under the general supervision of the dining room manager; in charge of one section of the dining room. Instructs, supervises, and gives help to the staff working the area when needed. Watches all the tables in given jurisdiction to detect any dissatisfaction; may make adjustments in response to complaints.

Dining Room Manager

Supervises all dining room staff and activities, including staff training, scheduling of staff working hours, keeping time records, and assigning workstations. Should be capable of working in a formal public atmosphere.

Director (film)

Uses knowledge of acting, voice, and movement to oversee the interpretation of plays and scripts for movies, TV, or theater.

Director of Escort Services

Responsible for the hiring, training, and assignment of tour escorts. Trains the escorts in the areas for which they will be responsible.

Director of Human Resources

Oversees the day-to-day activities of the human resources staff. Ensures that staff complies with policies set and approved by the Vice President of Human Resources and senior management. (See **Vice President of Human Resources**)

Director of Marketing and Sales

Supervises sales department. Coordinates sales and marketing departments to develop and an effective marketing effort. Responsible for increasing sales volume through direct sales efforts and by assisting sales reps in the field. Coordinates future market growth plans with regard to products, services, and markets. May plan and implement advertising and promotion activities.

Director of Marketing and Advertising

Plans and carries out advertising and promotional programs. Works with company's top-level management to prepare an overall marketing plan. Arranges with various suppliers regarding schedule and cost of brochures, advertisements, etc., being promoted. Responsible for the advertising budget.

Director of Media Advertising

Defines corporate media objectives. Provides media information and advice to the company. Measures media costs against industry standards. Searches for new, creative ways to use media. Recommends controls, quality, and cost of media purchases.

Director of Public Relations

Plans, directs, and conducts public relations program designed to create and maintain a public informed of employer's programs, accomplishments, and point of view.

Director of Public Safety

Responsible for the safety of the equipment in a city, town, or state.

Director of Recipe Development

Creates new recipes for the menus of larger restaurants or restaurant chains. Requires thorough knowledge of food preparation and the ability to apply this knowledge creatively.

Director of Research and Development

Directs and coordinates activities concerned with research and development of new concepts, ideas, basic data on, and applications for organization's products, services, or ideologies. Reviews and analyzes proposals submitted to determine if benefits derived and possible applications justify expenditures. Develops and implements methods and procedures for monitoring projects. May negotiate contracts with consulting firms to perform research studies.

Director of Tour Guides

Responsible for the hiring, training, and assignment of tour guides.

Director of Training

Oversees training function for an entire company at all locations. Responsible for approval of recommended programs and proposed budgets. (See **Training Manager**)

Display Coordinator

Designs and implements the window decorations and interior displays that are so important in promoting sales. Must work well within limitations of time, space, and money.

Display Director

Supervises the display of merchandise in windows, in showcases, and on the sales floor of retail stores. Schedule plans for displays and ensures staff follows store plan. Often responsible for several stores within a designated division.

Distribution Manager *(Retail)*

Oversees the routing of merchandise from one branch store to another on the basis of sales. Analyzes reports of stock on hand and kind and amount sold.

Direct Manager

Manages personnel for an assigned district, ensuring the development and accomplishment of established objectives. Trains, develops, and motivates staff. Recruits new hires. Maintains good business relationships with customers through periodic contacts and proper handling of administrative functions.

District Manager *(Food Service)*

Supervises smaller facilities in certain areas. Purchasing, negotiation, and supervision of area personnel are main responsibilities.

District Sales Manager

Actually carries out "cold calls," maintains reporting forms and proper business files, holds periodic meeting with sales staff.

District Sales Manager *(Travel)*

Administers city ticket and reservations offices and promotes and develops airline passenger and cargo traffic in the district.

Divisional Manager *(Banking)*

Responsible for the activities of a related group of departments in a bank, such as all departments involved with customer service versus operations or systems.

Divisional Manager *(Retail)*

Retail executive responsible for the activities of a related group of selling departments or divisions.

Doctor *(Medical)*

Examines patients, orders or executes various tests and X-rays to provide information on patient's condition. Analyzes reports and findings of tests and of examinations and diagnoses condition. Recommends treatment.

Document Examiner

Helps resolve criminal cases by using a variety of skills and tools to examine evidence such as handwriting samples.

Documentation Specialist

Makes computer technology accessible to people who have no computer background. Translates the technology into plain, comprehensible English. Writes promotional brochures and advertising copy.

Drafter

Develops detailed design drawings and related specifications of mechanical equipment according to engineering sketches and design-proposal specifications. Often calculates the strength, quality, quantity, and cost of materials. Usually specializes in a particular field of work such as mechanical, electrical, electronic, aeronautical, structural, or architectural drafting.

Drafter/Computer Assisted—CADD

Drafts layouts, drawings, and designs for applications in such fields as aeronautics, architecture, or electronics, according to engineering specifications using the computer. Locates file relating to projection database library and loads program into computer. Retrieves information from file and displays information on cathode ray tube (CRT) screen using required computer languages. Displays final drawing on screen to verify completeness, after typing in commands to rotate or zoom in on display to redesign, modify, or otherwise edit existing design. Types command to transfer drawing dimensions from computer onto hard copy.

Ecologist

Studies the relationships between organisms and their environment and among groups of organisms.

Economic Development Coordinator

Directs economic development planning activities for city, state, or region. Negotiates with industry representatives to encourage location in an area. Directs activities, such as research, analysis, and evaluation of technical information to determine feasibility and economic impact of proposed expansions and developments.

Editor

Reads the rough drafts and manuscripts of authors and other writers that are to be published in a magazine, book, or newspaper. Corrects grammatical errors and makes suggestions for improving readability and consistency of style.

Editor (Word Processing)

Helps design the overall package and rough out the information to be contained on each page of videotext display. Once the information is set up, the page creator takes over.

EDP Auditor

Monitors computer functions of the entire company and operational procedures and reports findings back to top management with recommendations for improvements. EDP Auditors make specific recommendations for improved accuracy, procedures, and security.

Education Consultant

Develops programs for in-service education of teaching personnel. Reviews and evaluates curricula used in schools and assists in adaptation to local needs. Prepares or approves manuals, guidelines, and reports on educational policies. Conducts research into areas such as teaching methods and strategies.

Educator/Administrator
(Food Service)

Designs and teaches courses tailored to students of food service, such as sanitation, food service management, and nutrition. Develops curriculum and hires staff. Works with designated budget to purchase equipment and materials needed to operate the school. Seeks support from industry with instruction and funding.

Electronics Engineer

Works on research and development, production, and quality control problems. Highly specialized may work in a specific area such as the design and implementation of solid-state circuitry in radar, computers, or calculators.

Electronics Technician

Repairs and maintains machines and equipment used in processing and assembly of electronic components. Starts equipment or machine. Reads blueprints and schematic drawings to determine repair procedures. Dismantles machine. Removes and sets aside defective units for repair or replacement. Starts repaired or newly installed machines and verifies readiness for operation.

Employment Agency Owner

Manages employment services and business operations of private employment agency. Directs hiring, training, and evaluation of employees. Analyzes placement reports to determine effectiveness of employment interviewers. Investigates and resolves customer complaints.

Employment Counselor

Screens and places professionals in available jobs.

Employment Manager

Oversees the recruiting function. This includes soliciting qualified applicants through various sources including advertising and college recruiting. Oversees screening, interviewing, and selection procedures. Responsible for overseeing the hiring of all personnel.

Employment Recruiter

Matches job seekers with job openings that employers have listed with placement firms, employment agencies, or governmental employment offices.

Engineer

Applies the theories and principles of science and mathematics to practical technical problems. Designs and develops consumer products. Determines the general way the device will work, designs and tests all components, and fits them together in an integrated plan. Evaluates overall effectiveness of the new device, as well as its cost and reliability.

Engineering Technician

Develops and tests machinery and equipment, applying knowledge of mechanical engineering technology, under direction of engineering and scientific staff.

Equal Employment Opportunity Coordinator

Monitors and enforces governmental regulations concerning equal employment practices in all levels of the organization. Maintains required record to verify adherence to approved affirmative action plan.

Executive Administrator
(Education)

Makes projections for future needs; oversees curriculum and policy decisions. Hires and supervises personnel; prepares school budget. Works with local groups to ensure the best interest of the community is being met.

Executive Chef

Coordinates activities of and directs indoctrination and training of chefs, cooks, and other kitchen personnel engaged in preparing and cooking food. Plans menus and utilization of food surpluses and leftovers, taking into account probable number of guests, marketing conditions, and population, and purchases or requisitions foodstuffs and kitchen supplies. Reviews menus, analyzes recipes, determines food, labor, and overhead costs, and assigns prices to the menu items. Observes methods of food preparation and cooking, sizes of portions, and garnishing of foods to ensure food is prepared in prescribed manner. Develops exclusive recipes and varied menus.

Executive Director

Develops and coordinates an administrative organization plan and staff to carry out the plan. Delegates authority and responsibility for the execution of the organization's many departments and functions. Establishes operating policies and procedures and standards of service and performance. Involved with fund-raising. Serves on various civic committees.

Executive/Administrator
(Telemarketing)

Directs the planning and operations of telemarketing function. Sets goals and objectives for telemarketing programs and establishes budgets as well as sales goals. Guides development of telemarketing programs and evaluates available systems applications.

Executive Assistant

Member of the management team who is responsible for overseeing the overall administrative functions of an office. Ensures productivity of office staff. Makes recommendations for improved systems. Supervises staff. Handles special projects and confidential materials. Assists executive. Represents the company at professional and community events on a regular basis. Often acts as a spokesperson for the executive.

Executive Director, Associations

Directs and coordinates activities of professional or trade associations in accordance with established policies to further achievement of goals, objectives, and standards of the profession or association. Directs or participates in the preparation of educational and informative materials for presentation to membership or public in newsletters, magazines, news releases, or on radio or television.

Executive Director, Chamber of Commerce

Directs activities to promote business, industrial, and job development, and civic improvements in the community. Administers programs of departments and committees which perform such functions as providing members with economic and marketing information, promoting economic growth and stability in the community, and counseling business organizations and industry on problems affecting local economy. Coordinates work with that of other community agencies to provide public services. Prepares and submits annual budgets to elected officials for approval. Studies governmental legislation, taxation, and other fiscal matters to determine effect on community interest, and makes recommendations based on organizational policy.

Executive Director, Convention Bureau

Directs activities of convention bureau to promote convention business in the area. Administers promotional programs. Coordinates efforts with local hotels, restaurants, transportation companies, exhibit centers, and other related facilities. Works within specified budgets. Serves on various civic and community boards to enhance the position of the bureau.

Executive Director, Department of Economic Development

Directs activities of the department. Ensures that demographic and economic information is maintained. Decides on research projects to be conducted. Directs publications prepared for public information. Works in conjunction with local and national agencies.

Executive Housekeeper

Supervises housekeeping staff. May hire and train new employees. Orders supplies, takes inventories and keeps records, prepares budgets, sees to needed repairs, draws up work schedules, inspects rooms. May be in charge of interior decoration.

Executive Secretary

Schedules meetings, takes minutes at meetings, and then transcribes and types them; composes letters; evaluates priority of incoming mail and telephone calls. Organizes and executes special projects and reports. May prepare budget reports. Works with a minimum of supervision; initiates much of own work according to office priorities.

Expeditor

Ensures that merchandise and supplies that have been ordered are received when and where needed.

Facilities Designer

Plans and designs utilization of space and facilities for hotels, food service operations, and other related properties. Draws design layout, showing location of equipment, furniture, workspaces, doorways, electrical outlets, and other related facilities. May review real estate contracts for compliance with regulations and suitability for occupancy. Suggests decor that is both practical and attractive to suit the purpose of the facility as well as maximize client business.

Farmer

Plants, cultivates, harvests, and stores crops; tends livestock and poultry.

Fashion Coordinator

Offers advice to the buying staff in large department stores on changing tastes, trends, and styles. Works with buying staff to be sure that the store's merchandise is completely up-to-date.

Fashion Designer

Creative specialist responsible for designing coats, suits, dresses, as well as other lines of apparel. Adapts higher-priced merchandise to meet the price range of customers.

Fashion Display Specialist

Responsible for designing display windows and display units within department or clothing stores. May have supervisory responsibilities as a coordinator for chain of stores.

Fashion Writer

Writes articles on the subject of fashion. Writes press releases and completes public relations projects. Writes about projected fashion trends, designers, new store openings. Writes newsletters for stores and buying offices. Covers fashion shows and does research.

Federal Food Inspector

Responsible for enforcing compliance with all regulations that ensure food safety for the consumer.

Finance Manager

Directs activities of workers engaged in performing such financial functions as accounting and reading financial transactions. Establishes procedures for control of assets, records, loan collateral, and securities.

Financial Analyst

Performs the quantitative analysis required for strategic planning and investments. Evaluates the financing and refinancing of certain projects and lines of credit. Prepares various reports for management. Collects data for financial comparisons with similar companies and securities.

Firefighter

Responds to fires and emergency situations where life, property, or the environment are at risk.

Fish and Game Warden

Patrols and protects public areas and wildlife.

Flight Attendant

Directly responsible for making passengers' flight comfortable, enjoyable, and safe. Ensures cabin is in order and that supplies and equipment are on board. Greets passengers as they board the plane. Helps passengers with carry-on luggage and with finding their seats. Instructs passengers before take-off in the location and proper usage of oxygen masks and other emergency equipment and exits. Serves meals and beverages.

Food and Beverage Manager

Responsible for compiling statistics of food and liquor costs, sales, and profits and losses. May also develop the procedures of portion control and item usage. May inventory bars as needed and prepare daily consumption reports that are forwarded to the auditing office. Takes inventory of foodstuffs with the chef, and works closely with chef on matters of buying and producing.

Food Director (Recreation)

Responsible for all food service areas at a particular theme park, amusement park, arcade, or other type of recreational facility. Supervises the procurement and preparation of food and drinks for concession stands, snack bars and dining halls, and rooms. Hires and trains staff. Maintains control of food costs and inventories. Deals directly with suppliers in ordering and paying for all food products. Enforces sanitation policies and health department codes throughout all food service facilities.

Food Production Manager

Responsible for all food preparation and supervision of kitchen staff. Must possess leadership skills and have knowledge of food preparation techniques, quality, and sanitation standards and cost control methods.

Food Service Consultant

Advises clients on site selection for food service operation, menu design and selection, interior décor, equipment, and overall design and layout of dining facility. Advises owner/operator of expected food and beverage costs, and helps to develop effective pricing strategy for all menu items.

Food Service Director

Exercises general supervision over all production areas in one or more kitchens. Also responsible for all the service that may be needed on counters and in the dining rooms. Responsible for the buying of food, its storage, its preparation, and the service necessary to handle large groups.

Food Service Engineer

Analyzes and creates efficient and cost-effective production processes, designs manufacturing equipment, or operates a plant's physical system.

Food Service Manager

Responsible for the operation's accounts and records and compliance with all laws and regulations, especially those concerning licensing, health, and sanitation.

Food Service Salesperson

Tells customers how a given item performs against the competition, how it will benefit the buyer, and ultimately, how it can increase profits and encourage repeat business. Demonstrates new products, gives customers actual product samplings, advises on menu ideas and serving suggestions, and even helps work out portion costs.

Forensic Scientist

Responsible for determining facts surrounding a crime based on physical evidence analysis.

Freelancer

Submits articles to editor for publication. Works independently. Initiates own stories and also writes specific articles or stories for publications upon request.

Freelancer (Visual Merchandising)

Initiates own designs and plans and offers services to designers and display directors.

Freelance Reporter
(Court Reporting)

Reporters who are in business for themselves. Develop their own contracts, follow up on recommendations of those for whom they may already have worked, and generally initiate their own assignments.

Front Desk Clerk

Responsible for direct personal contact with the guests, handling reservations, special needs, check in and check out. Familiarizes guests with a facility as well as the surrounding area. Prepares status reports on available rooms for manager. Receives guests' complaints and makes appropriate decisions about how to resolve them.

Front Desk Supervisor
(Hospitality)

Directs the front desk operations in the hotel. Oversees those responsible for guests' reservations, special needs, check-in, and checkout. Reviews status reports on available rooms. Ensures that guests' complaints are handled promptly and properly.

Front Office Manager (Hospitality)

Supervises front office operations of the rooms division of a hotel or motel.

General Accountant

Handles daily business needs, such as payroll, budgeting, accounts receivable, accounts payable, general ledger, and financial statements. Must pay close attention to all laws and regulations affecting daily business operations. Involved in sending out all payments, royalties, dividends, rents, and other necessary expenditures.

General Manager

Acts as overseer to all phases of a particular group, working with the management team to plan future accounts and solve day-to-day problems.

General Manager (Hospitality)

Establishes standards for personnel administration and performance, service to patrons, room rates, advertising, publicity, credit, food selection and service, and type of patronage to be solicited. Plans dining room, bar, and banquet operations. Allocates funds, authorizes expenditures, and assists in planning budgets for departments.

Geologist

Studies the physical aspects of the earth; searches for oil, natural gas, minerals, and groundwater.

Group Manager (Retail)

Supervises many departments within a retail operation.

Group Sales Manager

Concentrates on managing group sales efforts, including planning and forecasting sales and supervising sales staff. Identifies target markets and assigns specific groups to specific sales personnel. Devises and implements promotions and training programs.

Group Sales Representative (Travel)

Promotes sale of group season tickets for sports or other entertainment events. Telephones, visits, or writes to organizations, such as chamber of commerce, corporate employee recreation clubs, social clubs, and professional groups, to persuade them to purchase group tickets or season tickets to sports or other entertainment events, such as baseball, horseracing, or stage plays. Quotes group ticket rates, arranges for sale of tickets and seating for groups on specific dates, and obtains payment. May arrange for club to sponsor sports event, such as one of the races at horseracing track.

Guest Services Agent (Hospitality)

Works as a liaison between hotel guests and party providing desired services. Inform guests on services available to them in the hotel facility and assists them with making the proper connections. Concerned with any requests that guests may have and with providing answers to questions that concern guests.

Hazardous Materials Technician

Removes dangerous substances, such as asbestos, from buildings; cleans up contaminated areas; and responds to accidental releases of hazardous materials.

Head Bartender

In charge of the entire bar. Responsible for stocking and dispensing. Responsible for hiring and firing. Must know how to mix all drinks served in the bar. Establishes drink formulas and sets up portion controls for each drink. Coordinates inventory, requisitioning, and stocking needed items, proper accounting, and receipt of proper payment of bar items.

Head Cashier (Hospitality)

Oversees the duties of the hotel's cashiers, which include receiving guests' payments when checking out of the hotel. Approves the cashing of guests' checks and the processing of certain loans. Responsible for security of the safe deposit box.

Head Waitperson

Supervises and coordinates the activities of dining room employees engaged in providing courteous and rapid service to the diners. Greets the guests and escorts them to tables. Schedules dining reservations. Arranges parties for patrons. Adjusts any complaints regarding the food or service. Hires and trains the dining room employees. Notifies the payroll department regarding work schedules and time records. May assist in preparing menus. May plan and execute the details of a banquet.

Health Club Director *(Cruiselines)*

Oversees use of the health club on cruiseline. Ensures passenger understanding of use of the equipment and exercise available. Ensures safety and cleanliness of equipment. Supervises staff and approves recommended programs.

Health Technician *(Electronics)*

Performs the work of an electronics technician, specifically on various types of health equipment. (See **Electronics Technician**)

Hearing Reporter

Follows up and records all that is said during various types of proceedings, whether they be court trials or informal meetings. Hearings are presided over by a commissioner and there is no jury. Hearings may be conducted by various governmental agencies and departments with differing functions and responsibilities.

Highway Maintenance Worker

Maintains highways, roads, and airport runways.

Home Economics Teacher

Teaches everything from balancing menus to hygiene to food journalism.

Hostperson

Supervises and coordinates the activities of the dining room personnel to provide fast and courteous service to the patrons. Schedules dining reservations and arranges parties or special services for the diners. Greets the guests, escorts them to tables, and provides their menus. Adjusts complaints of the patrons.

Housekeeper

Ensures clean, orderly, attractive rooms in the hotel or related facility. Inventories stock to ensure adequate supplies. Issues supplies and equipment to workers. May record data and prepare reports concerning room occupancy, payroll expenses, and department expenses.

Incentive Travel Specialist

Travel specialists responsible for developing special packages for trips that have been won as a prize or premium.

Information Broker
(Word Processing)

Responsible for formulating specifications on the basis of which information is pulled from the database and then relayed to the client company.

Information Coordinator *(Travel)*

Coordinates organization and communication of travel information as needed. Responsible for providing accurate information to telephone inquirers and visitors about a destination, attraction, activity, or program. Participates in and conducts surveys.

Information Manager

Involves specializing in database management. Beside having a general knowledge of how organizations work and how information flows through them, knowledge of how to set up and improve information systems is important. Knowledge of library referencing and indexing systems is applied. Helps a technical expert set up an electronic filing system or corporate database. Sorts and updates database files, advises how to design the automated office system that would best fit with the organization's style, workflow, and procedures.

Information Packager

Edits word processing systems and their software, applies working knowledge of word processing and text, and finds imaginative opportunities in which to further apply that knowledge and those related skills.

Information Specialist
(Hospitality)

Provides specific information on area attractions and services to guests staying at the hotel. May work in conjunction with the concierge in providing guests with information on restaurants, shopping areas, museums, historical sites, theater, and local entertainment. Is well informed on the history of the area and information available at the area's Chamber of Commerce and Visitor and Convention Bureau.

Information Specialist *(Paralegal)*

Consolidates legal information after research for easy accessibility. Lists resources for future research by subject and sets up reference library to maintain information in sequential order. Advises users on how to extract the information they need quickly and efficiently.

Informer

Person assigned by an organization as the contact for the press or other media for obtaining desired information on an as-needed basis.

INS Investigator

Reviews applications for visas, determines whether aliens may enter or remain in the country, and gathers all information for the administrative hearings and criminal prosecution of immigration law violations.

Inspector *(Hospitality)*

Supervises cleaning staff and inspects hotel guest rooms, corridors, and lobbies. Assigns work to cleaning staff and trains personnel in housekeeping duties. Posts room occupancy records. Adjusts guests' complaints regarding housekeeping service or equipment. Writes requisitions for room supplies and furniture renovation or replacements.

Instructor *(Education)*

Instructs students in commercial subjects (typing, accounting, computer systems), communications courses (reading and writing), and personality development in business schools, community colleges, or training programs. Instructs students in subject matter, utilizing various methods, such as lecture and demonstration, and uses audiovisual aids and other materials to supplement presentation. Prepares or follows teaching outline. Administers tests. Maintains discipline.

Insurance Investigation Specialist

Examines insurance made by individuals and businesses to ensure that the claims being made are legitimate. Investigates false claims and determines appropriate course of action.

Intelligence Specialist

Conducts background clearances and work on security personnel matters.

Internal Auditor

Conducts independent appraisal from within the organization by analyzing, criticizing, and recommending improvements to internal financial practices. Ensures the safety and profitability of investments and assets, and seeks to uncover sources of waste and inefficiency.

International Account Executive *(Hospitality)*

Responsible for the development of and service of international client business coming into the hotel. May also be responsible for referring clientele to international properties in other countries. May assist with providing information to client on the foreign country, its currency, passport and customs regulations, and overall familiarization with the area.

International Group Secretary

Provides secretarial support for a team headed by an account executive. Duties include transcribing letters and memos from dictaphone tapes and typing comprehensive multi-country proposals for clients, preparation of travel arrangements, and assisting with clients, brokers, and foreign visitors.

Interpreter

Translates spoken word from one language to another. Provides consecutive or simultaneous translation between languages. Usually receives briefing on subject area prior to interpreting session.

Interviewer

Interviews job applicants to select persons meeting employers' qualifications. Searches files of job orders from employers and matches applicants' qualifications with job requirements and employer specifications.

Inventory Control Manager

Ensures that all stock units are in adequate supply, both components and finished goods. Responsible for overall quality of the product. Maximizes customer service levels, inventory investment, and manufacturing efficiencies.

Inventory Coordinator

Prepares reports of inventory balance, prices, and shortages. Compiles information on receipt or disbursement of goods and computes inventory balance, price, and costs. Verifies clerical computations against physical count of stock and adjusts errors in computation or count. Investigates and reports reasons for discrepancies.

Inventory Manager

Supervises compilation of records of amount, kind, and value of merchandise, material, or stock on hand in establishment or department of establishment. Compares inventories taken by workers with office records or computer figures from sales, equipment shipping, production, purchase, or stock records to obtain current theoretical inventory. Prepares inventory reports. Makes planning decisions.

Investigators

Investigates civil offenses within a city, county, or state and makes recommendations for appropriate action for the violators.

Investment Banker

Analyzes the needs of clients and makes recommendations to them on the best way to obtain the money they need. Obtains permission from each of the state governments to sell the issue in their state.

IRS Agent

Responsible for examining taxpayers' records to determine tax liabilities and investigating cases involving tax fraud or evasion of tax payments.

Job Analyst

Reviews all job functions within the company to continuously maintain updated details on job requirements, specific functions, and qualifications needed.

Journalist

Gathers information and prepares stories about world events for newspapers, magazines, radio, or TV.

Junior Buyer (Retail)

Performs duties of buyer trainee and also becomes involved in deciding on products for purchase and evaluating the store's needs. Learns to study the competition on a regular basis so as to evaluate and predict decisions.

Junior Copywriter

Studies clients from printed materials and past correspondence. May answer phone, type, file, or draft simple correspondence. May write some descriptive copy and come up with concepts for new ad campaigns. Works with art department on presentations.

Junior Drafter

Copies plans and drawings prepared by drafters by tracing them with ink and pencil on transparent paper spread over drawings, using triangles, T-square, compass, pens, or other drafting instruments. Makes simple sketches or drawings under close supervision.

Keypunch Operator

Operates alphabetic and numeric keypunch machine, similar in operation to electric typewriter, to transcribe data from source material onto magnetic tape and to record accounting or statistical data for subsequent processing by automatic or electronic data processing equipment.

Kitchen Manager

Supervises all the production personnel in the kitchen area. Oversees the buying, storing, and preparation of all food. Takes inventory and reorders when necessary. Usually employed in operations where chefs are not employed.

Labor Relations Specialist

Responsible for being fully knowledgeable of current contracts or established policies affecting the working environment of all personnel including such areas as hiring requirements, pay policies, performance standards, leave of absence authorizations, and disciplinary procedures. When dealing with bargaining units, negotiates contracts as needed.

Landscape Architect

Designs landscaped areas that are functional and attractive and that fit in with the natural environment.

Law Librarian

Ensures books and other legal materials are updated periodically. Conducts legal research as needed, frequently accessing database information.

Law Library Manager

Manages the ordering and organization of all materials to be housed in the law library. Responsible for keeping up-to-date on changes in the law and for obtaining new literature describing most current laws. Super-vises staff. Trains staff and library users on how to use the library. Oversees telephone information service.

Law Office Administrator

Designs, develops, and plans new procedures, techniques, services, processes, and applications in the office; plans, supervises, and assists in the installation and maintenance of relatively complex office equipment; plans production, operations of service for the efficient use of staff, materials, money, and equipment in the office.

Lawyer

Conducts civil and criminal lawsuits; draws up legal documents, advises clients as to legal rights, and practices other phases of the law.

Lead Agent (Travel)

A car rental agent responsible for answering customers' questions.

Lead Analyst

Assists higher level personnel in analytical studies of complex and important problems involving existing and proposed systems and their costs. Develops, examines, and implements reporting systems and procedures which provide significant contributions in terms of time saved and increased efficiency or reduced costs.

Lead Analyst

Assists in developing the data processing procedures for solving business or mathematical problems. Assists in analyzing and evaluating proposed and existing systems.

Lead Consultant

Develops flowcharts to establish logic of execution. Codes logic in programming language. Writes program language to initiate and control the program in the hardware. Reviews existing programs and effects changes as requested. Solves production hang-ups in existing system. Writes operating instructions for computer personnel. Reviews output for the user. Supervises other programmers and gives final approval on the programs they have written. Ensures senior management receives information as requested.

Lead Word Processing Operator

Coordinates work priorities and assigns work to word processors. May train and supervise word processors. Ensures quality of work output.

Legal Assistant

Oversees the work of other paralegals in a firm. Delegates work, handles personnel-related problems, writes appraisals of other paralegals, and supervises the hiring of paralegals when needed. Works on special projects.

Legal Assistant Manager

Acts as a liaison between management and legal assistants; responsible for hiring, supervision, review, and dismissals, if necessary, as well as budgetary responsibilities. Also assigns case work to ensure work distribution, quality and timeliness.

Legal Secretary

Schedules appointments, court appearances; prepares documents, billing, bookkeeping, and record keeping. Handles subpoenas, mortgages, deeds, closings, pleadings, briefs, wills, proxies, and abstracts. May also review law journals and assist in other ways with legal research.

Legal Technician

Initiates and composes standardized legal forms routinely as needed for specific legal actions. Accepts service of legal documents, reviews for correct form and timeliness, annotates case files and status records to reflect receipt due dates for responses. Establishes, maintains,

and closes case files or systems of legal records. Maintains tickler system, coordinates schedules with court clerks, notifies witnesses of appearances, and reminds attorneys of court appearances and deadlines for submitting various actions or documents.

Legislative Reporter

Records events, speeches, and debates that take place in the different state legislatures. Attends and reports committee meetings.

Line Cook

Responsible for any duties necessary in order to prepare and produce menu items efficiently. Duties may include cutting and portioning, cooking, and serving items.

Litigation Paralegal

Assists attorneys at trial, prepares for trail, digests or summarizes depositions, indexes or organizes documents, prepares simple pleadings and discoveries such as interrogatories.

Litigation Support Consultant

Provides consulting services in litigation support. Consultation areas include analyzing the project, designing a database structure, developing a database building plan, creating coding sheets, and writing report programs.

Litigation Support Manager

Responsible for computerized litigation support. Consults with attorneys about whether a certain case will require automation and, if so, how to design the document retrieval database.

Loan Manager

Supervises loan personnel and approves recommendations of customer applications for lines of credit when loan officer is not able to do so. Communicates changes in policies and regulations regularly to loan personnel and customer.

Loan Officer

Interviews applicants applying for loans. Prepares loan request paper and obtains related documents from applicants. Investigates applicants' background and verifies credit and bank references. Informs applicants whether loan requests have been approved or rejected. Processes the loans.

Loss Prevention Specialist

Guards the internal security of a business to prevent employee thefts and inventory loss.

Mail and Information Coordinator *(Hospitality)*

Coordinates the information and mail services, usually at the front desk. Responsible for ensuring that outgoing and incoming mail for the facility as well as for guests is properly routed. Advises guests on most efficient procedures for receiving or sending important mail. Ensures that messages get to hotel personnel and guests on a timely and accurate basis. May also provide guests with general information about the facility and the area.

Maître d'Hôtel

In charge of the dining room in a hotel or restaurant. Supervises a team of captains, waitpersons, and junior waitpersons.

Manager *(Accounting)*

Organizes and directs all general accounting activities. Maintains accounting systems that ensure the proper accounting and recording of company resources; provides financial statements, analysis, and other key management reports.

Manager *(Recreation)*

Manages recreation facilities, such as tennis courts, golf courses, or arcades, and coordinates activities of workers engaged in providing services of the facility. Determines work activities necessary to operate facility, hires workers, and assigns tasks and work hours accordingly. Initiates promotion to acquaint public with activities of the facility. Maintains financial records.

Manager of System Analysis

Evaluates advances in computer equipment and software capabilities in light of the company's future system requirements. Coordinates the formulation of short- and long-range technical system development plans, with special emphasis on technical feasibility. Organizes, schedules, and conducts training programs for data processing and users of computer services.

Manager of Tour Operations

Supervises support functions related to the execution of a successful tour. Areas of responsibility include the bookkeeping, secretarial, telex, and computer operations areas.

Manager Trainee

Performs assigned duties, under direction of experienced personnel, to gain knowledge and experience needed for management position. Receives training and performs duties in various departments to become familiar with personnel functions and operations and management viewpoints and policies that affect each phase of the business.

Manager Trainee *(Finance)*

Works with financial manager while gaining an overall exposure to all aspects of the finance function of the company. Assists with budgets, purchase options, and expenses. Helps review financial reports for different product lines and assists with consolidating financial data for updated reports. May interview other department heads, customers, vendors, and other key people dealing with the finance area.

Manager Trainee *(Food Service)*

Assists with all functions of the area assigned. Learns the overview of the entire operation before specializing.

If in a large operation, may rotate within one area of the facility, such as the production or purchasing area, to learn all of its functions if that is the area of specialty. Usually trains by rotating among various stations in the kitchen itself and among related areas such as purchasing, the storeroom, front of the house, etc.

Manager Trainee (Retail)

Works with store manager organizing and managing the store on a daily basis. Spends time on the selling floor, learning customer service techniques and computerized systems. Assists with managing, merchandising, and analyzing stock. Directs and physically puts stock out on the floor and presents merchandise. May work with buyer learning financial planning, vendor negotiations, and branch store communications.

Manufacturing Manager

Coordinates all manufacturing operations to produce products of high quality and reliability at optimum cost and in accordance with customer shipping schedules. Participates in the preparation of the manufacturing budget. Ensures safety of employees in their exposure to varied manufacturing process hazards. Resolves various manufacturing and production problems.

Market Manager (Food Service)

Responsible for compiling information on the age, sex, and income level of restaurants' potential clientele and their dining habits and preferences. Marketing managers consider customer preferences in order to suggest appropriate sales advertising techniques. This information provides the basis for success/failure projections in certain demographic areas.

Market Research Analyst

Researches market conditions in local, regional, or national area to determine potential sales of product or service. Examines and analyzes statistical data to forecast future marketing trends. Gathers data on competitors and analyzes prices, sales, and methods of marketing and distribution. Formulates surveys, opinion polls, or questionnaires.

Market Research Director

Oversees market research for a company. Sets goals and objectives for projects. Sets timetables for completion and assigns personnel to projects. Keeps appropriate administrators informed on findings and makes recommendations and proposes marketing strategies based on results.

Marketing Analyst (Paralegal)

Examines and analyzes statistical data to forecast future marketing trends in the paralegal field. (See **Market Research Analyst**)

Marketing Director

Directs and coordinates the development of marketing programs assigned to attain maximum penetration in the required market segments. Directs the creation, writing, and publishing of market and product plans. Explores development of product line offerings.

Marketing and Promotion Manager (Food Service)

Supervises any advertising or sales promotion for the operation. Works with food production staff to create menus and promotions with customer appeal. Often coordinates these activities with an advertising agency.

Marketing Representative (Paralegal)

Promotes and sells law-related books. Works in the marketing division of legal publishing companies.

Marketing Support Representative

Backs up the sales force by demonstrating the equipment and working with the customers after the equipment is installed; teaches the customers' word processing specialists to use the equipment and helps them find the best methods of doing the company's particular tasks.

Materials Manager

Studies receiving or shipping notices, requests for movement of raw materials and finished products, and reports of warehousing space available to develop schedules for material-handling activities. May confer with supervisors of other departments to coordinate flow of materials or products. Supervises activities of shipping and receiving personnel.

Media Director of Planning

Plans media relations in line with company goals. Reports and analyzes industry media trends. Communicates with product development to determine product market plans as they relate to media proposals and media scheduling. Oversees Media Planners.

Media Planner

Plans and administers media programs advertising department. Confers with representatives of advertising agencies, product managers, and corporate advertising staff to establish media goals, objectives, and strategy within corporate advertising budget. Studies demographic data and consumer profiles to identify target audiences media advertising.

Medical Assistant

Works in hospitals or clinics cleaning and sterilizing equipment, performing various tests, and helping to maintain records.

Medical Claims Examiner

Examines claims for the medical field. (See **Claims Examiner**)

Medical Claims Representative

Claims representative: the medical field. (See **Claims Representative**)

Medical Librarian

Records, arranges, and makes medical information available to people. Handles books, films, periodicals, documents, and other media related to the medical field.

Medical Records Administrator

Plans, develops, and administers medical record systems for hospital, clinic, health center, or similar facility to meet standards of accrediting and regulatory agencies. Assists medical staff in evaluating quality of patient care and in developing criteria and methods for such evaluation. Develops and implements policies and procedures for documentation, storing, and retrieving information and for processing medical/legal documents.

Medical Records Technician

Gathers all information on patient's condition and records it on permanent files that become the history and progress of treatment of a patient's illness or injury. Accumulates the results of a physician's examinations, information on laboratory tests and electrocardiograms and records these results in the files. Accuracy is particularly important because much of this information is referred to during malpractice cases, and it is also vital when processing insurance claims.

Medical Secretary

Processes many kinds of complex health insurance forms. Responsible for patient billing, records management, medical and office supply organization, and appointments. Takes dictation and transcribes on dictaphone. Deals with medical supply vendors and pharmaceutical houses. Prepares correspondence and assists physicians with reports, speeches, articles, and conference proceedings.

Medical Technician (*Electronics*)

Performs the work of an electronics technician, specifically on various types of medical equipment. (See **Electronics Technician**)

Meeting Planner

Establishes objectives of the meeting, selects the hotel site and facilities, negotiates rates, sets budgets, makes air and hotel reservations, chooses speakers, plans food and beverages, arranges for all audiovisual equipment. Arranges meeting registration, exhibits, promotion and publicity scheduling, and room set-up; and arranges postmeeting evaluation. Planners are involved with negotiations that save the organization money.

Membership Coordinator

Solicits membership for club or trade association. Visits or contacts prospective members to explain benefits and costs of membership and to describe organization of club or association. May collect dues and payments for publications from members.

Membership Secretary

Compiles and maintains membership lists, records the receipt of dues and contributions, and gives out information to members of the organizations and associations. Sends out newsletters and other promotional materials on a regular basis. Answers telephone inquiries and coordinates mass mailings.

Menu Planner

Works with the Executive Chef to select all items offered on menus. Must know food service costs, preparation techniques and equipment, customer trends and preferences.

Merchandise Analyst

Evaluates available merchandise in different locations and identifies when transfers might be appropriate. Evaluates quality of merchandise from the vendors for price paid with the buyer.

Merchandise Manager

Takes charge of a group of departments, usually organized by merchandise. Coordinates and oversees the efforts of the buyers. Develops merchandise plans, divides up the buyers' merchandise assignments, and reviews their selections. Visits

the manufacturers' showrooms and travels abroad.

Merchandise Planner

Allocates merchandise from distribution point to stores as requested by buyers and merchandise managers. Ensures that merchandise is shipped properly and on a timely basis from the distribution center.

Merchandising Supervisor

(Food Service)

Plans and carries out promotional programs to increase sales. Works with printers, artists, writers, and other suppliers. Must know employer's food service operations thoroughly and be able to apply market research techniques as well as budgeting and planning skills.

Military Investigator

Investigates all matters pertaining to military personnel and programs to monitor and/or discover illegal activities within the military. Also investigates outside threats to military personnel and programs.

Military Police

Operates on military bases, patrols areas where the military is located. Are generally limited in their jurisdiction to military personnel, or to persons involved in illegal activities aimed toward military personnel.

MIS Director

Recommends and initiates programs and/or systems that support the desired corporate profit objectives. Issues business data and management information that facilitate the businesses' planning and decision-making process at all levels. Responsible for total information services provided to user departments.

MIS Manager

Responsible for coordinating the short-term planning for MIS/EDP efforts in systems development and computer processing; for establishing guidelines for measurement of division activity to these plans; and for monitoring Division MIS/EDP performance to ensure that information is made available to all levels of management on a complete, reliable, economic, and timely basis.

MIS Specialist

Has specific knowledge of and provides service to a specialized area in the company. May concentrate on such areas as accounting, sales, production, or any other function requiring the services of the MIS department to meet its particular need.

MIS Supervisor

Ensures timely and accurate processing of incoming orders through the order preparation and data processing areas to assist in achieving a high level of customer service. Maintains external relationship with vendors of paper supplies and forms, equipment manufacturers, equipment maintenance representatives, and leasing companies. Maintains contact with all company departments using the services of the MIS department.

Mortgage and Real Estate Secretary

Works with real estate investment officers and provides secretarial support for an investment team. Prepares commitment letters and various reports, maintains files, and handles telephone communications.

Motor Vehicle Registration Coordinator

Coordinates all aspects of motor vehicle registration and follow-up, including motor vehicle inspections and driver and licensing examinations.

Musician

Plays musical instruments, sings, composes, arranges, or conducts musical groups.

National Sales Manager (Marketing)

Devises and implements sales strategies, forecasts sales, supervises in-house salespeople; establishes and attains sales goals; trains and develops sales personnel. Develops and implements marketing and advertising strategy.

Night Auditor (Hospitality)

Brings all of the establishment's accounts up-to-date so that a day's revenue report can be made to upper management. (In a hotel, a revenue report includes such items as a detailed account of room revenues, number of rooms occupied, average room revenue, percentage of occupancy figures, and the like.) The night audit process is usually augmented by a computerized system. The night auditor often plays the role of the night manager.

Night Shift Supervisor

Supervises work of department during the night shift. Schedules the staff for the shift. Prioritizes work that must be completed. Responsible for maintaining the equipment and resolving routine problems that may occur during the shift.

Nurse

Cares for ill, injured, convalescent, and handicapped persons in hospitals, clinics, private homes, sanitariums, and similar institutions. Observes patient and reports adverse reactions to medical personnel in charge. Administers specified medications, and notes time and amount on patient's chart. Performs routine laboratory work.

Nutritionist

Identifies the kinds and amounts of nutrients in food, translates this knowledge for schools and health care menus and restaurants and hotels; develops new foods and ingredients.

Occupational Therapist

Works with individuals to recover from conditions that are mentally, physically, developmentally, or emotionally disabling. Treats people of all ages, from infants to teens to the elderly. Helps patients to restore abilities and skills or to adapt to physical dysfunction and become independent; or treats people who are dealing with alcoholism, drug abuse, depression, or eating disorders.

Operations Assistant *(Recreation)*

Responsible for assisting with overseeing the general operation of a recreational facility. Solves problems that arise concerning facilities and grounds. Contacts vendors, contractors, and equipment repair technicians as needed. Obtains and renews necessary licenses and permits.

Office Manager

(See **Department Manager, Office**)

Operations Manager

(Computer Systems)

Ensures that all jobs adhere to established conventions and may cancel any job that deviates from these conventions. Controls the processing of jobs and is responsible for obtaining the maximum utilization of the computer.

Operations Manager *(Retail)*

Oversees all functions of store operations, which include personnel, credit, payroll, shipping and receiving, customer service, warehousing and distribution, security, and maintenance.

Operations Research Analyst

Conducts analyses of management and operational problems and formulates mathematical or simulation models of the problem. Analyzes problems in terms of management information and conceptualizes and defines problems. Studies information and selects plan from competitive proposals that affords maximum profitability or effectiveness in relation to cost or risk.

Outside Sales Agent *(Travel)*

Brings new business to an agency on a referral basis.

Owner/Operator *(Food Service)*

Coordinates all employees; may be responsible for buying food and supplies; may help with menu planning; keeps the restaurant within health and sanitation guidelines; oversees payroll function. In small restaurants, may oversee marketing and promotion effort.

Owner/Operator *(Travel Agency)*

Delegates responsibilities to qualified managers. Encourages creative marketing and sales activities. Manages budget for the overall operation.

Packaging Specialist

Selects and evaluates materials and develops packaging to fit specific products for industry needs.

Page Creator *(Word Processing)*

Composes actual pages of catalogs relayed to home television or telephones. Involves word processing, text editing, and formatting, together with computer graphics. The system plus its computer graphics is called videotext.

Pantry Person

Draws from the storeroom all the raw materials needed to prepare all the fruit or vegetable salads, seafood cocktails, canapés, and other cold dishes. Serves these items to waiters and waitresses. May slice and portion cold meats and cheeses. Serves desserts and side dishes such as bread and butter. Makes sandwiches and prepares garnishes for other departments.

Paralegal

Assists a lawyer with routine legal assignments. Maintains legal volumes to make sure they are up-to-date; assists with legal research. Helps administer estates, draft wills and trusts, complete federal and state tax returns, prepare initial and amended articles of incorporation, stock certificates, and other securities. Helps prepare court-related forms. Performs a variety of related duties upon request of the attorney.

Paralegal (Publishing House)

Assists the general counsel in the company's legal department with the areas of law that affect publishing, such as contract law and copyright law. May assist the legal publisher in planning new books about the paralegal profession or the procedures utilized by paralegals in the office.

Paralegal Assistant

Assists paralegals in large scale litigation with such duties as organizing and indexing documents, summarizing simple depositions, and performing assignments that enhance the overall organization of the case.

Paralegal Coordinator

Responsible for paralegal workload management, both as a resource for attorneys needing paralegal assistance and to ensure fairly divided workloads among paralegals on staff.

Paralegal Instructor

Teaches paralegal students the legal procedures used by paralegals in the law office.

Paralegal Manager

Responsible for hiring, performance reviews, salary administration, budgets, and work assignments.

Paralegal Supervisor

Oversees work of paralegals responsible for researching law, investigating facts, and preparing documents to assist lawyers.

Parole Officer

Helps clients find a place to live or work after being conditionally released from prison; must enforce the specific conditions of the client's release at all times.

Partner (CPA Firm)

Responsible for major audit accounts. Solves complex accounting problems for clients, using standard accounting principles. Also responsible for quality of client service and volume of new business brought in to the firm. Achieves objectives through the effective management of the technicians and sales staff in the firm.

Passenger Service Agent

Provides passengers with information; assists passengers with information, assists passengers when boarding the plane.

Pastry Cook

Prepares desserts (both hot and cold), ices, and cakes for both daily use and for special occasions.

Pastry Chef

Oversees the bread and pastry needs of all kitchens and departments in a large hotel, club, or restaurant. Supervises pastry cooks and bakers. Requires ability to coordinate the activity of others. Supervises the preparation of desserts, pastries, frozen desserts, fondants, fillings, and fancy sugar decorations. Creates new recipes and produces delicate items that require the mastery of fine techniques.

Peripheral Equipment Operator

Operates on-line or off-line peripheral machines, according to written or oral instructions, to transfer data from one form to another, print output, and read data into and out of digital computer. Mounts and positions materials, such as reels of magnetic tape or paper tape onto reader-sorter. Sets, guides, keys, and switches according to instructions to prepare equipment for operations. Separates and sorts printed output forms.

Personnel Assistant

Performs diversified duties in the processing and monitoring of employee benefits programs and maintenance of all employee personnel files. Sets up files on new employees. Records changes on all employee status as necessary and forwards to payroll department.

Personnel Clerk

Prepares job postings and determines eligibility to bid and successful bidder{s}. Prepares monthly absenteeism reports. Prepares monthly accident reports. Assists applicants with filling out employment applications appropriately. Acts as a backup for the department secretary; performs a variety of basic personnel and clerical functions.

Personnel Director

Supervises the hiring and firing of company employees. Prepares performance reports and sets up personnel policies and regulations. In a large corporation, oversees the entire personnel function.

Personnel Manager

Responsible for developing, implementing, and coordinating policies and programs covering the following: employment, labor relations, wage and salary administration, fringe benefits administration, indoctrination and training, placement, safety, insurance, health benefits, and employee services.

Placement Director (Paralegal)

Responsible for employment orientation and job development, and may act as a liaison between the employer and the paralegal graduate seeking a position.

Plant Manager

Responsible for manufacturing of products in the required quantity and quality and for performing this function safely at a minimum cost. Recommends improvements in manufacturing methods. Sets up and approves production schedules. Regularly reviews inventories of required materials. Directs and approves all requisitions for maintenance and repair of building and equipment and for machine parts and manufacturing supplies.

Plant Safety Specialist

Coordinates safety programs. Communicates policies, programs, and regulations to appropriate personnel. Ensures compliance with governmental regulations. Enforces safety policies for chemical use, fire codes, equipment, and ventilation systems. Ensures proper guarding of machinery to avoid operator injury. Maintains records as well.

Police Patrol Officer

Responsible for the enforcement of laws and ordinances for the protection of life and property in an assigned area during a specific period. Conducts preliminary investigations, assists in the apprehension of criminals.

Police Officer

Keeps public order, protects lives and property, and investigates crime.

Polygraph Operator

Tests victims, suspects, witnesses and others through the use of a lie detector machine.

Portfolio Manager

Manages non trust accounts, such as the pension fund of a corporation or a university endowment. Decides what stocks should be bought and sold within the portfolio.

Postal Inspector

Investigates losses and thefts of the mail or property owned by the post office. In addition, investigators and security force personnel protect postal buildings and installations.

Prep Cook

Responsible for any duties necessary in order to prepare food items for production.

President

Plans, develops, and establishes policies and objectives of a business organization in accordance with the board of directors and corporate charter. Plans business objectives and develops policies to coordinate functions between departments. Reviews financial statements to determine progress and status in attaining objectives. Directs and coordinates formulation of financial programs to provide funding for new or continuing operations to maximize return on investments. May preside over board of directors. Evaluates performance of company executives.

President/Owner

Acts as president of a business and owns and operates it as well. (See **President**)

Press Coordinator

Arranges meetings and special events with the press. Contacts press either by phone or mail to detail upcoming events.

Private

An enlisted person in either of the two lowest ranks in the U.S. Marine Corps or the U.S. Army.

Private First Class

An enlisted person ranking just below a corporal in the U.S. Army and just below a lance corporal in the U.S. Marine Corps.

Private Secretary

As the executive's administrative partner, duties vary according to the size of the organization and the executive's responsibilities. May outline day's work for the office, schedule duties to be performed by all who work in the office; keeps everything on schedule despite interruptions. Greets callers, handles mail, keeps track of financial records, and processes data.

Probate Paralegal

Oversees probate proceedings from beginning to end, prepares federal tax forms, assists at the sales of assets, and drafts wills and trusts.

Probation Officer

Responsible for compiling the presentence investigation for the court. Makes formal court reports and recommendations to the judge for case deposition. Works with caseloads of individuals to assist them with counseling, job placement, and traditional social work-oriented functions while at the same time enforcing the rules imposed on the client by the court.

Product Development Technologist

Technologist working in the food service industry conducting experiments to improve flavor, texture, shelf life, or other product characteristics; develops new products or packaging materials; compares competitive products; ensures that every item meets quality standards, and interprets and solves the problems of the food service operator.

Product Manager

Oversees the research, development, and production of a particular product. Assesses need for modifications on the product based on input from market research. Estimates timely and cost-effective procedures for implementing periodic modifications. Ensures that quality of product is maintained.

Product Support Representative
(Computer Systems)

Acts as the customer's liaison with the computer manufacturer. Assists with familiarizing the customer with the computer. Acts as part trainer, part salesperson, and part adviser to the customer.

Production Coordinator

Coordinates flow of work within or between departments of manufacturer to expedite production. Reviews master production schedule and work orders, establishes priorities and availability or capability of workers, parts, or material. Confers with department supervisors to determine progress of work. Compiles reports on the progress of work.

Production Manager

Supervises and coordinates activities of those who expedite flow of materials, parts, and assemblies and processes within or between departments. Takes leadership position in such production operation areas as engineering, scheduling, purchasing, quality control, inventory control, distribution, and human relations.

Production Planner

Ensures that inventories of stock items are maintained at reasonable levels and that orders for non-stock items are processed in a timely, effective manner. Works with plant supervisor to establish manning levels that are appropriate based on current and projected levels of activity. Requisitions all raw materials and supplies required to manufacture products.

Production Technician

Assists engineer in preparing layouts of machinery and equipment, workflow plans, time and motion studies, and analyses of production costs to produce the most efficient use of personnel, materials, and machines.

Professional Waitperson

Serves meals to the patrons according to the established rules of etiquette. Presents a menu to the diner, suggests dinner courses and appropriate wines, and answers questions regarding food preparation. Writes the order on a check or memorizes it. Relays the order to the kitchen and serves the courses from the kitchen and service bars. Garnishes and decorates the dishes prior to serving them. Serves the patrons from a chafing dish at the table, observes the diners to fulfill any additional requests and to perceive when the meal has been completed. Totals the bill and accepts payments. May carve the meats, bone the fish and fowl, prepare flaming dishes and desserts at the patron's table.

Professor

Designation of faculty rank used to refer to members of the faculty with extensive experience in their area of expertise. Teaches and advises students and may be involved in

administrative activity. This position is often marked by an emphasis on research work. (See **Associate Professor, Assistant Professor**)

Program Coordinator

Oversees programs after the planning stage. Takes appropriate action to initiate planned programs, service them while in progress, and arrange for program evaluation. May assist with recommending speakers, agendas, room setup, and promotional efforts.

Program Director

Plans and develops methods and procedures for implementing programs; directs and coordinates program activities, and exercises control over personnel according to knowledge and experience in area with which the program is concerned. Prepares program reports. Controls expenditures.

Program Director (*Education*)

Supervises the development of a variety of academic programs or other programs related to an educational institution. Such programs might involve parents, student organizations, industry, or other special interest groups. (See **Program Director**)

Project Director

Plans, directs, and coordinates activities of designated project to ensure that aims, goals, or objectives specified for project are accomplished in accordance with set priorities, timetables, and funding. Develops staffing plan and establishes work schedules for each phase of the project. Prepares project status reports for management.

Proofreader

Reads typeset (original copy) or proof of type setup to detect and mark for corrections and grammatical, typographical, or compositional errors. Reads proof against copy, marking by standardized codes errors that appear in proof. Returns marked proof for correction and later checks corrected proof against copy.

Proofreader (Paralegal)

Reviews the content of law-related manuscripts to verify facts needed in case preparation. Also can act as person who checks for improper usage or spelling or grammar errors in legal copy.

Proofreader (Word Processing)

Checks the work of the correspondence secretary and word processor for accuracy of copy.

Public Relations Specialist

Writes news releases, directs advertising campaigns, and conducts public opinion polls. Tries to create favorable attitudes about a client or its products.

Purchasing Agent

Responsible for buying the raw materials, machinery, supplies, and services necessary to run a business.

Purchasing Agent (Food Service)

Purchases foodstuffs, kitchen supplies, and equipment. Makes large contracts for several products. Purchases all supplies with the exception of capital goods such as furniture and fixed equipment.

Purchasing Assistant

(See **Purchasing Agent**)

Purchasing Manager

Responsible for the management of the procurement functions of the company. Establishes practices and procedures to be followed by buyers and other department personnel. Negotiates price and delivery. Selects the vendors, assesses vendor capabilities, develops alternate sources, and evaluates vendor performance. Ensures that department records are maintained.

Purchasing Manager (Food Service)

Responsible for the actual purchase of all supplies and equipment, usually coordinated through the Executive Chef or Cook. Required to monitor and control costs and to maintain accurate inventories. Supervises purchasing agents responsible for a particular product line.

Quality Assurance Manager

Develops and maintains a system to assure that all products manufactured by the organization meet customer specifications and achieve superior quality and reliability levels. Revises and updates quality control manual. Meets with vendors, customers, and quality representatives to discuss and resolve quality problems as required.

Quality Assurance Specialist (Food Service)

Analyzes ingredients and finished products and checks standards of production, packaging, and sanitation. May be assigned to a particular type of product or food item.

Quality Control Manager

Travels to various departments to inspect them and make sure they adhere to company and state standards. Usually responsible for more than one operation.

Railroad Police

Responsible for safety and security on the railroads.

Ramp Agent

Supervises baggage area to be sure baggage is sent to proper destinations.

Real Estate Manager

Supervises the negotiations for the acquisition and disposition of properties. Supervises staff engaged in preparing lease agreements, recording rental receipts, and performing other activities necessary for efficient management of company properties, or in performing routine research on zoning ordinances and condemnation considerations. Directs appraiser to inspect properties and land under consideration for acquisition and recommends acquisitions, lease, disposition, improvement, or other action consistent with best interests of the company. Negotiates contracts with sellers of land and renters of property.

Real Estate Paralegal

Prepares loan documents, oversees transactions from beginning to end, drafts and reviews leases, works closely with escrow and title companies, reviews surveys, and prepares closing binders.

Reception Manager

Supervises all activities of guest services, including registration of incoming guests and checkout of departing guests; provides guests with information about functions at the hotel and about the general area where the hotel is located; takes messages for guests and provides wake-up calls; handles guest relations, problems with rooms, billing, or any other routine difficulty.

Receptionist

Greets people who come into an office and directs them to the proper department. They may also do other tasks such as answering the phone and some typing. Learns the departments and key personnel in the company and what functions they perform.

Records Manager

Examines and evaluates records-management systems to develop new or improve existing methods for efficient handling, protecting, and disposing of business records and information. Reviews records retention schedule to determine how long records should be kept.

Recruiting Coordinator Administrator (Law)

Works with the firm administrator and the recruiting or hiring committee to hire new attorneys. Coordinates Summer Clerk interviewing.

Regional Director

May oversee a group of regional managers. (See **Regional Manager**)

Regional Manager

Responsible for overseeing the activities of all operations in a particular geographical area of the country.

Regional Sales Manager

Recruits in-house personnel, recruits general agents, and assists when needed with training new sales staff with "cold calling." Holds periodic sales meetings to strengthen competitive position and explain strategies for market penetration.

Registered Representative
(Account Executive or Broker)

Buys or sells securities for customers. Relays the order to members of the firm who are stationed on the exchange floors; if the security is not traded on the exchange, sells it directly in the over-the-counter market. Advises customers on the timing of the purchase or sale of securities. Counsels customers about tax shelters, mutual funds, and other investments.

Regional Vice President

Deals with new business development; senior management contact, both internal and external; pricing analysis; proposal development and presentation; and contract negotiations. Works with planning and achieving marketing objectives within the responsible geographic territory.

Rental Sales Representative

Negotiates car rental rates with travel agents, corporate businesses, and other commercial accounts and individual clients so as to remain competitive in the market.

Research Account Executive
(Advertising)

Researches printed literature. Drafts reports from research. Gets competitive bids from suppliers. Sits in on planning sessions. Suggests new methods of data gathering. Helps design surveys.

Research Analyst

Evaluates research findings and determines their applicability to specific projects within the company. Recommends needed research projects. Compares research findings with similar studies or surveys to determine reliability of results. Uses statistical data and measurement to examine and apply findings.

Research Analyst (*Financial*)

Researches and sells their research to institutional investors. Recommends portfolio managers to the stocks they believe should be bought and sold.

Research Assistant

Compiles and analyzes verbal or statistical data to prepare reports and studies for use by professional workers in a variety of areas. Searches sources, such as reference works, literature, documents, newspapers, and statistical records to obtain data on assigned subjects. May interview individuals to obtain data or draft correspondence and answer inquiries.

Research Assistant (*Paralegal*)

Performs legal research by operating a computer-assisted legal research system.

Research and Development Specialist (*Food Service*)

Conducts research on new product lines and equipment for the food service industry. May work with food products in test kitchens or with new equipment in operating food service establishments. Reports findings to manufacturers of food products and equipment and publicizes results in trade publications to inform the industry about the possible alternatives the findings may provide for food service professionals.

Research Director

May supervise a group of research projects at a given time. (See **Project Director**)

Research Manager

(See **Project Director**)

Research Technician (*Electronics*)

Performs research to evaluate new methods for the electronics technician. Tests findings. May pass recommendations on to research and development. Upon request, works with other researchers and engineers to test findings.

Researcher and Evaluator (*Travel*)

Investigates and evaluates public relations efforts of the organization. Responsible for making recommendations on public relations programs based on goals and objectives and competition's position in the marketplace. Evaluates needs for expanding public relations efforts. Researches and recommends best strategy.

Reservationist

Sells reservations and other travel products such as tours, hotel accommodations, car rentals; operates computer reservations equipment; assists passengers in solving their travel needs.

Reservationist (*Hotel*)

Responsible for confirming room reservations, either by mail or by telephone, and for writing or typing out reservation forms. Works with computer to keep guest reservations current and for billing procedures. May assist guests with other reservations for local transportation, dining, or entertainment, depending on the staff size of the hotel.

Reservations Manager

Supervises and coordinates activities of personnel engaged in taking, recording, and canceling reservations in front office of hotel. Trains front office staff. Reviews daily printouts listing guests' arrivals and individual guest folios received by room clerks. Approves correspondence going to groups and travel agents to answer special requests for rooms and rates. Evaluates computer system and manual record procedures for efficiency.

Restaurant Manager

Responsible for efficiency, quality, and courtesy in all phases of a food service operation. In large organizations, may direct supervisory personnel at the next lower level. In smaller operations, might supervise kitchen and dining room staffs directly. Knowledge of the responsibilities of all restaurant staff is essential to this position.

Revenue Officer

Investigates and collects delinquent federal taxes and secures delinquent tax returns from individuals or business firms according to prescribed laws and regulations. Recommends civil penalties when necessary. Writes reports on all actions taken.

Roasting Cook

Responsible for all meat preparation that is made to order. Also responsible for all items that are deep fried, shallow fried, sautéed, or broiled.

Robotics Technician

Performs the work of an electronics technician, specifically on various types of robotic device. (See **Electronics Technician**)

Rooms Attendant

Coordinates service for a block of rooms in a hotel. Ensures room service operations are running smoothly. Arranges for any special requests from guests concerning accommodations. Checks the room rack and key rack frequently. Oversees the operation of switchboard and messages going to guests.

Rooms Division Supervisor

Directs all activities involved with the rooms division of the hotel. This includes staffing housekeeping, occupancy, service, and promotion.

Rounds Cook

Replaces every member of the kitchen brigade who may be absent from each station. Must be efficient and versatile in cooking techniques.

Sales Assistant

Responsible for successful management of a selling area. Involves supervision of a selling area and customer service functions. In a large department store, may also direct inventory control and merchandise presentation and increasing the sales growth and profitability of an area.

Sales Director (*Hospitality*)

Responsible for research and analysis, short-term and long-range planning, determination of marketing strategies and tactics, setting of goals and objectives, budgeting, the booking of individual as well as group business, and the securing of business for the food and beverage department as well as for the rooms division.

Sales/Field Representative (*Electronics*)

Advises customers on installation and maintenance problems and serves as the link between the manufacturer and the customer.

Sales Manager

Coordinates sales distribution by establishing sales territories, quotas, and goals, and advises dealers and distributors concerning sales and advertising techniques. Directs staffing, training, and performance evaluations to develop and control sales programs. Prepares periodic sales reports showing sales volume and potential sales. May recommend or approve budget, expenditures, and appropriations for research and development work.

Sales Manager (*Food Service*)

Responsible for the development and operation of the sales department. Maintains files on past group business. Works with the social director and promotion office on contacts and may do some traveling to other area to bring new business into the establishment. Also trains and supervises sales representatives and some account executives.

Sales Manager (*Retail*)

Oversees the various sales departments in wholesale and retail companies. Directs promotional sales campaigns for their merchandise or services.

Sales and Marketing Specialist
(Food Service)

Plans, researches, promotes, and sells products to the food service industry.

Sales Representative

Secures orders from existing and potential customers by means of visiting the customer facility or calling by phone. Follows up on quotations submitted to customers. Submits weekly activity/call reports concerning customer quotes, orders, or problems. Provides a territory sales forecast on a monthly basis.

Sales Representative
(Computer Systems)

Calls on prospective clients to explain types of services provided by establishment, such as inventory control, payroll processing, data conversion, sales analysis, and financial reporting. Analyzes data processing requirements of prospective clients and draws up prospectus of data processing plan designed specifically to serve client's needs. May also sell computers and related equipment directly.

Sales Representative *(Hospitality)*

Follows initial lead on a prospective client. Responsible for explaining hotel's services to government, business, and social groups to generate interest in the facility as a site for a major function. Sales representative conducts "cold calls" as well as calls to a selected prospect list. The sales representative may pass the interested client on to an account executive, who will actually set up, service, and maintain the account.

Sales Secretary

Types drafts of newsletters; keeps track of company's dealings with outside printers, suppliers, and creative people. Types, files, answers telephones, and routes mail. Takes orders, books events, or handles whatever customer request comes in for the product or service being sold.

Sales/Service Manager
(Electronics)

Oversees both the sales and service efforts of a branch or many branch operations of a company. Ensures that the quality and customer service levels are maintained in the field. Receives feedback from customers through the sales and service staff. Determines what action should be taken with repeated problems.

Sales Supervisor
(See **Sales Manager**)

Sales Trainee *(Hospitality)*

Usually begins with front office experience to learn client relations and total product line offered by the hotel. May go on sales calls with sales representatives or assist an account executive with servicing an account.

Sales Trainee *(Insurance)*

Attends sales strategy sessions as an observer, or "tails" an experienced agent on calls. Assists established agents to service accounts.

Sanitation Supervisor
(Food Service)

Supervises porters, office dishwashers, kitchen persons, and pot washers. Ensures that dishes, cooking utensils, equipment, and floors are kept clean. Ensures that kitchen always meets health department to regulations and standards.

Sauce Cook

Responsible for all preparation of sauces to be used on main items on the menu. In a middle-sized operation, the sauce cook is also the Sous Chef.

Schedule Planning Manager
(Travel)

Approves and enforces scheduling recommendation for all air traffic coming and going into and out of the airport.

School Director

Plans, develops, and administers education the programs. Confers with administrative personnel to decide scope of programs to be offered. Prepares schedules of classes and rough drafts of course content to determine number and background of instructors needed. Interviews, hires, trains, and evaluates work performance of education department staff. Assists instructors in preparation of course descriptions. Prepares budget for education programs and directs maintenance of records of expenditures, receipts, and public and school participation in programs.

School Director (Vocational)

Directs and coordinates schools with vocational training programs. Confers with legal members of industrial and business community to determine manpower-training needs. Reviews an interprets vocational educational codes to ensure that programs conform to policies. Prepares budgets and funding allocation for vocational programs. Reviews and approves new programs. Coordinates on-the-job training programs with employers and evaluates progress of students in conjunction with program contract goals.

School Secretary

Handles secretarial duties in elementary and secondary schools; may take care of correspondence, prepare bulletins and reports, keep track of money for school supplies and student activities, and maintain a calendar of school events.

Script Writer

Provides the creative support in a telemarketing agency. Writes all material that is to be read by the telemarketing representative.

Seafood Cook

Prepares all seafood dishes, mousses, soufflés, etc. Also prepares the fish for cold display or for hors d'oeuvres and then sends to the manager for final decoration.

Secret Service Agent

Protects the president and vice president of the United States, along with their families, and protects the coins and securities of the government by enforcing civil laws pertaining to counterfeiting.

Secretary

Performs secretarial duties for a supervisor. Takes and transcribes dictation with speed and accuracy. Maintains correspondence and data files, arranges appointments, answers routine inquiries, and handles general office duties. Often assists in performing administrative details using initiative and judgment. Requires thorough knowledge of company policies, the organization, and how to operate in the channels of the organization. As part of the management team, must be ready to make decisions and provide relevant information to staff members on a daily basis.

Secretary (Food Service)

In large food service operations, performs a variety of administrative duties; works with customers on group business and with vendors on orders and supplies. Frees the employer to work on other areas outside the property.

Security Officer

Responsible for security in buildings and grounds.

Senior Drafter

Gives final approval to the plans drawn up by other drafters before presenting the plan to client. (See **Drafter**)

Senior Legal Assistant

Oversees the work of paralegals and legal assistants in the firm. (See **Paralegal** and **Legal Assistant**)

Senior Systems Consultant

Provides specialized advice on programming languages and documentation. Maintains up-to-date knowledge of all programming language. Makes provisions for the orderly processing of changes, updatings, and modifications of programs. Coordinates all company programming efforts. (See **Systems Consultant**)

Sergeant

In the U.S. Marine Corps. and U.S. Army, a noncommissioned officer of the fifth grade, ranking above a corporal and below a staff sergeant.

Service Representative

Goes out into the field upon customer's request to service problems with purchased equipment. May diagnose the problem, correct and test the equipment to see if it is working properly. Reports problem to research and development. Tells owners and dealers about new products, service techniques, and developments in maintenance.

Service Technician (Electronics)

(See **Service Representative**)

Sheriff

A constitutional officer who is an elected official. Supervises deputies and plainclothes investigators. Responsible for the administration of the county jail. Serves civil papers and orders of the county courts and transports prisoners.

Social Secretary

Arranges social functions, answers personal correspondence, and keeps the employer informed about all social activities.

Sous Chef

Principal assistant of the Chef de Cuisine. In a large operation, will assist the Chef de Cuisine in general administrative and supervisory duties and will implement every order given. Must have the same professional background as the chef but

not necessarily the same number of years of experience.

Special Education Teacher

Instructs students with physical, developmental, behavioral, or learning disabilities.

Special Events Coordinator

Performs basic function of the meeting planner and also is directly responsible for the advertising and promotion of the event, for the budget for the event, and for identifying the appropriate target market. Works with the press and media on promotion. Acts as the liaison between all participating parties.

Speaker

Person elected by an organization to present its views, policies, or decisions.

Speech Therapist

Treats and teaches persons with speech, language, and voice disorders.

Staff Accountant

Oversees the general ledger of a firm. Reviews cost center and chart of accounts structure. Makes recommendation as to cost center/account structure which will identify the nature of expenses to their proper areas; assists in controlling annual expenditures. Reconciles daily cash flow statements and reconciles to monthly bank statements. Reconciles payroll and cash disbursement accounts. Reviews accounts payable aging and vendor statements for problems.

State Travel Director

Promotes visitor traffic within the destination, whether for pleasure, business, or convention purposes, and from within or from without the state.

Statistical Typist

Works in all types of businesses typing statistical data from source material such as company production and sales records, test records, time sheets, and survey and questionnaires.

Stenographer

Takes dictation in shorthand of correspondence, reports, and other matter, and operates typewriter to transcribe dictated materials.

Steward (Food Service)

Supervises and coordinates activities of the pantry, storeroom, and non-cooking kitchen workers, and purchases or requisitions the foodstuffs, kitchen supplies, and equipment. Inspects the kitchens and storerooms to ensure that the premises and equipment are clean and in order and that sufficient foodstuffs and supplies are on hand to ensure efficient service. Establishes controls to guard against theft and waste.

Store Manager

An executive responsible for the profitable operation of the store. Has broad merchandising responsibilities, develops staff, contributes to the store's public relations effort, and supervises the maintenance of the store. Spends significant amount of time on the selling floor and supplies other areas of management with detailed information on the operation of the store.

Storeroom Supervisor (Food Service)

Responsible for supervising, receiving, inspecting, counting, and storing of all food and other articles delivered to the storeroom. Responsible for filling out all requisitions and, under the instructions of the house auditor, for keeping a journal in ledger of all goods received and delivered. Records names of purveyors, the costs and descriptions of articles, and other required information. Supervises monthly inventories with the auditor.

Summer Clerk

A law school student who works for a law firm during the summer break, usually so both parties can learn more about each other in making potential employment decisions.

Superintendent of Service (Hospitality)

Responsible for overseeing all functions providing guest services in the hotel. This may include the front office and housekeeping as well as food service operations. Ensures quality service while keeping informed about any client-centered problems that may affect new or repeat business. Solves problems related to guest services.

Supervisor (Banking)

Responsible for improving the overall productivity of a department or area, motivating staff, and staying within budget. Oversees production, product development, marketing, and systems functions in the bank.

Supervisor of Data Entry Services

Directs all data input activities serving the users of centralized data input facility. Directs the development of data input procedures, performance standards, and controls. Directs the evaluation of new data entry equipment. Ensures accurate and timely completion of projects.

Supervisor of Gate Services

Observes staff to ensure that services to passengers are performed courteously and correctly. Supervises and coordinates the activities of staff engaged in admitting passengers to airplanes and assisting passengers disembarking at terminal exits of commercial flights. Reviews flight schedules, passenger manifests, and information obtained from staff to determine staffing needs. Recommends alternate procedures if needed. Evaluates performance of staff.

Supervisor (Telemarketing)

Manages groups of telemarketing communicators and is directly responsible for their performance. May also be responsible for training and scheduling of staff.

Surveyor

Interviews people and compiles statistical information. Asks questions following a specified outline on questionnaire and records answers. Reviews, classifies, and sorts questionnaires. Compiles results in a format that is clear and concise and highlights findings relevant to the objective of the survey.

Systems Administrator

(Word Processing)

Involves systems maintenance and management and systems analysis and design.

Systems Analyst

Prepares detailed instructions for assigned programming systems or components enabling qualified personnel to proceed with implementation. Evaluates procedural and/or programming systems required to operate and support programs and systems. Solves the problems of adapting computer hardware and software to end-users' needs. Determines how the company can save money by adapting existing equipment. Coordinates and supervises the efforts of many computer professionals. Maintains quality control by assessing the system once it has been implemented.

Systems Consultant

Advises clients on developing, implementing, and maintaining automated programs for clients and for in-house use; on selecting hardware, writing software, and consulting with user/client when special programs must be developed. Writes the codes that make up a computer program, tests their programs, debugs them (eliminates errors) and sometimes writes the accompanying documentation that tells others why the program was written the way it was.

Systems Operators Supervisor

Directs operations for optimum use of computer and peripheral equipment. Coordinates between users and other data processing functions in establishing and maintaining processing schedules. Recommends hardware changes and directs the installation of new equipment.

Systems Programmer

Prepares the computers to understand the language that the applications programmers will be using and tells the computer what peripheral equipment, such as printers and automatic teller machines it will be controlling.

Systems Trainee *(Banking)*

Works in programming or part of a systems team project, refining the use of current equipment or developing systems for as yet unmet needs.

Tape Librarian

Documents and allots hardware space for all computer and peripheral equipment for schedules; produces debugging statistics and other statistical reports for the department management personnel.

Technical Secretary

Assists engineers or scientists. In addition to the usual secretarial duties, may prepare much of the correspondence, maintain the technical library, and gather and edit materials for scientific papers.

Telemarketing Center Manager

Responsible for executing the program once components have been assembled and script written. This involves either making or receiving calls in a way that achieves each client's objective.

Telemarketing Communicator

Delivers what everyone else sells. Coordinates or manages the allocation of the product to the proper sales and delivery channels.

Telemarketing Representative

Sells a product or "qualifies" customers for the field sales force by telephone.

Telemarketing Trainer

Instructs communicators about the product or services and how to use the scripts. Trainers also teach telemarketing efficiency, listening skills, and sales techniques.

Ticket Agent

Sells tickets to airline passengers at the airport and city ticket office; promotes and sells air travel; gives air travel and tour information; makes the flight and tour reservations; computes fares; prepares and issues tickets; routes baggage; and prepares cash reports.

Tour Director

Conducts the actual tour. Accompanies travelers as an escort throughout the trip. Solves problems and settles complaints. Has alternative plans set for the group so that tour will be successful even under adverse conditions. Coordinates the group to stay together and encourages questions about the area being visited.

Tour Escort

Assists passengers; generally assists with tours; accompanies the tour from start to finish; often handles large sums of money.

Tour Guide

Does complete narration; has specialized knowledge of a particular region or country; hired to accompany a tour only while it visits the area of special expertise.

Tour Operator

Puts together all the elements of a trip: transportation, accommodations, meals, sightseeing, and the like; negotiates rates and block space; coordinates details of the itinerary; markets the product.

Tour and Travel Account Executive

Responsible for the development and service of group tour business coming into the hotel. Brings travel and tour groups to the hotel. Consults with the tour operators and travel agents and collaborates with the hotel staff to find best strategy for servicing the group.

Tourist Information Assistant

Provides information and other services to tourists at state information centers. Greets tourists, in person or by telephone, and answers questions and gives information on resorts, historical sights, scenic areas, and other tourist attractions. Assists tourists in planning itineraries and advises them of traffic regulations. Sells hunting and fishing licenses and provides information on fishing, hunting, and camping regulations. Composes letters in response to inquiries. Maintains personnel, license sales, and other records. Contacts motel, hotel, and resort operators by mail or telephone to obtain advertising literature.

Trader

Matches buyers and sellers of securities.

Traffic Manager

Negotiates price and service issues of all modes of transportation carrier contracts and determines the appropriate transportation mode to be utilized. Develops, maintains, and disseminates logistical data.

Traffic Officer

Directs and controls the flow of traffic for both motor vehicles and pedestrians. Enforces parking regulations. Tracks stolen or wanted automobiles. Investigates traffic accidents. Provides motorists' assistance, escort duty, crowd handling, and rerouting traffic.

Trainer *(Word Processing)*

Trains correspondence and word processing secretaries to make fewer errors by checking their work.

Training Manager

Develops ongoing training programs new and experienced personnel. Conducts training seminars. Writes and coordinates training manuals, working with specialists for specified details. Prepares training videotape and/or films; maintains library of video and film training aids. Notifies employees of training sessions. Introduces topic specialists at the beginning of the program and the program agenda. Develops means of measuring the effectiveness of programs through testing.

Training Specialist

Develops and conducts training programs for specialized functions within the company upon approval of the training manager. (See **Training Manager**)

Training Supervisor

May supervise training manager(s) as well as the entire training function for the company. Responsibilities might include overseeing training programs at various divisions and performing all budgetary responsibilities pertaining to the programs. Also may evaluate existing programs and make recommendations for modifications or new or additional programs. (See **Training Manager**)

Transportation Manager

Responsible for all aspects of transportation including inbound, between facilities, and outbound. Supervises various functions and personnel. Negotiates rates with warehouses and transportation companies. Plans, monitors, and implements the distribution department's fiscal budget. Establishes the most beneficial routing of company shipments for satisfactory customer service. Determines price levels. Plans for the department on a quarterly, yearly, and five-year basis.

Transportation Specialist

Advises industries, business firms, and individuals concerning methods of preparation of shipments, rates to be applied, and mode of transportation to be used. Consults with clients regarding packing procedures and inspects packed goods for confor-

mance to shipping specifications to prevent damage, delay, or penalties. Files claims with insurance company for losses, damages, and, overcharges of shipments.

Travel Agency Manager

Supervises the day-to-day operations of the agency. Prepares sales reports and dictates office policies. Decides on promotion and pricing of packages. Supervises, hires, and trains employees. Attends trade shows to keep informed on latest computer systems, rates, and promotions being offered by the airlines, hotels, and other related services. Initiates advertising for the agency and keeps budget.

Travel Agent

Plans itineraries and arranges accommodations and other travel services for customers of the travel agency. Plans, describes, and sells itinerary package tours. Converses with customers to determine destination, mode of transportation, travel dates, financial considerations, and accommodations required. Books customer's mode of transportation and hotel reservations. Obtains travel tickets and collects payment. May specialize in foreign or domestic service, individual or group travel, or specific geographical areas.

Travel Counselor

Advises clients on best ways to travel, destinations, costs, and safety issues. Offers advice to clients on packages available, preparation for a trip, or availability of transportation or accommodations. Researches information requested by the client.

Travel Director

Client-contact person who actually goes out with the incentive groups and on site, coordinating sightseeing trips and trouble shooting.

Travel Secretary

Coordinates all aspects of the travel function. Researches options to maintain an economical, efficient travel program. Schedules personnel for approved travel on corporate jets. Schedules personnel from approved travel authorizations on commercial flights. Makes hotel reservations. Performs clerical and secretarial duties pertaining to all travel arrangements.

Travel Specialist

Develops specialized expertise about a particular area of travel. May work for a travel agency, tour operator, publications department, or other related areas using information mastered about a specialized area of travel. May specialize in a geographic area, type of destination, or any other specific area in the travel industry.

Treasurer

Directs and coordinates organization's financial programs, transactions, and security measures according to financial principles and government regulations. Evaluates operational methods and practices to determine efficiency of operations. Approves and signs documents affecting capital monetary transactions. Directs receipt, disbursement, and expenditures of money or other capital assets.

Trust Officer

Manages money and securities as well as real estate and other property. Decides how assets will be managed.

Underwriter

Reviews applications, reports, and actuarial studies to determine whether a particular risk should be insured. Specializations are usually in life, property, and liability, or health insurance.

Underwriter Specialist

Specializes as an underwriter in life, property, and liability, or health insurance. (See **Underwriter**)

Underwriter Trainee

Assists the underwriter. Usually spends much time on the telephone gathering information and verifying what has been reported before the underwriter makes final decisions. (See **Underwriter**)

Underwriting Supervisor

Oversees the underwriting department. Ensures staff is working within appropriate guidelines and regulations when reviewing submitted materials. Evaluates performance of the staff and hires new underwriters as needed.

Urban Planner

Works with city or state officials to produce plans for future building and construction projects. Must be able to project an area's future population and its needs and design facilities to meet those needs.

U.S. Marshal

Responsible for executing and enforcing commands of federal courts; processing federal prisoners; seizing property under court order; and protecting federal judges, witnesses and juries.

Vending Manager

Independent businessperson who places own machines in various installations in a community or facility. Responsible for locating new machine sites, developing good public relations for the firm by handling complaints, and maintaining quality control of the product and proper functioning of the machines. Handles cash funds and keeps required records.

Veterinarian

Studies, treats, and controls animal injuries an diseases.

Vice President

Plans, formulates, and recommends basic policies and programs for approval of the president which will further the objectives of the company. Executes decisions of the president and Board of Directors. Develops, in cooperation with the president and supervisors, an annual budget and operates within the annual budget upon approval. Recommends changes in the overall organizational structure to the president. Approves public relations programs.

Vice President of Account Services

Oversees the promotion sales, and service of a product line to a variety of customers within a defined geographical area. Develops and seeks out business of a highly complex nature and of importance to the company. Ensures efficient servicing of all accounts, once obtained. Prepares programs for training and development of the field managers and other new and experienced personnel.

Vice President of Communications

Ensures the development and execution of advertising, public relations, public affairs, and members' relations' programs, together with effective internal and external communications to promote understanding, acceptance, and support of corporate activities and objectives by employees and the subscribing public.

Vice President of Finance

Acts under authority and responsibility delegated by corporate executive office. Conducts management studies, prepares workload and budget estimates for specified or assigned operation, analyzes operational reports, and submits activity reports. Develops and recommends plans for expansion of existing programs, operations, and financial activities.

Vice President of Human Resources

Develops Human Resources policies and programs for the entire company. The major areas covered are organizational planning, organizational development, employment, indoctrination and training, employee relations, compensation, benefits, safety and health, and employee services. Originates Human Resources practices and

objectives that will provide a balanced program throughout all divisions. Coordinates implementation through Human Resources staff. Assists and advises senior management of Human Resources issues.

Vice President of Marketing
(Hospitality)

In addition to overseeing the sales function, also coordinates the advertising, public relations, publicity, and community relations for the hotel. (See **Vice President of Marketing**)

Vice President of Marketing/Sales

Represents the marketing functions needs in the development of corporate policy. Formulates sales goals, marketing plans, and strategy and directs the execution of these areas for the achievement of corporate marketing objectives. Manages the sales force to achieve marketing and sales goals for assigned products.

Vice President of Merchandising

Manages several divisions of merchandise. Responsible for planning and giving buyers both fashion and financial direction. Plans sales, inventory, and marketing by store, based on the turnover desires. Plans markups and ensures that inventory supports sales efforts.

Vice President of Operations

Directs the formulation of corporate policies, programs, and procedures as they relate to distribution, operations, research, production, engineering, and purchasing. Maximizes group and divisional short- and long-range growth and profitability.

Vice President of Production

Plans, directs, and controls production and related support functions to provide timely manufacturing and delivery of output at lowest possible costs. Manages, controls, and reviews all assigned resources: staff, technical, material, and financial. Manages budgets and expense control to ensure effective meeting of operating objectives.

Vice President of Sales

Responsible for the selling of the output of several different manufacturing facilities. Must develop effective sales policies that result in each plant's producing the optimum profit. Determines final prices and works closely with the sales staff, the production, scheduling, and traffic staffs and research and development personnel. After the initial sale is made, the sales staff assumes continuing sales effort to such accounts.

Wage and Salary Administrator

Maintains files of updated job descriptions. Ensures that responsibilities are appropriately compensated according to established standards. Participates in and reviews local and national salary surveys to set current salary standards and pay rates for each position within the organization. Processes salary increases or other changes for personnel according to established policies.

Warehousing/Operations Manager

Determines and develops distribution strategies and practices that will support the corporate objective. Responsibilities include: identifying areas within the company that offer some opportunity for improvement; optimizing investments in all locations, in inventor) facilities, and people; and matching the corporate distribution support capabilities to the outgoing marketing, business, and operational needs. Makes use of financial and computer expertise in evaluating projects and allocation of resources.

Web designer

Designs and maintains sites on the the World Wide Web.

Window Trimmer

Displays merchandise in window or showcases of retail stores to attract attention of prospective customers. Originates display ideas or follows suggestions or schedule of manager. Arranges mannequins, furniture, merchandise, and backdrop according to prearranged or own ideas. Constructs or assembles prefabricated displays.

Wine Steward

Administers scheduling of all bar personnel, both on regular shifts and for catering work, and keeps records of their hours. Responsible for hiring, firing, and training all bar personnel, keeping customer account files, maintaining liquor and wine storage, setting standards, and ensuring that they are maintained.

Word Processing Center Manager

Responsible for word-processing support given to a function or a number of departments. Trains and motivates personnel; maintains good working regulations with departments being serviced, and administers basic first-line management responsibilities. Develops new procedures, keeps records, and orders supplies.

Word Processor

Uses computers and specialized word-processing equipment to enter, edit, store, and revise correspondence, statistical tables, reports, forms, and other materials. Word processing systems include keyboard, a cathode ray tube (CRT) for display, and a printer. Some equipment also has telecommunications hookups and scanners to ready manuscripts.

Writer

Communicates through the written word in newspapers, magazines, books, advertising agencies, and radio and TV broadcasting.

INDEX

CREDITS

Cover Credit

Cover illustration by Mark Fisher/Laughing Stock

Photo Credits